The Change Game

The Change Game

How Today's Global Trends are Shaping Tomorrow's Companies

Peter Lawrence

**KOGAN
PAGE**

London and Sterling, VA

First published in Great Britain and the United States by Kogan Page Limited in 2002.

120 Pentonville Road
London N1 9JN
United Kingdom
www.kogan-page.co.uk

22883 Quicksilver Drive
Sterling VA 20166–2012
USA

British Library Cataloguing in Publication Data

A CIP record for this book is available from the British Library

ISBN 0 7494 3926 2

Typeset by Jean Cussons Typesetting, Diss, Norfolk
Printed and bound in Great Britain by Biddles Ltd, Guildford and King's Lynn
www.biddles.co.uk

To Autumn

Contents

Acknowledgements

This book is mostly based on visits to companies and other organizations around the world involving interviews with their senior officers and with business owners.

The first 15 or so of these interviews in my native Britain were done with David Smith, at that time Director of Research for the Business School at University College Northampton (UCN). We clearly benefited at the early stage from UCN's contacts and good relations with companies and other organizations in its area.

Some of the material for the book derives from company visits in Canada in four or five of the provinces. These were done with John Blake, of the University of Central Lancashire. Similarly experience from a research project in Scandinavia has helped to shape arguments introduced in this book; this research project was organized by Jette Schramm of the Copenhagen Business School and all the fieldwork was done jointly with her.

After the first 40 or so interviews in the UK I resolved to make the research a joint UK–US study. The first tranche of interviews in the United States was done with Sara Keck of Pace University, New York City. The subsequent research visits to the United States were massively assisted by my friends Jim Krueger and Douglas Ohmer at

Northern State University, Aberdeen, South Dakota, who found me an amazing selection of good companies to visit.

One of my PhD students at Loughborough University, Nicole Richardson, has been interviewing senior people at some of the healthclub chains in Britain, and I accompanied her on some of these assignments. Similarly I have jointly interviewed airline executives in the UK and in Continental Europe with another of my Loughborough University based PhD students, Gianfranco Cuccaro. Going beyond the interviews I have learned much of value about these two industries from Nicole and Gianfranco.

I probably did the majority of the research interviews on my own; but it is often more fun and more relaxing to work with friends/colleagues/students, and you get the benefit of someone to talk to about it afterwards.

The research project that underlies the book was not expensive in the sense that nobody was employed to do the fieldwork; I did all that myself, some of it with others as detailed above. But there has been a cost in terms of travel expenses. In this connection I would like to thank University College Northampton, where I have been a Visiting Professor since 1994, for covering the travel cost of many of the interviews in the UK. Similarly for the research in Canada I am grateful to a grant from the Canadian High Commission in London, held jointly with John Blake, and for financial support from the University of Central Lancashire (UCL) where I have been a Visiting Professor since 1997. UCL were also kind enough to fund attendance at the Eighth Annual International Business Conference organized by Northern State University of South Dakota at which John Blake and I presented some of the findings of the Canadian research.

Loughborough University Business School provided me with an annual research budget from the mid-1990s. This made it possible to visit some companies in Continental Europe, to participate in the Scandinavian project referred to above, and to make several research visits to the United States. This support has been decisive.

At the stage when I was planning the book I benefited from a discussion with Dave Hill and Dick Williams, and subsequently from helpful comments on draft chapters. I likewise benefited from ideas and stimulus from Vince Edwards at BCUC and from my former colleague at Loughborough University, John Piper.

While writing this book I have become a member of the international management organization TEC, which I have found generally enjoyable and stimulating. In particular I got a lot out of a TEC seminar on Customer Service Excellence given by Stuart Dalziel of The Results Company and from another on Acquisition and Merger Integration by Garnet Twigg of London Consulting, and have used some of what I learned in this book.

Taking a longer-term view I also feel a debt to Gerry Johnson now at the University of Strathclyde and to Roland Calori in ESC Lyon in France who variously inspired, directed and included me on two multi-country EU studies. Without this start I would not have developed the interests that led to this book.

But of course my most substantial debt is to the many managers, senior officers and business owners who gave up their time to talk to me about their organization. This turned into the most absorbing project I ever dreamed up.

Introduction

This is a book about the way business in the West has developed. It is about trends and issues, and their implications. It tortures the past, especially the recent past, to make it confess the origins of the present. And it chips away at the present for clues to the future.

It is a big picture approach, concerned with general trends and major issues, rather than with the perspective of any particular sector or industry. At the same time the discussion is supported by examples and illustrations taken from a host of companies visited or researched in the last two or three years.

The book has a starting point and a mainspring. This is the world-wide intensification of competition. This heightened competition is the context for all that follows, and it clearly drives some particular issues such as the struggle for cost reduction, the quest for flexible employee structures, an ethic of focus and core business, and of course, industry concentration. Sometimes these competition-driven strivings provoke unintended consequences, that may be depicted as paradoxes.

Some of the trends we look at are dynamic. That is to say the labels by which they are known are familiar, they have been around for some time, but the content of the trend has changed. Downsizing, for example, has been with us for 20 years but has moved across sectors and categories of workers, and is currently making its way up the skills and status hierarchy; and outsourcing, which in the beginning embraced very routine operations, has now developed mightily in sophistication and scale.

We try to adopt a common sense perspective, starting with what everyone knows, but sometimes are able to take the analysis further. Take merger and acquisition (M&A). Everyone knows it is there, that it generates a few big players in industry after industry. We chart all this, but have also managed to tease out some variations on the theme – cluster concentration, counter-concentration, and bi-polarization – all highlighted with current industry examples.

Business is a proactive affair. People do things for reasons, hoping to achieve certain objectives. It is not all rational, there is often sentiment and emotion and even sometimes fashion in there, but it is still purposeful. The deeds and decisions are meant to lead somewhere. There are means–ends relations in the minds of the actors. We have tried to understand and to depict these connections. Also we have tried to be alive to consequences which were not necessarily expected or intended. Consider the core business ethic. The case for focus/core business/core competence is widely recognized and generally persuasive, a view accepted here. At the same time the dynamics of core business have implications for employee status, for organizational solidarity, and for the relations of different companies aligned in the same value chain, and these were not always planned or intended.

Where it seemed to be helpful, to further understanding, we have synthesized. We have noted, for instance, how the level of competition has driven proactivity and purposefulness, a rise in the status of management, and a meritocratic search for the right candidates, and all this has led to general agreement on what the right qualities and mindset are. We have labelled this the managerial consensus, and tracked its progress across sectors and even national frontiers. Or again we have looked at a variety of business initiatives and employee measures which collectively impact on corporate cultures and work-force morale, and labelled this phenomenon the crisis of human capital.

Finally we have been interested in solutions as well as problems. Competition and focus together put restrictions on the expansion of revenue. But there are companies that are improving the top line by growth as opposed to the bottom line by internal economies, and we have seized on the examples encountered in the research and looked for patterns going across industries. We have canvassed solutions to the crisis of human capital issue flagged up above. We have gone back to the ideas of the unique business proposition and that of competitive advantage, and endlessly unpacked examples of these in smaller and newer companies, and struggled to define their basis, both as inspiration and as a diagnostic tool.

A natural history of business?

The author's obligation to explain 'where it all came from' is actually quite tricky. I did not start off with any theory, or any hypothesis to be tested, or any particular case to be proved. I began only with the conviction that competition had intensified and the rate of change quickened during the 20 years I had spent teaching in a business school. Plus the fact that I had taken part in the two EU multi-country research projects in the 1990s that had alerted me to some of the developments in train. But more importantly this EU research had shown me that there were forces at work that it is interesting to try to unpack. But I did not want to impose an order on it, at least not in the first instance; instead I wanted to let business reality to dominate me.

QUESTIONS

So the formula I came up with was to seek interviews with senior people – CEOs, directors/vice-presidents, occasionally general managers, and business owners – to whom I put these deliberately open-ended questions:

▌ Looking back over the last 10 years or so, what has changed in your industry?

▌ Similarly, what has changed in your own company or organization?

▌ What do you think will happen next, what trends do you expect to continue, what will be the next game?

As the series of interviews unfolded, and I did well over 100, there were two changes. First, I was no longer starting from scratch, I got an idea of the sort of things that would come up, did not need the underlying dynamics explained so often, and built up a working knowledge of a number of industries. All this had a mildly streamlining effect, and facilitated the second development. This was that I became more adventurous in the interviews, probed on relations with customers and suppliers, asked about competition, pursued questions of competitive advantage and how the companies saw themselves keeping ahead of the game, and asked about the overall business rationale. And throughout I kept it flexible enough to pursue 'targets of opportunity' in the interviews in the sense of pursuing anything interesting that came up even if it had not been on my list.

Sample

To speak of a sample is a bit pretentious. The term suggests something that is systematic or even scientific, rather than the intellectual smash-and-grab raid upon which I embarked. But for want of a better word, I will use 'sample'. These were the key features of my research into the sample:

▍ Carrying out interviews in over 100 companies or other organizations – about two-thirds of these were in the UK, and most of the rest in the United States.

▍ Deliberately going for a complete mix of industries; as much variety as possible.

▍ At the same time trying to get two or more companies from any industry represented to get a bit of balance; in several cases this match was achieved by having one UK and US company from the same industry.

▍ Deliberately including a 'sub-sample' of non-profit-making organizations – administrative, charitable, and educational – for comparison, and to check for 'trend migration'.

But the boundaries are more fuzzy than the above itemization suggests. As the project progressed I increasingly drew on other experiences and used other materials. For instance, in the early 1990s I visited lots of companies in several locations in the United States to collect material for a book on US management; I found myself going back to these sources and looking for continuities with the companies

I visited when preparing this book in 2000 and 2001. Similarly I had the chance to interview executives and business owners in several parts of Canada in 1998–99, thinking I might one day write a book about management in Canada to match the book on the United States. And in the period 1997–2001, as part of a different research project, I did multiple interviews in a small sample of companies matched by industry in Norway, Sweden and Denmark: as time went by on this Scandinavian study I found myself increasingly switching emphasis from organizational–management issues to strategic–business ones.

In short, all these sources helped me to shape the ideas that have found their way into this book, and I have used all these sources for illustrations wherever it seemed helpful.

OUT ON THE PRAIRIES

The following remarks are addressed particularly to US readers, but perhaps an anecdote will set the scene. One of the CEOs I interviewed in South Dakota told me that he had once gone to New York to make a presentation to a potential corporate customer. From the social chat beforehand he said that it was clear the New Yorkers did not have much idea about where South Dakota was: it is immediately below the State of North Dakota, which borders Canada. At the end of the presentation there was a pause, broken by one of the audience who observed: 'For a southerner, you don't have much of a southern accent!'.

The point of the story is that in subsequent chapters I have drawn quite heavily on businesses in the Dakotas, and especially on companies in the town of Aberdeen, South Dakota, as examples to develop ideas in the discussion. There is a reason for this.

Towards the end of the study in Britain I switched my attention from name companies to smaller and newer businesses, and found this very rewarding in terms of insight. So naturally I wanted to repeat this initiative in the United States, and preferably in an area where smaller companies would not be overshadowed by the Fortune 500. I chose the Dakotas because of a relationship with Northern State University at Aberdeen where I had friends who could set it up for me: having done it, I feel it was an excellent choice. The assurance I feel I should add is that I do know there is a world beyond the prairies; in fact I have been in 35 of the 48 continental states, in many cases professionally rather than as a tourist.

TIME FRAME

The last thing to add to the account of 'where it all came from' is the time frame. Before I had written a book myself I had always thought of books being produced at a unitary point in time. If it was ever important to know what that unitary point was I looked at the year of first publication on the copyright page. But now I know that it is unusual for academics to write books in less than a year, and they often take much longer. During the writing process their ideas may develop and their priorities change, and I have already noted some of these developments in my own case.

But the outside world changes as well as your thoughts, perhaps even that part of the outside world you are writing about. So one ought to make the time frame explicit. In March 2001 I began writing this book, and it was finished by early February 2002 (though with some correcting, amending and bits of rewriting continuing into May 2002). Quite a lot happened in this time.

2001 will be long remembered for the terrorist attacks in New York and Washington on 11 September. These had economic consequences, and not only for the United States. But there is a broader context. The world economic slowdown had already begun when I started writing, but seemed to be evaporating by the spring of 2002. The early part of 2001 saw the decline of the telecomms sector, which seemed to parallel the collapse of the dot.coms the year before. There was more bad news than good news during the period of writing.

In the period General Motors introduced 0 per cent financing, and Ford posted a loss in the last quarter of 2001. At the start of 2002 it was announced that L M Ericsson of Sweden recorded the first loss in its 127-year history. Profit warnings abounded. Advertising, other business services, much manufacturing, civil aviation of course, were all hit. Bankruptcies included K-Mart, three major airlines, the South Africa based health chain Healthland, and most famously Enron.

Jack Welch retired from GE, as did Lou Gerstner from IBM and Herb Kelleher, the founder of Southwest Airlines. The M&A rate slowed, though there were still some high-profile mergers including that between Allianz and Dresdner Bank in Europe, and between Hewlett Packard and Compaq in the United States.

China joined the World Trade Organization (WTO). Argentina's economy/fiscal structure cracked. And at the start of 2002 the Euro became the actual daily currency for the 12 participating EU countries (Denmark, Sweden and Britain stayed out at this stage).

Not a dull period, but not a very upbeat one. Also it rather contrasts with the bullish late 1990s when the idea for the research and the book was conceived. Yet though after the events of 2001 some industries will 'never be the same again' – UK agriculture as a result of the foot and mouth outbreak for example – most of the trends and issues discussed in this book are likely to be a continuing dynamic that transcends the downturn and the specifics.

So is this book a contribution to 'the natural history of business'? It is difficult to judge this in a balanced way. Yes in that I had few preconceptions, wanted to be told by those who know, and a lot of what it offered here is 'what they told me' out there. At the same time I synthesized, checked for patterns, decided what were 'the good bits', and reflected endlessly on the testimonies of those who gave up their time to talk to me. So the responsibility is mine.

Nor can there be anything conclusive about the ideas expressed here. As with all things, our understanding of the world will never catch up with out experience of it.

IN SHORT

▌ We have defined the scope of the book, a close-up look at the dynamics of modern business.

▌ Interviewing senior executives and business owners was the principal research method.

▌ The sample is well over 100 companies and other organizations, mostly in the UK and the United States.

▌ The time frame for writing the book was spring 2001 to spring 2002.

▌ The responsibility for the interpretation is all mine!

1

Pressure and trends

Samuel Gompers, founder of the US labour movement, once famously remarked that what the US working man wanted was ... MORE.

'More' has become something of a *leitmotiv* of what has been happening in business and management as we enter the 21st century. It is universally agreed that there is now more competition, more stress, more emphasis on doing everything quickly, more turnover among CEOs, more demanding customers, more corporate predators, more distribution channels, more players in many markets, more contingencies you have to take account of, more frequent profit reporting, more accountability, more transparency, more performance measurement, more you have to know about IT, more privatization and deregulation and more downward pressure on costs and prices.

COMPETITION AND PRESSURE

Where did it all come from? There are all sorts of causes, overlapping and mixed up with each other, and it all started in the third quarter of the 20th century, in what the French call *les trentes glorieuses*, the 30 glorious years of unprecedented economic growth in the West after the Second World War. In this period all national economies in the West did well, most companies prospered, wealth was more widely dispersed in society than ever before, and in John F Kennedy's phrase, 'all boats rose on a rising tide'.

Then somehow or other it all came to an end in the 1970s, though it was not really clear that it was ending until afterwards. Unlike a recession, when everyone knows it is happening, the 1970s at first seemed like an interruption of the growth and affluence norm. It began when the Yom Kippur war between Israel and some of its neighbours in October 1973, which led to massive, retaliatory, rises in oil prices by Arab states inflamed by Western sympathy for Israel. But in the event it was more than a blip on the radar screen. The energy crisis undermined Western (and Third World) economies, the energy shortages and price rises triggered inflation that persisted throughout the decade and in turn limited growth and sparked unemployment. And in case anyone thought things were getting better there was another energy crisis at the end of the decade triggered by the fall of the pro-Western Shah of Persia in 1979. By the start of the 1980s, it was clear that the post-war period, *les trentes glorieuses*, were over. Much of what has happened in the last quarter of the 20th century and beyond is a consequence of the passing of that golden age.

AFTER *LES TRENTES GLORIEUSES*

One consequence was that in the 1980s corporate orthodoxy started to change. In the golden age diversification had been favoured. After all, pretty much every industry was doing well, it made sense to have stakes in several of them or even in many as with ITT in the reign of Harold Geneen. But if easy growth was over then a more discriminating appraisal was required, companies increasingly wanted to specialize in what they felt they knew best and did best, not spread themselves wide and thin.

Similarly vertical integration had been favoured in the golden age. If the emphasis was on production, on 'getting the stuff out the door' because companies could sell all they could make, it was critical to control all the contingencies that could affect production. So it made sense for companies to internalize competencies, to acquire raw material and component suppliers, to own downstream activities including distribution and delivery. But when conditions changed there was a case for re-evaluating vertical integration, and over the last 20 years of the last century it largely evaporated.

The last two ideas – a move away from diversification and vertical integration – can be put more broadly. In the golden age, strategy was not an issue. Only US companies (and text books) had it and talked about it. In Europe the implicit view was that if everything went well anyway you did not need corporate strategy. After all, strategy involves trade-offs, prioritizing, making choices, allocating resources, doing this rather than that because you cannot do everything. The end of the golden age saw the incremental spread of strategy as a prerequisite of the successful company, not just in the United States but worldwide, to the point in the early 21st century where strategy is the priority of top management and the *sine qua non* of corporate survival.

At a more tangible level, the end of the golden age led to a concern with cost cutting, with wage controls, with clawing back benefits conceded to employees in more favourable times, eventually to a range of corporate options that have become all too familiar including:

▌ downsizing;

▌ de-layering;

▌ outsourcing;

▌ moving manufacture offshore to take advantage of lower wage rates in developing countries;

▌ similarly moving administrative processing work cross-border, with the help of developments in telecommunications and information technology;

▌ business process re-engineering (BPR), that is streamlining and simplifying administrative processes in the interest of efficiency, cost reduction, and better customer service.

All of these, and we will examine them in more detail later, flow from the heightened competition attendant on the end of the golden age. But these developments have been reinforced by another phenomenon – overcapacity.

OVERCAPACITY

The simple fact is that the world is suffering from industrial overcapacity, at least in relation to those people and countries able to pay for the goods generated by world industry. In some industries – iron and steel, ship building, textiles – this overcapacity has been obvious for decades. More recently a more diffuse overcapacity has been signalled by the hectic role of concentration, where in one industry after another M&A activity leads to industries being dominated by a smaller number of big players – this would apply, for example, to cars, confectionery, computers, white goods, chemicals, pharmaceuticals, brewing, publishing, professional services, airframe manufacture, financial services, and even to higher education.

All this provokes a simple question – how did this overcapacity come about? There are probably three constituent answers. First, and most important, the West has increased its output. The very competition discussed already has led companies to strive for competitive advantage via improved productivity and quality. Now productivity is, of course, a ratio not an absolute. It is about the relationship between inputs and outputs; not how many cars do you make, but how many cars per employee? But even with this qualification the 1990s saw an increase in manufacturing output in the United States and in most of Western Europe.

Second, much of what used to be called the Third World has also increased its industrial output. Back in the golden age of the 1950s and 1960s when many of the Asian and African countries came into existence as independent states as a result of de-colonization – the break up of British, French, Dutch, Belgian, Portuguese colonial empires – there was much talk about how these new countries would achieve industrialization, what would be the preconditions, and what stages they would have to go through. Looking back it seems that rather than do it themselves a lot of these countries have had it 'done to them' by Western FDI (foreign direct investment). A major manifestation of the enhanced competitiveness in the West has been the drive to reduce costs by manufacturing offshore in relatively low wage countries.

This phenomenon of offshore FDI seems to have come in waves. To start with Hong Kong, Taiwan, Singapore, Korea were the exemplars; then as they upgraded themselves, and became more expensive, the offshore FDI passed to another group including Malaysia, Indonesia, Vietnam and the Philippines. Some of these countries experienced colossal economic growth in consequence. Until the Asian meltdown of late 1997 Thailand, for example, was credited with a 10 per cent per year growth in GDP over 10 years, and China was able to claim much the same.

Nor was this an exclusively Asian phenomenon. Western and particularly United States FDI had a similar effect in various Latin American countries especially where low labour costs were conjoined with a large domestic market, as with for instance Mexico, Columbia, Argentina and Brazil. Indeed the world's most startling example of 'offshore' manufacture is to be found in the northern strip of Mexico where it abuts the US states of California, Arizona, New Mexico and Texas, where the famous *maquiladoras*, assembly plants, are to be found. These *maquiladoras* tend to be concentrated in a few key towns opposite US towns, Cuidad Jaurez opposite El Paso, Tijuana across the border from San Diego and so on. Indeed Tijuana, Mexico, likes to call itself 'the richest town in the Third World.'

The third development which 'bumped up' world industrial output was the fall of European communism in the 1989–91 period. The former USSR, the six Warsaw Pact countries allied with it (the German Democratic Republic, Czechoslovakia, Poland, Hungary, Romania, and Bulgaria) and to a lesser extent Albania and Yugoslavia largely traded sub-standard goods and underpriced raw materials with each other in non-convertible currencies. Their impact on the West was small. They bought Western industrial goods with scarce hard currency when there was no alternative, they sold a few niche products to the West (Czech glass, Russian caviar) and violated Western patents whenever they had the chance – but nobody cared very much because they would not try to sell the stuff back to the West. Then with the fall of communism all this totally unneeded industrial capacity that had been so splendidly kept under wraps for nearly half a century was dumped on world markets – just in time to make the early 1990s recession worse.

MATURITY AND ITS FALLOUT

The diffusion of affluence in the post-war Golden Age, exacerbated by overcapacity, has produced mature markets. This is most obvious, of course, in consumer goods, though there is a business-to-business version of it, where the goods and even services consumed by companies becomes routinized, commoditized, and supply is thrown open to competition.

At its simplest, mature markets means no one is buying anything for the first time. Everyone in the West has one or two cars, a refrigerator and a dishwasher and more besides. So the consumer product industries concerned find themselves selling in a replacement market, selling upgrades, trying to enhance the product with some additional capability or embellishment that will render it more appealing, or trying to enhance product with service.

Internationalization

This heightened competition spurs internationalization. If domestic markets are mature, growth may be sought abroad. If there is world overcapacity in many industries this will drive concentration via M&A activity, some of it cross-border, so that more companies will find rivals abroad as well as at home. As competition intensifies, individual companies will 'lock horns' with each other in more places. This drive to internationalize has been enhanced by some other considerations:

▌ R&D (research and development)/new product development costs rise;

▌ so do associated marketing costs;

▌ at the same time product life cycles are tending to reduce; that is, a product or model becomes outdated, or simply unfashionable, that much faster.

So the drive to internationalize is irresistible. It is helped by some of the developments reviewed in the last section – by the enhanced purchasing power of many of the 'developing countries', and even by the growth of income inequality, for example, where Western consumers aspirations arise in the former European communist countries. The whole question of international demand is rather beguiling. Often the demographic mass and income inequality give so-called developing countries an unsuspected allure for Western exporters.

Consider chocolate. If you are a manufacturer of up-market confectionery, Switzerland is not your best market. Never mind that Switzerland has the world's highest GDP per capita (and is one of the homes of up-market confectionery). The fact is that the population is only 7 million, barely half the population of Cairo or Mexico City. The key to corporate wealth is not provided by 7 million wilfully unpretentious consumers. If you are selling some Western luxury product, including Swiss watches, there are probably more people who want this product and can pay for it in India or in Brazil than in Norway or Austria, Belgium or Denmark.

Nor it is just an argument that applies to consumer goods. What Western company is buying machine tools or computers or forklift trucks for the first time? But companies in Malaysia, Mexico, and Thailand are doing so. And the governments of some of these developing countries, especially when they have oil revenue, may also have spending aspirations and a considerable appetite for civil engineering projects, consultancy services, and infrastructure development. More cement is being poured in Bombay than in Boston. More surfaces need to be painted in China than in Canada.

International competition has come to assume a 'war games' character. If you are an international company you need to engage in all the key (geographical) markets, typically in those of what has come to be called the triad – the United States, (Western) Europe, Japan. If you do not, you may be vulnerable to an attack from another player in your industry which has a tryad presence. Consider, for instance, how some Japanese companies invaded US markets and outflanked US companies in consumer electronics. It goes like this.

The Japanese company enters the United States market with a product that is perhaps a bit better in, say, the 1970s or 1980s, and which is certainly cheaper; the Japanese can afford to do this because they are also selling in Europe and in the Far East where they are not for the moment fighting to establish themselves and so their profit margins are intact. In the face of this invasion of US markets by price-competitive Japanese products the domestic companies have no option but to reduce their prices, but they are not selling in Europe and Japan, or not to the same extent, so they cannot afford this price reduction. Their profits are eroded, they exit the industry eventually, leaving it all to the Japanese who are then free to raise prices and clean up.

So your company needs to be in all important geographic markets so that:

I It can do it to them if they do it to you.

I Which probably means they won't try to do it to you.

▌ If any companies in your industry come up for sale abroad best snap them up, to stop someone else doing it, and to increase your potential leverage.

Branding

One of the responses to the enhanced competition is branding. While branding has been with us for a long time it is now seen as increasingly important. It is being spread sideways, moved out from its consumer goods heartland to embrace services and business-to-business operations, as well as being moved up and down the value chain. In an age of intense competition, branding is important in that it attaches customers to particular products and services, it engages loyalty.

Traditionally branding has been seen as filling a number of functions. First of all, it may be said to reduce anxiety. Faced with a choice of goods and services buyers experience uncertainty. This may be relieved by encountering a known brand, something they feel they can depend on, something that they know from experience will answer their need, so that the decision is in a sense made for them by the lustre of the brand. Second, running through branding is the idea, beloved by public relations and advertising agencies, that familiarity will lead to favourability, that which is known will become that which is liked. Third, the brand should signal functional adequacy to buyers, it should communicate the idea that the product or service is 'fit for function' and will do what it is supposed to do, confer the benefit that is anticipated, and indeed do all of this better than the offerings of rivals. Fourth is the idea that the brand will have emotional appeal. As Ind (2001) puts it: 'Does it (the brand) appeal to me emotionally? Does the product tap into my needs and desires and sense of self?' (Ind, 2001: 25).

Ellwood, another commentator, takes the idea back a little further, suggesting that a key reason for the contemporary importance of branding is individualism: 'Western societies recognize the fragmentation of our personal and social identities and this encourages self-identity construction through the consumption of material goods and services – you are what you buy.' (Ellwood, 2000: 10).

Finally, branding confers identity, and thus serves to differentiate the identified branded product or service from other offerings in the same category.

Of this set of arguments to explain the function and importance of brands it is the idea of emotional appeal which has excited the most interest, and provoked the most discussion both by enthusiastic analysts and by detractors seeking to develop a radical critique. The emotional appeal argument, of course, relates especially to a group of consumer goods and services – cars, clothes, cosmetics, fashion goods and drinks, recreation and travel – that it is nice to have, fun to talk about, and everyone can play in the sense of not being debarred by lack of specialist knowledge.

For half a century or more critics have homed in on the scope consumer goods branding offers for psychological manipulation by marketeers and brand promoters, on unnecessary need creation, inauthenticity and the trivialization of human spirit. It is particularly easy to make the charge stick with clothes/fashion/accessories, as is demonstrated by the success of Naomi Klein's book *No Logo*, 2001). She is at her most devastating showing brand promoters tracking through the ghettos of US cities to discover what black youth thinks is cool so that it can be embodied in a cultish style offering to the whole age group. Indeed she gives the argument a new twist by linking the increasing cross-border outsourcing of production noted already in this chapter with the obsession with branding. The idea is that as new companies do not have to worry about the production, at least they do not do it themselves any more, they can give their whole attention to marketing and promotional activity – branding as a corporate *raison d'être*.

This emotional appeal argument is convincing for a particular range of goods and services. Yet we would like to suggest that the identity and differentiation justification for branding is both more fundamental and more widespread. This view is consistent with:

▌ Greater competition, leading to a more desperate struggle for buyer loyalty.

▌ Greater internationalization.

▌ The demonstrable endeavours of companies to engage in brand extension, to embrace new products, associated products, and sometimes quite unrelated products with the halo of the brand.

On this key issue of brand extension Kapferer (2001) argues that this extension is viable as long as the newly embraced goods or services are consistent with the brand's values. Not all companies seem to heed this advice, however, and Ellwood condemns some for going too far in the scramble to exploit a loyalty attaching advantage:

At the other end is the vast range of goods that fall under the Pierre Cardin brand, which has been stretched too far and has now been devalued. In a similar move the Gucci brand is extending from luxury clothes to household items like oven gloves, cooking aprons and dog toys. (Ellwood, 2000: 37)

We have quoted Ellwood both to show the two poles of the argument, consistent brand values versus value dilution, and to flag up the temptation generated by fiercer competition. The pervasiveness of branding can also be seen in the effective branding of services, in the attempts to brand industrial or business-to-business goods, and in the generation of retailer and distributor brands superimposed on producers' brands. It is indicative that we have come to take it for granted that retailers that do not actually make anything have successfully branded complete product ranges manufactured by others.

MARKETS NOT INDUSTRIES

At the start of 2000 the UK newspaper *Evening Standard* carried the front-page story: Ferry Firm to Import Bargain Price Cars.

For reasons British citizens do not really understand new cars in the UK cost more than in many of the countries of Continental Europe. The ferry firm in question, P&O Stena Line, was announcing its intention to import cars from Continental Europe and sell them in the UK at discounts of up to 18 per cent.

For example, an imported Peugeot 206, 1.4XL with a sunroof, which cost at the time £10,450 in the UK, would sell for £9,102. Or at the top of the range a Mercedes CL500 which cost £83,045 from a dealer in the UK, would cost via Stena Line £63,000 taxed and on the road – a saving of £19,145.

If one would pause to ask, what has automobile retail got to do with a company that (principally) transports people (and their vehicles) between the UK and France, the answer is pretty much nothing: but it is doable, and it will make money. There is a moral here. Over the last 10 years or more, competition has shifted incrementally from industries to markets.

Once upon a time, if you made, for example, paint, your competition was other companies who also made paint. It all happened in what was called 'the paint industry', and this was a meaningful concept. This, in fact, is 'the world we have lost.' Now, if you are an auto retailer, your competition may well be a cross-channel ferry company.

It is not entirely new, even if we have produced an eye-catching cross-industry example to highlight the phenomenon. The essence of this move from industry based to market based competition is caught in the now rather old-fashioned British expression 'the leisure pound.' The idea is that the prototypical member of the general public has money, a pound say, to spend not on a specific product or activity, but on 'leisure': maybe on tenpin bowling, or perhaps eating out, or it could be gambling, or spectator sport, or a visit to a health/leisure club, or forget being healthy and just hire a video and watch it with your six-pack to hand!

But neither leisure expenditure nor the vagaries of the new car market in the UK are isolated examples. Consider mortgages. Again, once upon a time in the UK mortgages were provided by institutions called building societies, mutual organizations for the most part owned by their members. But now you can get mortgages from the clearing banks, from grocery chains such as Sainsbury and Tesco, from insurance companies such as Standard Life and the Prudential, even from British Gas and from Virgin (primarily known for its record stores and a transatlantic airline). Of course you can still go to a good old-fashioned building society, but most of them in the UK have now demutualized and become public companies quoted on the London Stock Exchange (and the ones that are still mutual societies are likely to fall since the societies have cross-shareholdings in each other, and those that have already been demutualized and have to satisfy rapacious shareholders will want the other players in the industry to face the same demand)

Nor is this in any way an exclusively UK phenomenon. One of the banks whose CEO we interviewed in the United States rather pithily raised the same concern of cross-industry competition with the remark: 'Microsoft may enter financial services – What will the telecomms industry do?'.

Or consider books, and take the UK as *point de repère*. In the old days bookshops competed with other bookshops. But now supermarkets, especially grocery chains, heavily discount the most popular titles. And of course there is also competition from the Internet companies. One can buy a book on Amazon quicker than one can drive to Borders in the US or walk to W H Smith in the UK.

Or take another example – builders merchants, the companies that supply tools, materials, and various artefacts to builders, big and small. In the UK this industry has seen consolidation. The top three builders merchants have 42 per cent of the market. But if you are one of the Big Three, with whom do you compete? There is an interesting variety of answers:

I With the other two of the Big Three, but only residually.

I More importantly, with regional builders merchants; the Big Three compete with a variety of independent builders merchants strong in each of the different regions; for example Travis Perkins, the industry leader, would compete in Cambridgeshire/East Anglia principally with Ridgeons.

I Competition also comes from some of the DIY (do it yourself) stores, in the UK, for example B&Q and Wickes, who are in part supplying builders as well as the general public, or increasingly aspire to.

I The manufacturers who supply the builders merchants in some cases are trying to 'disintermediate' the merchants and supply big construction companies direct; this is not a risk free option – the builders merchants may seek to discipline the suppliers by de-listing their products or by looking for alternative suppliers (most suppliers in this industry are not sole suppliers, and on what in the trade is called 'the light side' – tools and small items rather than tons of sand and cement – there are often cheaper suppliers in developing countries).

If one wants an idea of where it might be going one might look to Home Depot in the United States, one of the fastest growing firms in the world and the world's second largest retailer after Wal-Mart (Home Depot's turnover is bigger than the UK market) and its share of non-food retailing wealth in the United States went from 1.8 per cent in 1988 to 13.9 per cent in 1998. But there are two key issues: Home Depot offers other services, for example, supply and fit, surveying for construction companies; and it supplies both the DIY market and the trade.

Imagine that you are a partner in a firm of surveyors. Your competition now is not only other surveyors, but the world's second largest retailer.

So the trend whereby competition moves from industries to markets, although not universal, is not restricted to any particular industry – one can make the case from financial services to airlines, from books to builders merchants. In turn it is reasonable to ask, are there any general causes, valid across industries?

Well, one such cause is certainly that information technology (IT) is a solvent of industry boundaries. By programming core operations IT renders these more transparent and easier to replicate. As the general manager of a business-to-business components supplier operating in several Western European countries comments:

> The ability to maintain clear blue water between the competition and ourselves is more problematic. When you have got up to stocking 60,000 components and have got distribution into place, you can be imitated. The warehousing technology anybody can buy, ditto the computer system; all you need is the money to buy these things.

Another clue is distribution. With overcapacity and ease of production the emphasis shifts downstream to marketing and distribution. If you have distribution in place the marginal cost of distributing something else, beyond your core range, is small.

In this spirit European visitors to the United States are beguiled by the range of things one can buy at petrol stations – work clothes and tourist accessories, hot and cold food, and in country areas all sorts of farm and DIY related items. I have been in gas stations in Texas that have more to offer than a European departmental store, though Europe is fast catching up; and the 1990s in the UK saw site alliances between oil companies and grocery chains.

The Internet may be first harnessed to provide a secondary distribution channel for the core business, but then be used for something new. The UK's leading academic bookseller, Blackwell Ltd, with outlets on many college campuses, for example, speak of using the Internet to sell students travel services and insurance products. So if you are a travel agent, you may be in competition with an academic book chain.

Diffuse competition, of course, is driving these developments.

DENOMINATOR MANAGEMENT

Beyond the developments discussed in the last few pages – brand extension, cross-industry market entry, the enabling effects of the Internet and so on – intense competition has provoked a number of more mechanical responses that may be grouped under the general heading of denominator management. This is a metaphor derived from school arithmetic where in sums with fractions the bit at the top is the numerator and the bit below the line is the denominator!

The starting point is that many measures of business performance for instance ROCE (return on capital employed), RONA (return on net assets) or earnings per employee, are ratios. The capital or assets or workforce are the denominator. The ratio can be improved by expanding the numerator – getting output, turnover, or profits up, or by working on the denominator.

This denominator management leads us to a number of 'old friends' that have been around for 20 years or so, though as we shall try to show, some of these are dynamic, changing in substance and manifestation. Consider downsizing.

Downsizing

Probably the most staggering examples of downsizing occurred in the early 1990s, in the former communist countries of Central and Eastern Europe. Tracking these events in the former communist German Democratic Republic in the 1991–94 period I found that reductions of 30–80 per cent of the workforce were common, where the companies did not actually go bankrupt (Edwards and Lawrence, 1994). But then the SOEs (state owned enterprises) of communist Europe were mostly hugely overmanned to start with.

In Western Europe downsizing or de-manning made its appearance most obviously in the UK in the early 1980s recession. It was the period in which Britain's industrial base contracted and those who were 'downsized' were typically blue-collar workers in manufacturing industry. More than 20 years later the downsizing phenomenon is still going on, it has spread from blue-collar workers to white-collar employees, from the private sector to the public sector, from manufacturing to financial services, and incrementally from the UK to the other countries of Western Europe.

But the most dramatic change is from downsizing when times are bad, during a recession, when companies are in difficulties and have to cut costs, to a state of affairs where downsizing, like the poor, is always with us. MIT economist Lester Thurow drew attention to this phenomenon in the United States, where in his view, reducing the headcount is invariably regarded as a desirable outcome whatever state of the economy (Thurow, 1996).

Thurow's verdict on the United States would apply equally to the UK. Indeed it has now become common for favourable results and redundancies to go hand in hand. Lloyds TSB, for example, one of the UK's leading retail banks, announced in February 2000 a 16 per cent increase in profit and 30,000 redundancies at the same time (a scenario repeated more modestly in February 2002). In March 2001 Britannic Assurance announced that it would give up door-to-door sales (2,000 redundancies) bringing to 6,000 the number of sales staff made redundant in a three-week period. Sun Life of Canada and the Prudential had made similar moves to restructure the salesforce. In the case of Britannic they announced a 7 per cent increase in operating profit at the same time, and the dividend went up 11.6 per cent.

To return to the United States for another example, in March 2001 Heinz announced its net income for its third quarter, ending January 31, 2001. It had risen to US $270.5 million from US $171.1 million a year earlier. At the same time it announced that it intended to eliminate 1,900 jobs, or about 4 per cent of its global workforce.

Which brings us to another twist. As the likes of Thurow (1996) and Luttwak (1998) have pointed out, if you are going to make 30,000 people redundant **do it in one go**. Investors will love it, the stock market will react favourably, and share prices will rise. Turbo-capitalism, as Luttwak calls it, has its own code as shown in Figure 1.1.

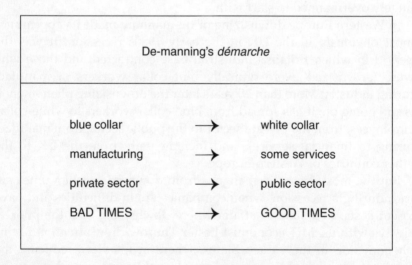

Figure 1.1

At the same time there is usually a reason for these joint announce-ments by companies, whatever one thinks about the balance between what is good for business and the distress experienced by many employees who lose their jobs. Of course door-to-door selling has little future for insurance companies in the age of the Internet; Lloyds-TSB is the result of an earlier takeover so that some branch and personnel rationalization was always to be expected. Or the Heinz redundancies are to fall on its struggling tuna and pet food lines – Starkist tuna and 9-lives pet food – as the *International Herald Tribune* reported in March 2001.

The other fascinating thing about de-manning is the way that it keeps popping up, not always intended, often as an effect of some-thing else. It also occurs among unlikely groups of employees. Consider for example salespeople.

Several developments are serving to reduce the importance of tradi-tional salespeople, the manufacturer's representatives, and to trim their numbers. For instance:

▌ Consolidation among retailers, especially grocery retailers, means there are fewer organizations to be sold to; the United States because of its size and the relative absence of national as opposed to regional chains is not the most compelling example, but in some of the European countries their concentration is spectacular; in Norway, for example, four grocery chains have a 99 per cent share of the market.

▌ The phenomenon of overcapacity discussed at the start of the chapter has the effect of shifting the balance of power from suppliers to retailers (the phenomenon of retailer as opposed to producer brands mentioned in the previous section is another manifestation of this shift in power down the value chain to the retailer) and thus retailer proactivity will tend to constrain the role (and need for) sales representatives.

▌ More generally, in business-to-business operations the establish-ment of Internet buying portals bypasses the need for representa-tives.

This idea of de-manning as an unintended effect first struck me at a Saturn Auto dealership in Dallas. By way of background it might be helpful to say that Saturn is a subset of General Motors models launched in 1990. The brand is managed separately, the cars are made at one of GM's leading plants, in Tennessee, south of Nashville, rather than in the traditional auto-industry area around Detroit, and the Saturn works is known for having better labour relations than is often the case in this industry. The owner of the dealership mentioned that he liked to hire sales staff who had no prior experience in car selling, to try to give the operation a better image, to get away from the 'If I can, would you?' ethos of auto trading. Fine, instantly comprehensible. On impulse I asked if there was any particular aspect of the performance of sales staff that was measured. Just one thing, it emerged, the proportion of potential customers seen by appointment. Again it makes good sense. An appointment system will tend to screen out the non-serious showroom visitor, those who just want to fantasize about the cars and enjoy the air-conditioning in the showroom. It is also a much more efficient way of using the salesperson's time; avoid the peaks and troughs, be busy all the time, and with more serious sales prospects. But of course if your salespeople are working more efficiently, you need fewer of them.

Or consider brewing in Sweden. Sweden has three major brewers – Pripps, Spendrups, and Falcon. At Falcon I was told that the company aimed to differentiate itself by projecting a more professional image, in part by concentrating on beer whereas Swedish breweries have traditionally been expected to supply the trade with a mix of products including soft drinks. But more than this in the HORECA (hotels, restaurants and catering) sector Falcon sent out its sales staff armed with a laptop and software package that enabled them to make instant and definite price quotes to customers, checking availability, inputting the order, and factoring in any discount. In the pre-laptop age, I was assured this would often be a long drawn out iterative process. Not liking to presume, I asked if this would lead to more or less sales representatives being employed, and was told that over time far less would be needed.

The interesting thing is that neither of these cases are de-manning initiatives. Both serve the ends of enhanced efficiency and better customer service. But de-manning still results.

De-layering

De-layering, taking out organizational layers, is the twin of de-manning. It has had a similar genesis and development to de-manning; again its initial Western European manifestation is de-layering in the UK manufacturing industry in the early 1980s recession. An early manifestation was that where companies had two levels of worker supervision, say a foreman and a senior foreman, common for example in the motor industry, one of these would go. But by the end of the decade one could observe this de-layering phenomenon in retail banks and in the public sector as well as in manufacturing: 'the flat pyramid' had become an article of faith.

De-layering did not for the most part start at the top, but tended to focus on supervisory and middle management grades. This has some important consequences.

First, by the late 1980s in the UK surveys and studies of middle management were showing greater job satisfaction. The de-layering and de-manning meant that the survivors were more accountable, which was often seen as a plus, they got enlarged responsibilities, got control over activities that had previously been performed by staff echelons, and generally felt themselves to be more in control.

But that was not all they felt. They also complained of more stress, pressure, performance measurement, and the downside of transparency. And certainly for the British all this has surfaced in surveys ever since.

Second, the supervisor and middle management de-layering was one force leading to empowerment at lower levels. There were simply not enough middle managers and supervisors left to exercise the kind of direction and control of blue-collar and routine white-collar workers that had been normal since the outset of industrialization. Empowerment was an answer.

Third, the greater transparency meant that while middle managers continued to be responsible up the line they were less interpersonally focused on their superiors. Their concerns were more exclusively operational, and less relational and political, which marked them off more sharply from general management. This in turn seemed to make general management more general, to give it a more pronounced 'upwards and outwards' orientation, and a more strategic focus.

Outsourcing

Outsourcing occurs at the point where two forces interact:

Get costs down

×

Concentrate on key activities

Like de-manning outsourcing has been going on for 20 years or more, but the content is being ratcheted up.

In the early days it was very straightforward things that were outsourced from manufacturing companies, such as:

▌ catering;

▌ cleaning;

▌ security.

This happened as the earlier philosophy of the golden age, 'keep everything in-house, you will have more control that way', was incrementally reversed.

Then less routine and non-qualitative things were outsourced. IT is a good example. Every organization needs it, none relishes paying for it, and both the equipment and the personnel come dear. In Europe the Anglo-French company SEMA, subsequently acquired by Schlumberger, has played successfully to this, approaching other companies and offering to meet their IT needs. The client company that buys this deal has its IT staff taken over by SEMA, they actually become SEMA employees on SEMA's terms and benefits. This is really quite seductive. The client company gets the benefits of outsourcing and de-manning at the same time; it also manages to avoid the standard objection to outsourcing more qualitative and discretionary activities, namely that 'they' will not understand our business.

On its side SEMA of course gets economies of scale together with cross-business transferable know-how. SEMA is not an isolated example. This initiative would be common to the generalist management consultancies with probably Accenture (ex Andersen Consulting) in the lead.

HRM (human resource management) is another example. For some time now companies have had the option of outsourcing the more routine HRM work, what would once upon a time have been known as personnel administration. More recently some of the more discretionary activities may be outsourced too, for example graduate recruitment. Certainly in the UK one can find consultancies such as Norman Broadbent who are able to handle the new graduate recruitment assignment, sometimes approaching potential client organizations in a SEMA-like style – we know you have to do it, we can figure how much it costs you, and we can do it cheaper! So they will take on board the job specifications from the client, write the advertisement, send out the forms, do telephone interviews, have applicants in for psychometric testing, and end up sending, say, six candidates to the client with all the preliminaries done and with the simple message, 'pick the one you like best'.

A further twist to the outsourcing scene is that one now finds cases where management itself has been outsourced, not just a particular process or function. In a way this is not new. For most of the 20th century it was taken for granted that oil extraction facilities in the Middle East and, say, Venezuela would be run by US and UK engineers. But what is perhaps new is that it is now possible to find examples of cross-border outsourcing of management as between countries in the West. So that for example the international airport at Naples, Italy (Napoli Capodichino) is run by the BAA (British Airports Authority). BAA also run the airports at Indianapolis and Pittsburgh in the United States. Water provision in Buffalo, New York State, is run by Anglian Water, headquartered in Huntingdon, near Cambridge (England). Interestingly Anglian Water on being asked about this assignment claimed that their expertise was in 'change management.'

At the risk of being a little fanciful one might argue that this trend is symbolized by the presence of CEOs of high profile companies who are non-nationals with respect to the companies they run. Consider that at time of writing (spring 2001):

▮ Ford was run by an Australian (until Bill Ford took over in the autumn of 2001).

▮ British Airways is run by an Australian.

▮ Air Canada is run by an American.

▮ But Barclays Bank in the UK is run by a Canadian.

▮ Carlos Ghosn, heading Nissan Motor, was born in Brazil.

▮ And Marks & Spencer, the UK's much loved store chain, is run by a Belgian (until summer 2002).

▮ But Belgian based brewery Interbrew (most famous brand Stella Artois) is run by Hugo Powell, who has both Canadian and UK citizenship.

▌ Pret à Manger, which sounds French but is British, is run by a South African, Andrew Rolfe, but L'Oreal which really is French is run by Welshman Lindsay Owens-Jones!

▌ And British Telecomms is run by Dutchman Ben Verwaayen.

Just a few random examples. Perhaps the most stunning cross-border management buy-in is one that concerns the Savoy Hotel off the Strand in London. While the Savoy may not be a Fortune 500 company, it is exactly the kind of UK institution where one would expect to find an Old Etonian with previous (commissioned) service in a Guards regiment; yet the present incumbent is in fact a Spaniard with an MBA from Harvard. More remarkable, he once attracted media attention by shortening the wine list at the Savoy in the interests of inventory control.

BPR

Standing of course for business process re-engineering, BPR is another weapon in the armoury of denominator management. But here we are entering new territory where something that is done for positive reasons – to promote internal efficiency, to enhance customer service – turns out, typically, to impact on the denominator.

While the details of the BPR operation clearly vary from case to case, there are some recurrent elements. BPR:

▌ Critically reviews the business process concerned, this review typically being led by an outside consultant but involving employees directly concerned.

▌ Simplifies the process, usually taking out stages, collapsing these stages into each other.

▌ Ensures that the employees involved are multi-skilled so they can do more than one bit of the process; a common example is with the customer interface over the telephone where the pre-BPR employee used to say 'I can take your order for fried eggs, but you have to talk to my colleague about the bacon'.

▌ Support the change with improved IT.

But while the aims are enhanced efficiency and service levels BPR invariably impacts on workforce size. I recall an amiably cynical business owner who had declined to establish a personnel department telling me in jaunty explanation: 'No one ever asked to see their job description in the hope of doing more work.'

A corresponding *bon mot* for the BPR era might be: 'No company ever inaugurated BPR in the hope of employing more people!'

Consider another example, which shows both sides of the equation, that of a smallish UK construction company. The CEO comes up against the fact that the company uses 14 different kinds of cement, graded by quality and price. A lot of this grade variation comes from site managers following tradition, using old-fashioned denominations, doing what they did in the 1980s. The CEO cuts through this and reduces the 14 grades to 3, but his next move is more radical.

This is to suggest to their suppliers that there should be a single price for all (grades of) cement. Not so unreasonable. It is not a move to get the dearest grade for the price of the cheapest; after all, these suppliers have had the construction company's business for years, they have their records, they can compute a fair single price from their data knowing what mix of grades has been supplied over time.

There are three principal cement suppliers, all of them high-profile companies. In the first instance all three refuse the single price invitation. But a senior executive at one of them makes their misgiving explicit: 'If we do this, what will happen to our 40 salesmen?' That is to say, they will go the way of the sales personnel at the Dallas auto-retailer.

But there is another twist. The construction company is not doing this to get the price down, but to get simplicity up. It wants to take work out of its accounts department. It wants a situation where all the accounts department has to do is say, we had y tons so pay the supplier $y \times z$ (price per ton). The construction company spells it out: 'A company of our size would normally have one, maybe two, people handling purchasing – but we don't.'

In short BPR leads to simplification that in turn leads to potential downsizing – in the two organizations that make up the trading relationship. More generally, as the construction company CEO put it: 'Everyone wants to shorten the supply chain – that means bigger orders with fewer people.'

Cross-border administrative outsourcing

Offshore manufacturing, typically moving manufacture and especially assembly operations to developing countries with lower labour costs, has been with us for 20 years or more and is familiar to all. More recent is shifting administrative work cross-border, aided by developments in IT and telecommunications. So that, for example, a lot of routine data inputting for Western companies is performed in developing countries: much of the routine credit card work, for instance, is done in the West Indies. It is possible for professionals in the United States to outsource copy-typing; doctors, for example, may have their case notes typed up in a developing country at a fraction of US secretarial costs; India, with its surplus of well-educated citizens including many English speakers, has come to be known as 'the back office of the world!' Speedwing, British Airways consultancy subsidiary (sold off in the spring of 2002), has much of its financial administration done in India; Lufthansa does its ticketing in India; much IT development is outsourced to India.

Offshore manufacture

While the phenomenon is very familiar this does not mean that it is static. Looking back over 10 years or so one thing that has changed, albeit incrementally, is that offshore manufacture has become less of a trade-off between quality and cost, where the former was sacrificed to the latter. Talking to manufacturers in the early 1990s I was conscious that they regarded offshore manufacture as a very precarious business. On one occasion (in 1992) I sat in on a meeting at a manufacturing plant in Nashville, Tennessee, where a major component was made for them in Mexico. The group strove to put together a set of work processes and quality control measures to reduce the recurrent defects in this component. At the end of the meeting the exasperated manufacturing vice-president declared: 'We'll get new Mexicans if we have to' – (ie, go elsewhere).

For the most part those days are past. The offshore operations have been up and running longer, local enterprises have got better at the tasks involved, employees in developing countries have moved down the learning curve, and Western managers have gained experience in managing these operations.

Something else that I have become aware of visiting companies during the last 10 years or so is that some companies have offshore manufacturing, like greatness, thrust upon them. That is to say companies do not always set out to go down the offshore road, but are led by circumstance. A UK vertically integrated retailer-manufacturer, for instance, decided to take its retail chain cross-border and chose as the two target countries Holland and Thailand. Then it established local manufacturing in Thailand to supply the new retail outlets. Then the company saw how much cheaper production was in Thailand, and began to re-import Thai production for sale in the UK and Holland. Another UK company had all its manufacturing in Britain, but acquired a French company producing a comparable range of products for the French market. The interesting thing was that this French company already had offshore manufacturing in Algeria and Tunisia. Taking advantage of this was dismissed by the company chairman on the grounds that UK levels of craft skill were required, but it is not inconceivable that 'the Thai effect' would click in at some stage.

Causing the unintended!

In this discussion of denominator management there is perhaps a suggestion that it is all drearily predictable, that we can all see the signposts and know where the road is headed. This is not necessarily so – things done for a purpose, where there is a known cause and effect relationship, may generate some unintended consequence. Consider as a puckish example airline pilot salaries around the world.

Many airlines are members of multi-company strategic alliances (a fuller account of this phenomenon is offered in Chapter 2). These alliances are attempts by the airlines concerned to increase revenue, and to enjoy some of the advantages of M&A, which is not in fact possible in an industry that is heavily controlled, and sometimes still owned by the various national governments. The unintended consequence is cross-border solidarity among employees (pilots) in airlines belonging to the same alliance.

So, in the spring of 2001 Lufthansa pilots got a substantial rise. They were helped to 'prepare their case' by their partners in the Star Alliance, United Airlines of the United States. And what is the interest of United's pilots? They fear that because US pilots are the best paid in the world, in an age of globalization their employers might 'outsource' in the sense of recruiting pilots from other countries (say, Germany) where salary expectations are more modest.

Not an isolated case. Korean Air pilots have been similarly assisted by pilots from their American Sky Team alliance partner, Delta Air. Or again the pilots of Iberia of Spain announced a series of strike days to take place in July and August 2001; they were believed to be taking advice from their colleagues at their One World United States alliance partner, American Airlines.

This is what economists call factor price equalization, but working in reverse where globalization leads to a levelling up, to protect the interests of the best paid occupational group in the richest country. It is worth keeping in mind this idea of unintended consequences; in Chapter 6 we take up more systematically the issue of the effects of denominator management upon organizational solidarity.

STEPPING BACK

We have looked at a number of recent and contemporary initiatives under the loose heading of denominator management. They all have a clear business rationale. Depending on both macro economic and individual company circumstance they may be desirable, necessary, even essential, sometimes the only way to assure corporate survival.

But they buy time rather than future success. They deliver a cost advantage in the here and now. But they do not confer long-term competitive advantage for two reasons. They are the tools of retrenchment rather than of expansion; the growth they create is exterior to the companies concerned, and benefits the likes of outsourced service providers, and underemployed graduates in developing countries. Also, the measures are transparent, any company can copy them, the only 'barriers to entry' are consultants' fees and redundancy payments.

So, such measures have a cause that we have explored at the start of the chapter, and they have a place in business operations. But they are not a substitute for creativity, for imagining the future, for seeing possibilities on the matrix of change.

2

The joining and unjoining of companies

If we start with the joining, most of it has been by means of merger and acquisition activity (M&A), a *leitmotiv* of the last 20 years or so, and in some industries longer.

To get a feel of it take a high profile industry we can all identify with – cars:

▌ **In the United States**: General Motors, itself created by at that time unprecedented merger activity in the 1920s, also acquired Vauxhall in the UK and Opel in Germany at the end of that decade; it began its takeover of Saab of Sweden in 1990, owns Izusu of Japan, and Suzuki of Japan is its affiliate.

Ford's cross-border expansion was originally organic, it opened its own plants in other countries, but in the last 15 years of the 20th century it variously acquired in the UK: Jaguar, Aston Martin and Land-Rover; and acquired Volvo in Sweden. Ford also has a stake in the Japanese car manufacturer Mazda.

Chrysler merged with Daimler Benz in 1999 (hence the American joke, how do you pronounce Daimler-Chrysler in German? Answer: the Chrysler is silent!) and Daimler-Chrysler also has a one third stake in Mitsubishi.

▐ **In Japan**: Honda, Subaru, and Toyota are independent, but Toyota owns Daihatsu.

▐ **In Europe**: Renault has a 36.9 per cent stake in Japan's Nissan. If one sorts through this little maze only three of Japan's eight well-known car firms are really wholly independent.

▐ **In France**: PSA is a fusion of the earlier independent companies of Peugeot and Citroën.

▐ **In the UK**: Rolls Royce kind of disappeared; BMW own them but cannot use the name, though some of the Rolls Royce models have BMW V12 engines and BMW are building a new facility for producing Rolls Royce, but at the moment at least Volkswagen own the name.

Austin Rover has been variously owned by British Aerospace, then in part by Honda of Japan, by BMW of Germany, and is now (2001) back in British ownership under Mercury.

▐ **In Germany**: VAG is a fusion of Volkswagen and Audi; it bought SEAT of Spain in 1986, and acquired Skoda of Czechoslovakia in the 1990s after the fall of European communism.

▐ **In Italy**: Fiat owns/absorbed Lancia, Alfa Romeo, Maserati, Ferrari, and at one stage acquired SEAT from Spain before selling it to VAG (Volkswagen-Audi) of Germany, as mentioned above.

The above is not an exhaustive summary but the main lines are clear.

There have been many whole or part changes of ownership in the car industry. These are in the direction of concentration; there are fewer manufacturers left, and they are bigger. A lot of the acquisition, both outright and of ownership stakes, has been cross-border.

Furthermore, M&A in the motor industry has a patterned design/production effect, namely the next generation of cars from the junior partner are based on the floor PAN and other parts from the bigger company. For example Saab models are now based on GM floor PANS, and cynics say the new Jaguar is basically a Ford Mondeo.

The main thrust of the first part of this chapter is that this concentration is a rather general phenomenon, not just something to which the auto industry with its emphasis on production volume and economies of scale lends itself.

Let us take as a second introductory example, a service industry – airlines. In a way airlines are quite a good test case of the hypothesis that there are strong forces conducive to concentration. First, as an industry, civilian aviation is a quarter of a century younger than automobile manufacture. Second and more important, airlines are typically:

▌ A focus of national esteem; they are 'national flag carriers'.

▌ Government owned, at least in Europe.

▌ Or, governments used to own them, and have only recently privatized them, not always completely (in Europe British Airways, fully privatized in 1986, is an exception).

In Europe it is unusual for foreign ownership above the 49 per cent level to be allowed; in the United States this limit is 25 per cent, the theory being that in time of war the Defense Department might want to sequestrate civilian airlines in the national interest.

All this makes cross-border acquisitions in civilian aviation rather difficult, in contrast as we have seen to the car industry. So what do we have?

▌ **In the United States**: American Airlines has acquired TWA, and one or two regional carriers. Delta bought some regional airlines, and own a low cost airline, and acquired some of the 'remains' of Pan Am. Both American Airlines and United Airlines have bought shares in DC Air. United Airlines tried to buy US Air in 2001 but failed.

▌ **In Canada**: Air Canada acquired Canadian International (and moved it from one global alliance to another).

▌ **In the UK**: British Airways over the years acquired Dan Air, British Caledonian, Brymon Airways and City Flyer; they also have a majority stake in Deutsche BA; in summer 2001 they sold GO to 3i, from whom they previously bought British Caledonian and City Flyer.

▌ **In the Netherlands**: KLM own City Hopper and KLM UK, as well as Buzz, the low cost subsidiary that started up in January 2000 flying out of Stanstead, England.

▌ **In Spain**: Iberia owns Inter Canarias and Binter Mediterraneo, and has a majority stake in the National carrier of Argentina; it is rumoured to want to sell Binter.

▌ **Norway, Sweden and Denmark** jointly own SAS (Sweden has the biggest stake). SAS acquired Braathens (Norwegian) before selling it to KLM and is expected to sell Malmö Airlines (Swedish) and Widerøe (Norwegian).

▌ **In France**: Air France acquired Air Inter plus a few regional carriers; Air Inter was transformed into Air France Europe.

▌ **In Switzerland**: Swissair acquired a big stake in Sabena of Belgium as well as the Swiss domestic carrier Crossair, and three French regionals – Air Litoral; Air Liberté; AOM – but then disposed of them, in the face of hostility from the labour unions, and from Air France and the French government. This of course was all before Swissair's brief bankruptcy in the autumn of 2001 and subsequent bail out/transformation. Sabena also went bankrupt in the autumn of 2001.

But maybe these dry facts about acquisition do not give a sense of the impact that may be felt in the industry. We will consider a small example in a small country – Switzerland.

Geneva is Switzerland's second airport after Zürich. In 1996 Swissair decided to concentrate its long haul flights in Zürich, taking all but one of these, a daily flight to New York, away from Geneva. This is devastating for Geneva.

Then along comes the UK's low cost airline easyJet and buys a Swiss charter company based in Basel. EasyJet switches most of its operations to Geneva, which has a regenerating effect. In 2000 Geneva airport's revenues went up by over 11 per cent, and easyJet became Geneva's second biggest customer.

There is another possible twist. It is folk wisdom in the industry that the low cost carriers in Europe, or the 'no frills' airlines as they prefer to be known, can only do short haul – journeys up to a maximum of two to two and a half hours. But it has never really been put to the test, and easyJet is regarded as the industry innovator in this market, implicitly modelled on South West Airlines in the United States. And if they did do it, where would they do it from?

But acquisitions in this case are only part of the story. We should also take note of ownership stakes:

▌ British Airways has a 20 per cent stake in Quantas of Australia, 10 per cent in Spain's Iberia, and a majority stake in Deutsche BA as already noted. During 2001 there was an industry rumour that British Airways might be seeking to buy a stake in Ireland's national carrier, Aer Lingus, perhaps the 30 per cent of Aer Lingus owned by the Irish government, but this initiative evaporated after the events of 11 September in the United States.

▌ Lufthansa has stakes in SAS and in British Midland.

▌ KLM of the Netherlands and Northwest of the United States are the oldest alliance partners in the business, and exchanged equity stakes; KLM also has stakes in Transavia and Martinair in Holland, as well as in Braathens of Norway and in Kenya Airways.

▌ Singapore Airlines has a 49 per cent stake in Virgin Atlantic and stakes in Air New Zealand and Ansett Australia. As of July 2001 Singapore Airlines is trying to buy more (than the 25 per cent stake they already have) of Air New Zealand, which in turn would give Singapore Airlines control of Ansett Australia since Air New Zealand already bought Rupert Murdoch's 50 per cent stake in Ansett Australia. Unfortunately Ansett went bankrupt in September 2001, before the 11 September attacks in the United States.

This is not an exhaustive list, but it shows the pattern. There is yet another element to this sketch of relationships between airlines, the plethora of strategic alliances. The first of these in the industry, the alliance between KLM and Northwest mentioned above, dates from the late 1980s. It is now known as the Wings alliance, and has been enlarged to include Continental of the United States and Kenya Airlines, and until talks broke down in the early summer of 2000 it was expected that Alitalia would be integrated into the alliance as well. In fact by the summer of 2001 Alitalia had instead joined the Sky Team alliance, led by Air France and Delta of the United Sates.

Two big alliances, however, stand out – One World and the Star Alliance. The big players in One World are American Airlines and British Airways and this alliance also includes Aer Lingus, Cathay

Pacific, Finnair, Iberia, LanChile, and Qantas. The Star Alliance on the other hand is dominated by United Airlines and Lufthansa plus Singapore Airline is given new consequence by its 49 per cent share in Virgin Atlantic (above), and Star also includes Varig of Brazil, British Midland, Air New Zealand, Tai Airways International, All Nippon Airways, Mexican Airlines, and Air Canada – Canadian International before being acquired by Air Canada was a member of the rival One World Alliance!

While these two, One World and Star, are far from being 'the only games in town' they are the biggest and most inclusive, and both include a major airline from Europe, Asia, and the United States. They tend to embrace:

▌ shared advertising and marketing;

▌ code sharing;

▌ reciprocal lounge access;

▌ consolidated frequent flyer programmes.

These alliances are at their best in offering 'seamless travel' to passengers flying different airlines in the same alliance on one journey, especially in the case of first class and business class passengers. And because Germany and the United States have an open skies agreement, but the UK and the United States do not, United and Lufthansa in the Star Alliance enjoy anti-trust immunity and can go further in initiatives such as schedule coordination and operational integration. At the time of writing (July 2001) British Airways and American Airlines had launched a joint lobbying offensive to move to a US–UK open skies agreement, which if successful would have conferred the same advantages on these two key players in the One World alliance, but at the start of 2002 it was clear that this initiative had failed, at any rate for the time being.

We have pressed the example of airlines because here we have an industry ripe for concentration in terms of:

▌ thin profit margins;

▌ ownership of expensive assets;

▌ world overcapacity, especially after the 1997-plus Asian meltdown and the 11 September 2001 terrorist attacks in New York and Washington.

Yet cross-border acquisition is impeded by government regulation and national sentiment, so that what we have in practice is:

▌ a lot of consolidation and ownership of subsidiaries, for example, KLM and British Airways buying up small carriers in their own countries;

▌ plenty of cross-border ownership stakes, but mostly minority stakes;

▌ loads of cross-border alliances (One World, Star Alliance, Sky Team, Wings, as well as Swissair's one time Qualifyer Alliance), as a proxy for cross-border acquisitions.

There is a school of thought that suggests that if governments come to relax foreign participation and ownership rules, there will be real cross-border consolidation along the lines of the present ownership stakes. The alliances also serve as surrogate acquisition activity with the emphasis on increasing market share and going for market dominance, rather than exploiting to the full the possibilities of cost saving.

In short, in their frustrated incompleteness the endeavours of the airlines are a testimony to the global force for concentration. This conviction that concentration, usually achieved by M&A activity, is a general phenomenon, by no means limited to the two industries just reviewed in snapshot style, is very much borne out by the companies visited in preparing to write this book. I always asked senior executives and business owners to comment on developments in their industries and concentration was mentioned with regard to:

Accountancy firms	Furniture retailing
Advertising agencies	Grocery retailing
Agricultural coops	Health care products
Air transportation	Health and leisure clubs
Autocomponents	Higher education
Auto manufacture	House building

Bed making	Ink-jet industrial products
Book publishing	Law firms
Book retailing	Machine tools
Beer brewing	Pharmaceuticals
Building materials	Road transport
Car retailing	Ship building
Charitable organizations	Shoe retailing
Chemicals	Steel
Civil engineering consultancy	Tableware and crockery
Computers	Textiles (domestic)
Corn merchants	Textile retailing
Farming	Waste disposal
Financial services	White goods
Food processing	Wholesale operations
Furniture manufacture	generally, especially in
	the United States

The above may not be an exhaustive list of industry sectors in the West, but there are enough positive examples for it to be telling evidence. What is more, the companies or organizations visited were picked on the basis of interest and accessibility, and above all in order to have a nice mix of 'shapes and sizes' – a lot of different industries, old and new, big and small companies, public as well as private sector, and spread across several Western countries though with most of the companies in the UK. In other words the companies were not picked with the intent to show the presence or absence of concentration, but the trend was identified by representatives of most of the industries included. And many interviewees identified their own companies as being part of this industry trend, as being engaged in M&A activity, being the product of M&A, or being constantly on the lookout for acquisition targets.

These M&As of course bring increased market share, but perhaps more important are the much talked about synergies. Sometimes these synergies can be new channels to market for existing products using channels already established by the M&A partner. But often the synergies are mainly cost savings based on people reduction, closure of duplicate production facilities or service outlets, and simplification of the supplier network together with administrative and IT harmonization.

CONCENTRATION IN CONTEXT

This widespread and continuing process of concentration clearly results from the 'big picture' forces outlined in Chapter 1 where:

▌ the end of *les trentes glorieuses*;

▌ overcapacity;

▌ mature markets in the West;

in turn lead to intensification of competition and internationalization of competition; which in turn drive concentration through M&A.

To put it another way these forces make it more likely that stronger companies will want to:

▌ dominate their industries;

▌ grab market share;

▌ expand internationally, and compete in all major world markets;

▌ absorb weaker rivals;

while the weaker companies are at the same time more vulnerable than they would have been in earlier times.

VARIATIONS ON A THEME

While the cause and effect may be clear, this does not mean that concentration is a simple phenomenon, standardized in its manifestation. Underlying some of the variation is the idea that it is dynamic not static, its manifestation varies over time, it is configured differently from situation to situation. In practice there are lots of quirks and anomalies.

One strand is that consolidation may range over different corporate size strata. Consider for example the house building industry in the UK. There is no doubt that it is consolidating. For example, as of June 2001 some 55 building companies accounted for 85 per cent of output; some 25 companies for 65 per cent; and the top 10 or 12 for around 45 per cent. But here is the interesting thing: in the 1990s consolidation was in the form of top tier companies taking over regional builders, but now it is about top tier firms acquiring each other. Indeed in the spring of 2001 there was even a case of a second tier company, Taylor Woodrow, buying a top tier builder, Bryant. And there is a general expectation that top tier consolidation has further to go, albeit some-what restrained by the fact that the stock market tends not to like the construction industry, which leads to construction company shares being undervalued. This in turn impedes takeover activity ('paper deals', shares for shares, are more difficult if your shares are under-rated).

Another variation is that concentration may occur in different corporate size strata of the same industry perhaps overlapping in time. Consider brewing in the UK. Until the mid-1990s it was common to speak of the 'big six' brewers in the UK having a national market share of around 80 per cent. These brewers were:

Bass plc;
Allied-Lyons;
Whitbread;
Grand Metropolitan;
Scottish and Newcastle Breweries;
Courage.

Less than 10 years later these six have been transformed by M&As (Scottish and Newcastle merged with Courage) while others variously gave up their public houses, sold their brewing interests, and diversi-fied into (other) leisure activities and into the hospitality industry so that by 2001 it was a question of the Big Three, namely:

I   Carlsberg-Tetley (Danish);

I   Interbrew (Belgian) – Stella Artois plus other acquisitions including Labatt of Canada and Becks of Germany plus Bass of Britain, renamed;

I   Scottish-Courage (British).

From six to three, and only one of them British, in a traditional beer-drinking country, the land that invented pubs!

But this is not the whole story. Micro-breweries, brewing up to 200 barrels a week, have also been flourishing, and there are a lot of them.

Again there is stratification among the micros, with some 80 per cent of them producing (only) up to 50 barrels a week. The problem is that a lot of these micros are privately owned by enthusiasts, who will tend to hang on, relatively indifferent to profit levels. What they are enthusiastic about is top-brewed, cask-conditioned (ie secondary fermentation of the beer in barrels, resulting from injected yeast and sugar) real ale, having a darker hue than lager. So the expectation in the industry at the micro-level is that there will be a corresponding shakeout at the bottom-end, with enthusiast driven, small output, thin margin micro-brewers eliminated, with only a dozen or two micros, the bigger and better equipped ones, surviving.

Another twist is that there are sometimes clumps of concentration, where several related industries – typically related as component suppliers to end-product manufacturers – 'concentrate'. The first time this phenomenon caught our eye was in the furniture industry. Visiting in quick succession one French and one UK company that made beds, the testimony was that:

▌ there was concentration among bed manufacturers;

▌ and among producers of flock (the stuff you put in mattresses);

▌ and among spring-manufacturers, led by Leggett and Platt of Carthage, Missouri; Leggett and Platt are legendary in the industry having bought spring-makers and/or relevant machinery-manufacturers in the UK, Denmark, and Switzerland.

BI-POLARIZATION

ESC Lyon, a distinguished business school in France, organized a study of business trends in the early 1990s across four industries – banking, publishing, brewing, and the car industry – in seven of the EU countries including all the big players – UK, France, Germany, and Italy. This study has an interesting implication for the present discussion of the dynamics of concentration. The research identified the phenomenon of bi-polarization, as a reality and as a trend.

Bi-polarization refers to the tendency for industries to break down into big companies on the one hand and small companies on the other, with the middle ground of medium-sized companies being progressively eliminated. The big companies get bigger, more powerful, and fewer in number – the key theme of the first part of this chapter. But at the same time some small companies, typically serving rather particular niche markets, continue to flourish. What lies between these poles, the medium-sized generalist companies, decline.

A good example thrown up by this French study is the brewing industry in the UK. As we have already seen there is concentration at the top, a plethora of micro-breweries, and a progressive decline in the regional brewers, ones that are more than local, but serve only a part of the UK national market and are or were often identified with a particular area, like Tetley's in Yorkshire or Wolverhampton and Dudley in the West Midlands. Until the early 1990s, these regionals were a significant part of the industry, but now many are gone, or live on as part of the portfolio of brands offered by the big players.

As one of the European interviewees, a senior manager in a French brewing company, said back in 1990:

> The first phenomenon is the phenomenon of size. I think that for breweries, the intermediary size will not exist anymore. Either you are a small brewer, not in direct competition with the big ones, and you install yourself in market niches which are too small to interest the big companies, or you have to be big. This logic leads to two poles, on the one hand very large companies, and on the other, small focused dynamic companies. I do not believe in middle-sized companies between these two extremes.

But if all you have is examples from four industries and from a study that is no longer recent, it is a bit risky to talk about a trend! For this reason, and because I had taken part in the French study doing some of the company interviews in the UK and in the Netherlands and writing the book that presented the findings (Calori and Lawrence, 1991), I was keen to look for examples of bi-polarization in other industries 10 years later, but I did it gently, raising it as a possibility in interviews with executives and business owners. The trend was often confirmed, and in a variety of industries.

Let us start with a non-European example, farming in the upper mid-west of the United States. Figure 2.1 shows the response I got from the head of an agricultural cooperative when asking about different sized farms.

Nice example, yet may be it seems a bit circumstantial. But sometimes there is a special reason driving the bi-polarization. Consider the house building industry in the UK. Building the houses is not that difficult, the tricky bit is getting hold of the land and the planning permission to go with it.

Small farms	Guy has another job; probably a factory job; farms on the side; OK, can pay us (the coop) to do the application services
Mid-sized farms	Not OK; not scientific; not moved with the timesn no non-farm income
Big farms	Fine; business-like; Economies of scale

Figure 2.1

To buy the land you need either local knowledge or big company clout. Local knowledge will allow you to get at small lots, maybe even buying them before they come onto the market. But bigger companies will be able to buy in bigger blocks, and actually build up 'a land bank'. And some of the land deals are huge, and are bought by consortia, and only big companies will be taken seriously as consortia members. A fairly recent (June, 2001) example of a consortium purchase would be the USAAF Upper Heyford airforce base (both US and UK airforce bases are coming onto the market as a result of the end of the Cold War).

In short, land acquisition favours the big or the small, for different reasons, but not the medium-sized builder. The struggle for planning permission, granted or withheld by local authorities, breaks the same way, and is often the subject of black humour in the building industry. As one interviewee put it: 'The typical planning officer is called Mildred, and she has just gone on maternity leave!' This is a reference to planning departments being understaffed. When local government has had to make cost-saving cuts, planning was an obvious victim – after all, you cannot cut welfare administration or refuse collection, an idea expressed by another interviewee:

> It's like MAFF (the British Ministry of Agriculture, Fisheries and Food, very much in the news during the 2001 foot and mouth disease outbreak) trying to fight foot and mouth with seven vets when they need about fourteen thousand.

Again, there is a big solution and a small solution. The small company solution is local knowledge and contacts. The big solution is 'buying' planning officers from the local authorities, massively increasing their salaries and at the same time exacerbating the shortage in the public sector – a nice competitive move this, like one side buying up the world's supply of ammunition before the other shoots. At the same time the big builders, of course, will have a myriad of ongoing planning applications in different regions, where there will always be one deal on the point of completion.

But if US agriculture and UK house building have their zany touches, there is a common and comprehensible dynamic which runs through bi-polarization. It goes like this. Companies will have to choose between being big players in their industries, reaching an overall critical size, or focusing on one or two niches or segments to reinforce their competitive advantage. The choice between big and small tends to be decided by:

▌ Increased market segmentation; formerly homogenous markets that start to break down into different segments serving groups of buyers with different wants and needs;

▌ which development is fuelled by the maturity of many markets (an idea considered in Chapter 1);

▌ and by increasing product development and marketing costs;

▌ sometimes accompanied by shortening product life cycles in some cases.

All of the above activity will take place in the context of deregulation and enhanced competition.

So the essence is that the big players will strengthen their advantage by reaching a critical mass and serving the whole market, where 'whole' is increasingly understood internationally. These companies should enjoy economies of scale, that is reduced unit costs, thanks to higher volumes. And also economies of scope, economies arising from sharing resources and skills and from synergies between businesses. Their relatively greater size should also allow them to exploit their bargaining power with suppliers, and sometimes also with customers.

Whereas some other companies will strengthen their competitive position by focusing on one or two niches and serving them with perfectly adapted products or services.

This classic dynamic was clear in a number of industries researched in the run up to writing this book. Examples are shown in Figure 2.2.

Retailing often offers nice easy-to-grasp examples of bi-polarization in action. We might windup this discussion with a look at a homely, US small town. The town of Aberdeen, South Dakota, has a population of around 25,000, though it would be fair to say it has a standing beyond its size because:

▌ It is a college town (home of Northern State University).

▌ It is a medical centre.

▌ It benefits from being 'the town' in a thinly populated area (South Dakota's total population is about 700,000; cf. Minnesota, South Dakota's next door neighbour, with 4.4 million).

Aberdeen has the usual edge of town mall, with departmental discount clothes retailers, but it also has an independent up-scale men's clothes shop, in the original downtown area, appropriately named The Main. There used to be six of these independents, The Main is the only survivor.

The advantages of the chain stores are obvious, but how has The Main survived? Part of it is that The Main is a story of endless upgrading since it opened in 1951:

army and navy surplus → work clothes → sportswear
→ suits and jackets

In particular, going upmarket has been The Main's response to the opening of the mall. So it is offering a better range, and better quality, including some classy brands from Canada that do not usually get exported; and in part neutralizes its size disadvantage via a buying consortium representing some 400 independents. In addition:

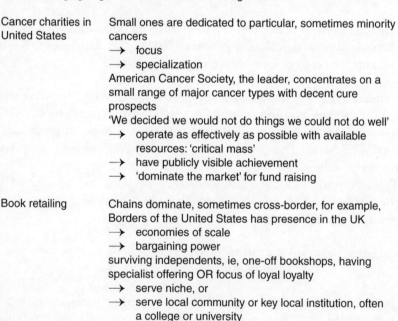

Civil engineering	Small firms specialize, for example in bridge design, and tend to be specalist structural firms → specialist know-how and quality service. Big consultancies do everything, or at least can take on a range of loosely related assignments → economies of scope → enhanced bargaining power → access to bigger clients wanting 'one stop' service.
Road haulage	Big operators can provide nationwide/worldwide service → economies of scale and scope → bargaining power Small operators offer → flexibility → availability can oblige local customers with irregular needs; sub-contract work from large operators.

This bi-polarization in road haulage is also driven by what in the industry is known as 'back-haul percentage', that is, the extent to which trucks make the return journey with a new consignment paid for usually by a second customer, not the receiver of the outward journey load. A big fleet operator can get up to 85 per cent paid back hauls, whereas the smaller specialist operator usually returns empty unless managing to get a sub-contract from a large haulier.

Cancer charities in United States	Small ones are dedicated to particular, sometimes minority cancers → focus → specialization American Cancer Society, the leader, concentrates on a small range of major cancer types with decent cure prospects 'We decided we would not do things we could not do well' → operate as effectively as possible with available resources: 'critical mass' → have publicly visible achievement → 'dominate the market' for fund raising
Book retailing	Chains dominate, sometimes cross-border, for example, Borders of the United States has presence in the UK → economies of scale → bargaining power surviving independents, ie, one-off bookshops, having specialist offering OR focus of loyal loyalty → serve niche, or → serve local community or key local institution, often a college or university

Figure 2.2

I The premises are quite new; and big, certainly for a small town.

I It has good customer relations, including a relaxed regime on returned goods.

I It is the natural choice for the 30–50-year-olds wanting newer and neater clothing.

I Its sales staff are older, better paid, more formally dressed than other sales staff.

I It sales staff are often long-serving, with superior product knowledge.

I It has enhanced its image by advertising in the right places.

Finally, if you want the services of an independent men's clothes retailer, the next nearest options are in Fargo and Sioux Falls, both about 200 miles away. (Never underestimate the power of a big catchment area: Wal-Mart's top store by sales per square foot is the one in Laredo, Texas, with a catchment area of a 150 mile radius, both sides of the border!)

But The Main is not the only example the town of Aberdeen has to offer. At the intersection of State Street and Sixth Avenue is Kessler's, a third generation, family-owned, up-market independent grocery store. Finding Kessler's is like finding Fortnum and Mason's set down on the US prairies. There are live lobsters in a tank, a remarkable delicatessen, a range of cheeses unusual in the United States, an extensive meat section, and loads of staff to serve you and answer your queries.

Again, it is a case of a mix of advantages, in Kessler's case they include:

I location;

I quality and range;

I service;

I one-stop features, including liquor store and in-store bank;

I being the focus of local affection.

Kessler's faces all the usual chain-discount competition, including a Wal-Mart in the edge of the town mall. Yet its surveys show a 62 per cent customer loyalty, that is, this is the proportion who say they 'would not shop anywhere else'.

This is how the niche players do it in the age of bi-polarization. Both these retailers are appealing to a section of the market that wants quality/choice/service, rather than recourse to the chain store alternatives, and both have put together a web of competitive advantage. I have deliberately picked examples from a quiet, rural part of the US rather than from Rodeo Drive, Beverly Hills, for greater impact!

Franchises occupy a tantalizingly difficult to pin down role between the big and the small in the bi-polarization debate. If you take McDonald's or Starbucks, or hotel and motel chains like Best Western or Super 8, or in Europe retailers such as Spar or Aldi or Londis, such franchises enjoy many of the advantages associated with the big player, variously including:

▌ central support for the brand;

▌ heavy promotional expenditures;

▌ advantages of bulk buying, enjoying (vicarious) clout with suppliers;

▌ administrative integration;

▌ standardized business plans;

▌ central reservations systems; and so on.

Yet at the same time by definition the franchisees are the small players, the bottom stratum in the bi-polarization model. We would like to suggest that franchising reinforces the idea of bi-polarization, even if the bottom layer is cross-fertilized with the upper layer.

COUNTER CONCENTRATION

In business competitive advantage is a zero-sum game. You can only enjoy it at someone else's expense.

So when industries are juxtaposed – in the value chain, in the distribution system, in supplier–manufacturer or manufacturer–retailer pairs, or whatever – there is a tendency for concentration in one industry to provoke or at least to be accompanied by concentration in the associated industry.

Again the brewing industry in the UK is a good example. The concentration in this industry has already been noted. But side-by-side with this is a high level of retail concentration, that is to say of concentration among those places where beer is sold – English pubs.

In order to stimulate competition in 1989 the then Monopolies and Mergers Commission promulgated the Beer Orders, requiring the UK brewers to divest themselves of (most of) their pubs. This had several consequences:

▌ Some of the brewers closed their brewery interest and became concentrated pub-owners/operators.

▌ A lot of pubs came onto the market, and that led to entrepreneurial activity, particularly in the form of MBIs (management buy-ins) with managers with experience acquiring (mostly smallish) pub and pub–restaurant chains.

▌ But most of the pubs were formed into big blocks, with non-traditional (non-brewing) owners, and the blocks were securitized against their rental income; the biggest owner of UK pubs for some time was the Japanese bank Nomura with some 4,000 pubs.

So, for the most part, a consolidated brewing industry confronts a consolidated beer retail industry. It is a tense situation, with the brewers protesting that their produce has been commoditized, their margins depressed, that the balance of power has swung to the retailers, and that they, the brewers, have no choice but to engage in the denominator management practices outlined in Chapter 1. Perhaps indicatively, one of the major brewers claimed to have reduced the cost of its distribution operation by 25 per cent, mainly by actual wage reduction rather than by reducing the headcount among distribution workers.

Publishing and book-retailing is another example. Cross-border consolidation among publishers was revealed by the French study of the early 1990s, referred to earlier, and this consolidation among publishers is very much in evidence in the UK, especially the growth area of business and management books. But again this concentration in publishing has been matched by concentration in book retailing, where for the most part independent bookshops have declined to be replaced by chain retailers. And again it is a very tense situation, with the publishers often claiming that the retail chains:

▎ Demand advance information on forthcoming books, in months not weeks, but don't do anything with it.

▎ Expect the publisher to do the selling and the promotion.

▎ Want to handle everything on a sale or return basis, and then abuse the trade credit terms.

▎ This sale and return policy is made easier by EPOS (electronic point of sale) monitoring, so that it is easy for bookshops to know how many copies they have sold of each title; some publishers say that this does not lead to more discriminate buying by the bookchains, but to just a crude mechanism for getting rid of unsold books.

▎ It is now increasingly difficult for publishers to sell 'back-list titles' (books that already exist as opposed to books newly published) unless the publisher can pitch some story to the book chains – a link to a TV series, or an adoption by a university, or whatever.

But if you talk to the bookshop chains you hear different things, of course:

▎ That there is competition from the growing supermarket chains who now have 11–12 per cent of the retail book market, selling top fiction titles and a few popular non-fiction items such as Delia Smith's cookery books – all heavily discounted, of course.

▎ That there is also competition from Internet companies, and Amazon, it is said in the trade, discount up to 50 per cent.

▎ That publishers have an annoying habit of printing the price on the book or dust jacket even though the net book agreement (a species of industry specific retail price maintenance) was abolished in 1995; this makes it more difficult for the book retailers to engage in imaginative and flexible pricing or to try their hands at category pricing.

▌ That publishers are always wanting to send their sales reps into the bookshops; there are too many of them, and it wastes the time of local management; one book chain with decentralized buying, ie, buying decisions made at branch not corporate level, spoke of ordering its branch managers to limit calls to reps from the top 10 publishers for each branch; the reps who are excluded get to put their books in a newsletter sent to all branches.

▌ That universities are selling bookshop space more keenly, and switching between book chains for a better deal, which puts up the retailers' costs.

▌ That publishers should not moan if they are faced by mega book chains; after all, the publishers encouraged this counter concentration in book retailing by offering discounts for volume when they could have been subsidizing independent bookshops.

A final twist to the story is that there is now a third tranche of related concentration, the formation of library (and particularly of university library) buying consortia, to put pressure on all the previous links in the chain and try to neutralize the market dominance that derives from up-the-chain concentration.

This industry-pair example has been worked through in detail because it illustrates the dynamics rather nicely, as shown in Figure 2.3.

overcapacity and enhanced competiton

→ concentration;

→ counter concentration;

→ a tense interface, with mutual recrimination

Figure 2.3

There seems to be no natural reason why even longer chains of counter concentration among interfacing industries should not occur. Consider the chain of concentration in Figure 2.4, based on practitioner testimonies from some related industries in the UK.

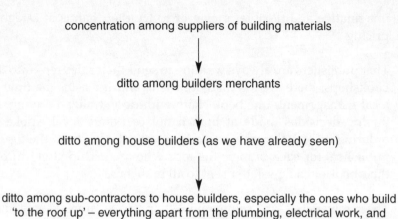

concentration among suppliers of building materials

↓

ditto among builders merchants

↓

ditto among house builders (as we have already seen)

↓

ditto among sub-contractors to house builders, especially the ones who build 'to the roof up' – everything apart from the plumbing, electrical work, and kitchen fitting

One might eventually be able to add concentration among home loan providers and home insurers to this chain of related concentration.

Figure 2.4

STOCKTAKING

We began this chapter by arguing that concentration is a near universal phenomenon, and offered some evidence and examples. Bi-polarization and counter concentration are not universal, one can find industries and businesses where they are not occurring, but they are not common. And we have tried to unveil the dynamics driving them, and these suggest they are likely to become more widespread.

UNJOINING

The last 20 years have seen a lot of unjoining of companies in a quite literal sense. As diversification became unfashionable and the idea of core business became more and more *de rigueur*, companies increasingly sold off non-core interests.

We have already noted breweries getting out of soft drinks, or in the UK selling their pubs to concentrate on their brewing, or selling their brewing capacity to concentrate on pub–restaurant chains. But this 'core business leads to sell-offs' is not just a feature of traditional industries with stable technologies. Consider for example Alcatel of France. In 1995 when CEO Serge Tchuruk took over, Alcatel was a conglomerate. It encompassed high speed trains, nuclear power plants, magazines, radio stations, and even a few vineyards. But by 2001 it has become a streamlined supplier of telecomms equipment that might be ranked alongside such North American stars as Cisco, Lucent, and Nortel. That means a lot of sell-offs.

Or to take a UK example, the Glasgow based engineering group Weir announced in July 2001 its intention to close three of its non-core businesses, and to sell a fourth. Slated for closure were:

I tooling products in Hampshire;

I G Perry (auto parts) in Leicester;

I Strachan and Henshaw (nuclear engineering) in Manchester.

Attempts to sell these three had not come to anything, but Weir announced it would sell another non-core business, Weir Systems, its software and IT division.

The declared purpose of all this as reported in the *Financial Times* was: to concentrate on its core pumps and valves operation, where it enjoyed significant market share. In further pursuit of this objective the COO anticipated strengthening pumps by acquisition, and disposing of more non-core business in the future.

The core business movement, given a big boost in 1982 with the publication of *In Search of Excellence* with its emphasis on 'stick to the knitting' (Peters and Waterman, 1982), is in part fad, fashion and ideology. Yet like the typical fad and fashion that catches on, it does have a rationale. Quite simply if a company does only one thing, seeks to be a player in a single product market or at most in some related product/market segments, then more people will have more focus, there should be more corporate critical mass, the company has a better chance of becoming a key player, of coming to dominate its market.

This is not to say that core business like the poor will always be with us, but when the fashion changes so will the rationale. Visiting companies in the run-up to writing this book, however, I noted some more subtle versions of 'unjoining', of things being taken out of companies, being given up, or being delegated forward or backward along the value chain.

SHALLOW MANUFACTURE

US consultant Hermann Simon coined the term 'deep manufacture' (1996) in a book celebrating the achievements of a group of mid-sized, mid-tech companies in Germany. The companies in his sample were ones that dominated their market, often a niche or series of niches. I have chosen one or two examples that may help to give the sense of the thing, picking companies I have also visited. Hauni Werke Koerber, a company a little way outside Hamburg, makes cigarette-making machinery. It is the world's only supplier of complete systems for processing tobacco. All the filter cigarettes in the world are made with Hauni machines. Maschinenfabrik Rudolf Baader, on the edge of the city of Lübeck close to the Baltic coast, makes fish-processing equipment. Simon gives their world market share as 90 per cent. Another example is Brita which invented point of use water filters and has a world market share of 85 per cent.

In Simon's view *Technik* is in the foreground: 'Technology is the single most important factor behind the competitive advantages and global market leadership of the hidden champions.' (Simon, 1996: 124). Developing this idea Simon argues that part of his company's attachment to *Technik* is that they do as much as they can of the operation in-house, including on occasion making their own manufacturing tools and testing equipment. This inclination to do all they can is what Hermann Simon means by deep manufacture.

Fine so far. Homage to Germany! And where else would machines for taking bones out of fish have been identified as such a mega business opportunity?

But among the companies I have visited in the last two to three years exactly the opposite trend has been observable. From Texas Instruments in Dallas, to the Black Sheep brewery in Masham, Yorkshire, I have been given examples of things now done by others that were formerly done in-house, or at least that normally would be in the industry in question.

Take brewing. Maybe I ought not to be proud of this but I have now visited breweries in Australia, Belgium, Canada, Denmark, Germany, Holland, Norway, Sweden, Switzerland, the United States, and lots in my native UK. Something I have noticed over time is an increasing tendency, especially among the UK breweries, to outsource the bottling operation. That is to say the brewery makes the beer but some other company puts it into kegs, barrels, cans, or bottles.

Or take UK furniture companies. One making beds used to make their own springs, but now buys them in. The CEO of another observed: 'We have become more of an assembly operation. We used to have our own woodmill; I closed it. It is more effective to buy units ready machined.'

The same phenomenon could be observed in the (UK) house building industry, at this stage as much an aspiration as a trend, where it was argued that quality and efficiency would be improved by buying in more complete and ready to fit units from factories rather than trying to make or assemble them on site, often in poor weather conditions.

A *leitmotiv* here is a tendency for producers of the finished item to push more responsibility back onto their suppliers. A machine tool company in the US West is a good example of a supplier at the receiving end of this trend. Its CEO claimed:

> We are doing design, development and modifications for customers. We want to know the customer's business. We ask them 'What do you want it for?' We are helping them to find solutions, to reduce their manufacturing costs, and to make more profit.

Another interesting development at this US machine tool company is that some of the machines they produced were not sold at all but retained on-site to do work for end-manufacturers who in earlier times would have bought the machines and done the work themselves.

The motor industry offers another example, or more properly a vision of this phenomenon taken further. Industry spokesmen suggest there may come a time when although they will continue to own the factories and operate the assembly lines, the suppliers, instead of delivering the bits to the back door and leaving, would come through the front door and fit them. Successive waves of suppliers doing this would magically produce whole cars, leaving the car manufacturers (Ford is a particularly good example) to concentrate on what they do best – design, styling, marketing, and, above all, financing.

German performance car manufacturer Porsche, as profiled in *Forbes*, is a neat example of the trend in that up-market part of the industry where one would least expect it (Meredith, 2002), a source that throws up some fascinating facts:

▌ Porsche is big on outsourcing; 75 per cent at least of every Porsche is manufactured by suppliers.

▌ For the ever popular, long running Porsche 911 the outsourced parts total 80 per cent of each unit; axles, hoods, brakes, doors come from suppliers; Britain's GKN supplies all the constant-velocity joints for the drive-line.

▌ The outsourcing led to a 17 per cent reduction in the Porsche workforce in the early 1990s.

But the best bit is the arrival of a Porsche SUV (sports utility vehicle) in the autumn of 2002, the Cayenne. It will only be assembled in a Porsche factory, not the traditional factory in Stuttgart but at a new one in Leipzig in the former East Germany. Only 12 per cent of the Cayenne's content will come from Porsche, principally the V8 engine. And Porsche has cooperated with Volkswagen to develop a joint platform, on which the two companies will build somewhat different SUV models. Whatever impression all this makes on traditionalists it is certainly putting costs down and profits up. What is more it is probably raising quality as well.

One of the companies visited was a component supplier to several auto-manufacturers. These, the company chairman claimed, would encourage the supplier to be innovative, to come up with embellishments that will give the end product a little competitive advantage. So the supplier concerned does the development work, comes up with something good for the manufacturer who buys it and then drives the price down. The chairman commented dryly: 'There is no such thing as partnership!'

There is another variation on this theme of shallow manufacture, that is nicely illustrated by UK academic publishers, by which we mean UK publishers who are primarily selling to universities – to university libraries, to professional academics, and above all to students. There is good news and bad news from a business standpoint.

First the bad news: from 1981 successive UK governments have reduced university funding in real terms. Libraries have ever tighter budgets, and as we have seen are forming buying consortia to get leverage over the suppliers of books. At the same time students have seen their traditional grants converted into repayable bank loans, have had to pay fees from 1996, and are unbelievably resistant to the idea of spending money on books that could be better spent on fun.

Now the good news: there are more of them (students)! Over 30 per cent of the age group eligible to enter higher education was doing so by the end of the 20th century. The result:

massive classes → standarization → dependence on a
single textbook

The publishers have responded. Away with research monographs and the scholarly reflections of academics, up with textbooks, strive to commission them, fight for market share. So these academic publishers are commissioning fewer titles, are concentrating their endeavours, selling more of less. This is the paradigm:

BEFORE	AFTER
monographs	textbooks
more titles	fewer titles
dispersed sales	concentrated sales
CRAFT INDUSTRY	MASS PRODUCTION

DISPERSING THE VALUE CHAIN

Finally we would like to put down a marker for a more metaphoric manifestation of 'unjoining'. This is that there is a tendency for the sequence of activities that have traditionally constituted the value chain in particular industries to get dispersed, broken up or re-arranged in some way.

As we saw in the previous section the manufacturing part of the chain is most vulnerable. Manufacturing is variously:

▌ simplified or slimmed down as in 'shallow manufacture';

▌ passed back to component or sub-assembly suppliers;

▌ outsourced;

▌ outsourced cross-border.

Just consider all the Silicon Valley firms that conceive, design, test, and market but do not actually make anything.

Another candidate for dispersal is the distribution part of the chain, even in businesses which are really about providing *and delivering a* product or service, though this was a trend more common in the UK than in the United States.

Perhaps the more general point is that one needs to be alive to the possibility of value chain dispersal, wherever it may be. It is clearly driven by the idea that companies:

▌ do some things better than they do others;

▌ make more money on some parts of the operation than on others;

▌ derive more competitive advantage from control of some links in the chain than from others.

As one distribution-outsourcing CEO put it: 'If it does not give you advantage, you have to ask why you are doing it.'

THE GRAND CONCERN

▌ Concentration, more industries dominated by fewer but larger companies, is near universal.

▌ This proposition was illustrated by a quick look at car manufacturing and civil aviation.

▌ Concentration is linked to overcapacity in many industries, and to enhanced competition.

▌ The dynamic of bi-polarization has been explored and illustrated – the big get bigger, the small hang in, and the mid-sized disappear.

▌ The phenomenon of counter concentration has been explored, where concentration in one industry provokes concentration in an adjacent and interdependent industry.

▌ Divestment in line with the emphasis on core business has been reviewed, together with the dynamic of 'shallow manufacture'.

In the next two chapters we would like to take up a new theme, that of the emergence in the West of a more unified view of business and management.

First we will try to evidence the growth of this view, showing how the values of private sector business have increasingly come to dominate the public sector and the operations of non-profit-making organizations at a time when the state is reducing its responsibilities and activities. We also seek to illustrate the spread of this unified view of management, which we call the management consensus, to countries that previously espoused distinct, non-Anglo-Saxon views of management.

Second we take four very different organizations, different kinds of operation from different countries, and profile their recent developments. Then we argue across the four cases to suggest common elements, the essence of a new management deriving from the consensus.

3

Managerial consensus

The increase in competition explored in Chapter 1 is a universal phenomenon. We want to suggest here that it has evoked a near-universal response in terms of a cross-border, cross-sector view of how organizations should be run, of what both the mechanics and dynamics should be.

PUBLIC AND PRIVATE

One obvious manifestation of the managerial consensus is that the public sector has been taken over by the private. Deregulation and privatization have been real forces over the past 20 years, more obvious in the UK in the 1979–97 period of Conservative governments, then in the 1990s, and still in progress in the countries of Continental Europe. Even the United States with its smaller initial public sector has seen some moves in the same direction with, for example, airline deregulation in 1978, and telecommunications deregulation in 1996. Typically, in the West, gas, electricity and water utilities have been privatized, so have mail services, telecomms and rail transport; civil aviation is deregulated and national carrier airlines are privatized (some of the Continental European airlines are still part owned by their national governments). Nothing is safe: the United States has privately run penitentiaries, there is talk in the UK of privatizing jails, privatizing air traffic control, and for ages loans to college students in the UK have been provided by banks, as in the United States.

'HONEY WE'VE SHRUNK THE STATE'

Behind all this privatization and deregulation there is something larger, a changed conception of the role of the state, especially in Europe. This change is part ideology, and part objective circumstance.

The ideology is loosely part of the managerial consensus we are endeavouring to unpack. The ideas of 'tax and spend', government indebtedness, the mission of governments to reduce socio-economic inequality among their citizens, governments as the provider 'of last resort' for all who are needy – all this is out of fashion. And there is a fashion element here. For a period that stretched from the end of the Second World War until the 1980s all these dispositions were in fashion – but no more.

But as with all changes of ideology (fashion) one can find 'good reasons'. Consider:

▌ Government indebtedness was much more acceptable in the period of *les trentes glorieuses*, the period of post-war economic expansion, where today's indebtedness could be offset against tomorrow's growth.

▌ Higher inflation in earlier decades eroded some of the indebtedness anyway.

▌ National economies tended to be more compartmentalized; now the 'no man is an island' dictum applies more to states than to individuals; a kind of global transparency has arrived.

As a tangible working out of the last point consider the Single European Market measures of 1992–93, the attempt to make more of a reality of 'the common market' by eliminating non-tariff barriers within the EU – a movement given a further thrust by the introduction of the Euro (the Single European Currency). Without fiscal harmonization states have become competitors both for corporations and for talented individuals.

This is a serious issue for some countries. Consider Sweden. Sweden has low FDI (foreign direct investment) because of the tax régime, but there is a readiness on the part of non-Swedes to buy shares in Swedish companies. Some 20–40 per cent of the shares of telecommunications giant LM Ericsson, for example, are said to be owned by guess who – the UK and US pension funds.

At the end of the 20th century an 'ebbing away' of the Swedish corporate state was observable. Again, Ericsson had for some time had a substantial R&D operation in Crawley, southern England – sufficiently sizeable for there to be a Swedish language school for the children of employees. In October 1998 Ericsson announced it was introducing performance-related pay, and was hammered by the trade unions for this initiative. Not long after Ericsson announced that it was moving the head office to London – though the company continues to be incorporated in Sweden.

Not an isolated case. Pharmacia of Sweden merged with Upjohn of the United States, and moved the head office to London in the first instance. Nordbanken, one of the big three Swedish banks, merged with a Finnish bank and it now has headquarters in Finland. Ingvar Kamprad, founder of Ikea, now has his corporate office in Denmark. Car makers Volvo and Saab, as we have seen, have passed into foreign ownership, and so it goes on. Sweden is simply an easy case to illustrate, but this ethic of global transparency and inter-country comparability is general.

The whole idea is neatly caught by UK economist McRae in an article under the title I have used as a heading to this section (McRae, 2001). He gives government spending as a proportion of GDP for a group of Western countries over the period 1980–2002 (the last bit of the period is a projection). McRae's diagram plotting the development over the period is fascinating and shows that:

I   The proportion is lower in the United States than almost anywhere else mentioned.

I   In 2000 it was lower in the UK at 38 per cent than in any of the Continental European countries considered (for example, France 51 per cent; Italy 47 per cent; Germany 43 per cent).

I   The proportion in Sweden was highest in 1980 at 60 per cent, and still is, although it has come down.

▌ All the countries have registered a fall against 1980 (though with one or to of them tilting up at bit at the end of the period).

▌ The Netherlands and Ireland show the most dramatic reductions; particularly remarkable in the case of the Netherlands which back in the 1970s was seen as a more southerly version of Sweden with its public affluence and welfare provision.

Demographics and medical advance are also likely to propel this trend. Ageing populations are a burden on the tax-paying, wealth-generating portion of the population, and the emergence of ever more resourceful, and costly, medical treatments pushes up the health care budget.

But the takeover of the public sector by the private is not just a matter of economics. There is also a change of mindset, whereby the public service has bought into the managerial consensus.

Public service ethic?

Cleaning out the office recently I came across a book I wrote in the 1980s entitled *Invitation to Management*. The impetus for it came from the publisher, it was part of a series, and the publisher's exhortation at the time was to write a book that would 'turn on' students going into business administration courses. It was to be something they might read the summer before going to college. I looked eagerly to see what, if anything, I had said in this book on the public sector–private sector distinction, and found it revealing. Back in the 1980s I made a strong case for difference between public and private using some arguments that are relevant to the discussion here.

First, I suggested, every decision in business organizations has two elements – one about do-ability, feasibility, technical viability and so on, and the other element is the impact on profit. This differentiated business organizations from public sector or non-profit-making ones. Second, I suggested that there is a marked difference in ethos with the public sector and especially the state administration emphasizing probity, procedural rectitude, impersonality, and an ethic of public service. Whereas business organizations, of course, are emphasizing getting it right rather than being in the right, exploiting opportunities, competitive advantage and commercial success (Lawrence, 1986). Do those ideas not sound wildly dated (quite apart from the fact that then I referred in the book endlessly to 'industry' where one would now say 'business')?

Budgetary pressure on the public sector has largely eliminated the distinction I once argued between public and private. While purists might object that 'staying within budget' is not the same as striving for profit, downward budgetary pressure in the public sector has:

▌ put efficiency gains and cost reduction centre stage;

▌ meant that initiatives (and expansions) are increasingly funded from 'surpluses';

▌ stimulated public sector organizations to find sources of revenue beyond government funding.

With so much taken out of the public sector as we have seen (with privatization and deregulation) these trends are now most observable in the health service, in education, and in a variety of non-profit-making organizations. UK universities, for instance, would be a good example of non-profit-making organizations struggling to stay out of debt by finding additional income streams, and when successful, funding their development from such privately sourced surpluses.

Remuneration in much of the public sector is increasingly moving away from graduated salary scales to performance-related, meeting objectives specified in advance, and to institutional efficiency gains. There is more control and less administrative or professional discretion, more performance measurement and formal appraisal, and more talk of 'customers'.

Whether one thinks these developments are desirable or deplorable my point is rather that they have happened. Managerialism has blurred to near extinction the difference between public and private.

Charities and change

In developing ideas for this book I deliberately sought to include some non-profit-making and public sector organizations, both out of real interest and to have something with which to compare the business organizations – though in the event this contrast is less sharp than I might have expected. Among this non-business subset are several charitable organizations, in both the UK and the United States. In a way charities are a nice test case of assimilation to the managerial consensus. They do aim to make money, but:

▌ They make money in support of good causes, not as dividends for shareholders.

▌ Much of this money comes from the general public.

▌ When it is given by companies it is at least not a commercial transaction; the donor companies are not 'buying' anything more than goodwill and reputation.

▌ Charities have been steered by unpaid, often amateur, trustees at the top.

▌ Charities have depended on the massive involvement of unpaid volunteers at grass roots level.

Certainly in the UK they have been viewed traditionally as sporting a culture of devoted, well-meaning, genteel amateurism. Not any more.

The first charity director I interviewed began with the remark: 'Being worthy is no longer enough' and went on to argue that charities in the UK are now sensitive about their administration costs, in part a result of Oxfam being slammed in 1979 for its high costs. So cost reduction is an acknowledged objective for many charities, and indeed when asking for donations charities often indicate the small proportion of the gift which will be absorbed by running costs.

The second interviewee, the deputy director general of one of what are known as the Big Five in the UK, said that the biggest change in his working lifetime in charity management was the growing professionalization of staff together with the fact that they treated working for the charity as the career, not as a kind of post-career after 20 years of military or civil service.

This thought was echoed by others, together with the notion that the trustees at the top were changing, and so were attitudes of the salaried staff to them. As one commentator put it: 'In 1980 staff did not speak at Council meetings unless asked. The chairman was a Brigadier-General.' (The current chairman, it emerged, was from an investment bank!) Others suggest this change at the top is normal. Trustees used to be 'the great and the good'; now they are people who demonstrated career success in their own organizations, often business men or women. The business connection was mentioned in a different way by one of the US interviewees, saying that the fundraising staff at charities would make diagonal career moves between the charities and business organizations.

Regarding revenue generation, the charities in the UK tended to the view that whatever part of their income came as a subvention from the government would decline, that the emphasis had to be on fund raising not fund receiving. None the less all the charities visited were concerned about how money was raised. The possible tension between commitment and commercial success was raised by one of the US interviewees who remarked: 'You get one dollar from each of a million people, that is good involvement; you get a million dollars from one person, that's good business!'

The British tended to be less circumspect, declaring frankly that they had seen 'revenue generation increase well above the rate of inflation'. But the key emphasis was on the analysis of revenue-generating alternatives. Another of the British interviewees bemoaned the recent past, before she took office. 'In the past it used to be a scatter gun approach. But now we measure and evaluate an event. We do a SWOT on anything before we do it.'

And as one might expect there was talk of cost-effective fund raising and concentration in fund raising. The best single episode of concentrated fund raising I came across was US $2 million raised at the Cattle Barons Ball in Dallas by the American Cancer Society!

A new phenomenon in this context is the charity 'turnaround'. One of my UK interviewees was an ex-oil industry executive appointed to sort out a major charity with a £3 million deficit. The organization concerned uses an army of volunteers to provide a humanitarian service, free nationwide. It is marked by a high level of decentralization, a massive property portfolio facilitating local service provision and even a substantial vehicle fleet. The twin themes of the turnround are centralization and rationalization, starting with a proper management control structure. Particular initiatives included:

I A centralized computer system, seen as rather novel by 'old hands' out in the provinces.

I Centralization of funds previously held locally, and a professional approach to their investment (surpluses placed overnight on the London money market, and so on).

I Charging for service provision where commercial organizations were the beneficiary.

■ Rationalizing the property portfolio: sell-offs, some lease-backs, better utilization; plus an amazing switch of the head office from a long lease (re-leased of course) site to a newly purchased site on which premises were constructed, some for the charity to occupy, and some for the generation of rental income.

This enterprising CEO even found ways of using the vehicle fleet for commercial subcontract work in the quiet periods when they were little needed for the charity's own work. It all makes perfect sense, but the beguiling thing is that though the subject of the story is a charity it reads like a success story from *Forbes* or *Fortune*.

As noted in Chapter 2 there is M&A activity among charities in both countries considered here. There is also bi-polarization, again as explored in the last chapter. In the UK, for instance, there were two very big cancer charities – Cancer Research Campaign and the Imperial Cancer Research Fund – whose merger under the title Cancer Research UK was approved in late 2001, but there were also some 60 small cancer charities, though not very much in between, it was suggested. Another of the UK interviewees took up the theme of bi-polarization. Her argument was:

> The Big Five are gaining funds, enjoy growing public awareness and growing budgets. The very small charities with under £500,000 are thriving, and on a percentage basis are getting a better return on their events. But the middle group of charities, those with £1–10 million income are being squeezed hard; as the big grow they are imposing on the middle ground.

Another twist was that no one I asked had any difficulty doing a rough market segmentation job on the general public vis-à-vis the purposes of charity. One interviewee, for instance, produced the following typology:

'The young give time; the young married, give nothing; the middle-aged and successful give more money but not much time; the retired give more time, but usually less money.' The young, it emerged, are worth their weight in gold when it comes to marathons, abseiling buildings, and jumping out of aeroplanes.

Finally it was suggested that all this had sedimented in the minds of the new commercially aware trustees. They in turn were concerned to appoint as charity managers people who combined PR and external skills with strategic thinking.

None of these reflections on the ethos and operation of charities is meant as criticism. The driving force for the charities is clear, and much good comes of their 'more business-like' orientation. The point is rather that apart from the ends served these charitable organizations are just like business organizations. They have come to embrace this pervasive view of how things should be done, to buy into the managerial consensus.

Around the world in search of sameness

So far we have argued that consensus has been promoted by governments seeking to reduce their responsibilities, and within society this consensus has made two parallel journeys: private sector → public sector; commercial organizations → non-profit-making bodies. Now we want to go a step further and suggest that managerialism has become an international force, not merely the property of any particular Western country, even if we continue to think of the forceful management values as belonging more to the United States than anywhere else.

To pursue this idea we might take one or two countries that are decidedly un-American, and run a quick check on managerial attitudes by taking advantage of a publicly accessible source – corporate job adverts. In picking one or two countries on which to run the argument, I have been guided by these considerations:

▌ knowing the country well enough to be able to context the findings;

▌ having taken an interest in it for a while, so as to be sensitive to change over time;

▌ having slight knowledge of the language, so as to get into the angling and emphasis of the job adverts.

Let us start with Holland.

GOING DUTCH

In 1985 I took a fellowship at a Dutch university, largely to find out about business and management in the Netherlands. I talked to business academics and consultants, visited loads of companies and interviewed managers, and ended up writing a book about it (Lawrence, 1991).

Holland, like the United States, is a 'what you see is what you get' society. If you ask, what was Dutch management like in the late 1980s, the answer is it was just what you would expect from a knowledge of Dutch society in general. That is to say, Dutch management was low profile, unpretentious to a fault, consensual and collectivist, rather egalitarian, pragmatic, a strange mix of international and parochial, and with a focus on detail within organizations.

Net salaries for managers were rather low (lower than say France, Germany or Switzerland), and salary levels between different ranks were small, in the sense of relatively small gaps between president and vice-president and so on down the hierarchy (remember Holland was second only to Sweden in 1980 according to McRae's figures cited earlier).

As soon as I had picked up enough Dutch to make it viable I became an enthusiastic student of the jobs section in *Intermediair*. This is the hefty, newspaper format publication that comes out on Friday and has a near monopoly on managerial and professional posts (it is a Dutch joke that you won't be allowed into a first class railway compartment on a Friday without *Intermediair*). These job adverts were striking in several ways:

▌ They usually did not mention salary; or just said salary was according to the CAO (collective agreement – these CAOs were not just for manual workers but went a long way up the professional hierarchy); the implication being that outstanding achievement does not attract outstanding remuneration;

▌ There was not much mention of benefits; the Dutch expression for benefits is *secundaire arbeidsvoorwaarden*, and it does not exactly trip off the tongue even in Dutch.

▌ Companies did not boast – about their size or eminence or market dominance.

▌ The things that were emphasized were decency, pleasant working environment, cooperative and agreeable colleagues, and also training opportunities.

The striking thing generally was that these advertisements made no appeal to greed or to competition.

In the summer of 2001 I got hold of a current copy of *Intermediair*. On the first page, the job spec demanded the following qualities from applicants:

▌ They must have strong personality and be good communicators.

▌ A proactive orientation is a must.

▌ They must be capable of coping with stress, and be energetic, independent – keen to initiate.

The next advert was for a *Change* Manager, that was the actual job title; Change Manager – proactive, resolute, and with analytical grasp. This advert went on to enthuse about 'a vast capacity for responsibility'. It also referred to *uitstekende secundaire arbeidsvoorwaarden* – outstanding benefits; as I read on I found a lot of the adverts now mention benefits as a plus, and sometimes actually list what they are! Also many of the adverts are citing gross monthly or yearly salaries. Probably the most striking bit so far was finding an advert asking for someone who is *stressbestandig*, capable of dealing with stress. In my time in Holland stress would have been seen as a problem for the organization, and their obligation would have been to get rid of it; put out the fire, not issue asbestos suits.

Something else that is new is Dutch companies boasting about themselves. In an advert for a tax manager for the Netherlands, Heineken describes itself as 'the most international brewing group in the world' (a very fair claim, but not one that would have been made in the old days) and goes on to talk about the company's 'bold vision for the future' (the bold vision is not a traditional Dutch artefact). This Heineken advert also talks about wanting someone who is 'results oriented' (very sensible you may feel, but I never saw the phrase in 1985). Another company speaks of its head office team working with 'full enthusiasm over the future of the company'. Yet another, an investment company, describes itself as 'one of the greatest' and speaks of it going from nought to IPO (initial public offering) in a mere three years.

This is very un-Dutch. As a language Dutch is a little treasury of proverbial expressions condemning pride, boasting, idiosyncrasy, sycophancy, and setting yourself apart. Something has got to them.

Another development is adverts that now explicitly appeal to the desire for career advancement, for example:

▌ The assistant controller post will lead to the controller rank.

▌ There will be six-monthly career reviews that will address the individual's needs.

▌ As Senior Finance Specialist in 3–6 years you will grow towards being Manager: Finance and Control.

This really is a disposition that does not come naturally to the Dutch. The old view was that you didn't talk about personal ambition in case God struck you down for overweening pride.

And so it goes on, with repeat references to being *stressbestandig*, a self-starter, results oriented, an initiator, a convincing persuader, a 'get things done' type, even 'a driver through of change'.

The features in the *Intermediair* edition I used include a pie chart showing that organizational rank is the biggest single determinant of salary (this is not a self-evident proposition to the Dutch). Also included was a survey showing that an MBA is worth more in starting salary terms than a first degree in general or even than a PhD (and that the superior earning power of the MBA rose faster than that of the other qualifications in the period 1998–2001). The cover story is about the newly appointed CEO of NS, the Dutch railways, who is described as 'a crisis manager with dirty hands!' The potted CV of this individual also makes it clear that he worked for four, yes four, other organizations before joining NS: in 1985 this level of intercompany mobility would have been seen as evidence of emotional instability and put him beyond the pale.

Still, maybe you think Holland is too easy. Just white space left over from the 1970s, waiting to be written on in the bold hand of economic realism. OK, try France.

After all France is a country with a strong image. It is not one of those wishy-washy places you have to grope around to find some way of characterizing.

Avec nous, conduisez le changement dans l'entreprise. This heading: join us and drive change in the company, is taken from an executive job advert in *Le Figaro Entreprises* (11 June 2001). This is the new France. Traditionally French managers have not joined companies to 'drive change' but to confirm their status, advance their careers, and realize their lifestyle aspirations.

The most important thing to know about French managers is where most of them come from, educationally rather than socially. France is unusual in having a two-tier higher education system. At first sight it is like the system in other countries. Students at selective secondary schools or the selective stream of comprehensive schools take an examination at 18, the Baccalauréat, which admits them to university, and this is what happens to the majority of those who pass the bac. But a more ambitious and typically talented minority go on after the bac to spend one, two or more years working very hard at an *école prépara-toire*, *prépa* for short, which culminates in their taking a nationally competitive exam, the *concours*, for admission to the *grandes écoles*. These *grandes écoles* are very élite institutions, and while there are about 140–60 of them, they admit only small numbers not the thousands that go to (mere) universities. A lot of the *grandes écoles* are schools of engineering, another sizeable block are business schools, and there are a few special grandes écoles such as the one which trains the upper level of secondary school teachers.

The system is front-end loaded. The toughest time is that spent at the *prépa*, the *concours* is the big hurdle, if you can get in you will certainly graduate three years later, and then you are made, on the *voie royale* as the French say, the royal route to success (see Figure 3.1).

Most French managers from any company one is likely to have heard of are ex-*grande école*. So for that matter are all the other élites in France – the political élite, the administrative élite, and the intellectual élite.

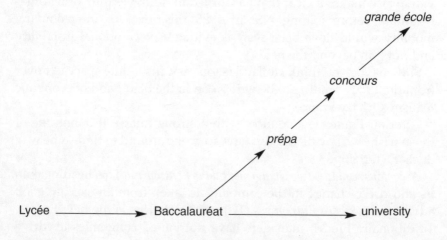

Figure 3.1

This educational background has given French management a cerebral quality. Being clever is what French managers are best at. Literate, numerate, articulate, at their best drafting the clever exposé or proffering a logical analysis in stylized French. And all this used to be clearly reflected in management job adverts. Indeed Jean-Louis Barsoux, a leading writer on French management, focused on the management recruitment job application process in the late 1980s, and made the following observations:

▌ Management job adverts show a low emphasis on drive and initiative, certainly by Anglo-Saxon standards; indeed several commentators on French life have noted a French preference for using nouns rather than verbs where possible.

▌ The things that are emphasized are mental qualities, *l'esprit critique*, *la rigueur, la capacité de synthése* (analytical mind, intellectual rigour, the ability to synthesize) and so on; indeed Barsoux argues that the French seem to focus on qualities of reception (passive cleverness) rather than on qualities of emission (charisma, pugnacity, ability to motivate).

▌ Formal educational qualifications are decisive, as we have suggested.

▌ The letters applicants write for management jobs are more deferential and more indirect than in the Anglo-Saxon world; they use passive expressions such as *être embauché comme* (to be placed as), *chercher un emploi de* (to seek employment as), *collaborer, aider* (to be involved, to assist).

In Barsoux's view the key to the whole thing was educational qualifications. If applicants have the right qualifications in this formal sense the rest does not seem to matter; if they do not have them they are not viable candidates anyway (Barsoux and Lawrence, 1990).

That was then.

In the summer of 2001, with the Barsoux analysis in mind, I looked at a sample of job adverts in French newspapers. The first thing that struck me was that verbs are now in! The first advert I looked at for a commercial engineer was all about developing clients, prospecting for new clients, recommending solutions, taking account of technical and financial imperatives, responding to requests to quote, and working in liaison with commercial partners.

The second thing I noticed is that experience has become important. In the 1980s there used not to be much mobility between companies. If you had not been to a *grande école* you did not get into the system, but if you were ex-*grande école* once in you could expect to be promoted internally; with a *grande école* diploma you did not need to change companies, without one you would not be able to. But now lots of the advertisements ask for experience – specific experience, x years, in this or that function, in particular industries, experience of particular developments or processes. It all suggests that there is a lot more inter-company mobility, that this mobility is socially acceptable, and that the companies doing the hiring know what they are looking for – particular competencies rather than general brain power.

Third, foreign language ability and particularly knowledge of English has assumed an importance it did not have in the late 1980s. Phrases like *anglais impératif, l'anglais serait un plus, vous parlez couramment l'anglais, le candidat sera parfaitement bilangue francais/anglais* abound.

There is also a new customer focus. In the late 1980s customers had little part in management job adverts which seemed to imply that successful candidates would enjoy themselves, in an intellectually rigorous way of course, focusing on the managing of the organization not the gratification of the customers. But now phrases along the lines of 'resolutely customer facing', 'we are looking for women and men who are passionate about service', and 'you have a sense of customer service and results …' are common.

Again, if one goes back little more than 10 years human qualities did not get much 'air time'! The presumption was rather that clever people (managers) would make rational decisions that would be implemented by hierarchic subordinates. The book *The One Minute Manager* was a flop in France; French managers were not turned on by the idea of a boss making heavy eye contact with them – giving them 'a one minute praising'. Others have suggested that the French actually like bureaucracy because of its impersonality – one is controlled by rules and procedures rather than by bosses and colleagues.

Now one hesitates to say that all this has changed, but again looking at job adverts in French newspapers in 2001 there are plenty of references to interpersonal skills that were not there before. Indeed *relationnel* seems to have become a standard expression, as in *votre excellent relationnel, votre professsionnalisme alliés à vos aptitudes relationnelles*. A line in one of the advertisements that seems indicative of the change deserves to be quoted in full:

qualités relationnelles alliés à un réel sens des responsabilités ...vous permettront de vous imposer auprès de vos interlocuteurs (human/ relational qualities allied to a deep sense of responsibility will enable you to 'take people with you' or get close to them).

Now I have translated this a bit freely, going for the spirit of it not the letter. But the interesting thing is that 10 years ago managers used to impose themselves (take people with them) by issuing orders, not by deploying their human skills.

But above all a perusal of the adverts today conveys an impression of proactivity and ambition. There are references to pragmatism (hardly a traditional French quality), passionate engagement in work, stirring teams into action, success-ambition, developing commercial instinct, constant progress, mission, the appeal of working for a market leader, strong growth, young and ambitious teams, charisma, and more besides. I even found one advert asking *'idéalement pour un MBA'* (ideally for an MBA): it does not make it sound as though the MBA is common yet, but it used to be either completely unknown or regarded as an US aberration.

Now, we have perused these management job adverts in Holland and France for two reasons. First, they allow a comparison with the past, and with the rather recent past at that. In both cases this comparison gives us a move away from national distinctiveness and towards a more Anglo-Saxon understanding of management, a move in fact towards a global or at least a Western consensus.

Second, the qualities flagged up in their adverts are indicative. We do not know if all these would-be employing organizations get what they ask for (or even if they like it when they do). But these adverts do tell us what companies think they need, what they feel they ought to ask for.

Two other factors both reflect the consensus, and have helped to shape it. The first – just mentioned in connection with one of the French management job adverts – is the MBA. Before 1980 MBAs were rare in Britain and unknown in Continental Europe. But in the last 20 years of the 20th century the MBA has become widespread and domiciled in the UK. There are many institutions offering it, and it can be taken on a full-time or part-time basis. There is also a conversion course version of the MBA, sometimes with the MSc title, for the benefit of newish graduates in non-business relevant subjects who would nonetheless like to embark on careers in management or administration. One often hears now of having or not having an MBA being a filtering mechanism when large numbers of applications are received for posts for applicants in the bottom third of the age range. Having an MBA, or having it as an aspiration, as part of the career development plan, is now the norm for the younger generation in the UK.

What has happened in the UK has also happened in Continental Europe, albeit in the 1990s and not (yet) on the same scale – remember here references to the MBA in Holland and more recently in France. Perhaps most telling is that there are now several institutions offering the MBA in Germany, the country that with its strong *Technik* orientation is the least sympathetic to the generalities of management and the dynamics of business.

While there are semi-specialized versions of the MBA, typically referred to in the UK as 'badged MBAs' there is a common core, and it tends to reinforce the management consensus depicted here.

The second factor is the pervasive influence of what have come to be called management gurus, and it probably is significant that while we may have had them 50 years ago the term was certainly not in use. Perhaps more than that the management luminaries of the late 19th century and early 20th century tended to be seen as 'founding fathers' and people associated with particular schools and approaches. It is only in the last decades of the 20th century that we have had block-buster management books, the genre pioneered by Peters and Waterman (1982). In addition there has been a tendency for leading writers on management, business and strategy to be known and talked about widely, those having at least 'some idea' including age groups beyond the MBA generation and practitioners whose formal education was not in business administration. We are suggesting here that this is all part of the consensus.

THE CONSENSUS REVIEWED

In this chapter we have argued that there is a growing consensus in the West about the nature and mission of management. The mission is to pursue its objectives with ever greater conviction and resolve. In a variety of Western countries the state has retreated, has spread the dynamic of management by privatization and deregulation, and we have seen the ethos and imperatives of the private sector come to dominate the public sector. Not-for-profit organizations, at least in the UK and the United States, have a *modus operandi* that is difficult to distinguish from that of commercial organizations. And countries that not so long ago exhibited a national distinctiveness and a disinclination to 'buy into' the Anglo-Saxon model now shows signs of espousing it.

The management consensus we have posited sees management as:

▌ hands on;

▌ focused;

▌ efficiency conscious;

▌ proactive;

▌ results oriented;

▌ confident in its own logic;

▌ impatient of the past, of tradition, of the claims of other élites and professionals.

It all reflects a consciousness of the enhanced competition, the causes of which were explored in Chapter 1. The model is loosely Anglo-Saxon, and more particularly identified with the United States.

The case for this increasingly universal model is self-evident. But that is not the whole story. In the next chapter we want to try to do two things. To look at some instances, in different countries, of the working out of the model. Then to examine it more critically; to ask in effect, is there a downside?

4

The new management in action

One of my former PhD students told me that there is a joke in French: I know it works in practice, but does it work in theory?

But for the non-French, a bit of practice is always welcome. So we want to begin this chapter by moving from the general discussion of the managerial consensus in terms of what one might call its indicative manifestation in Chapter 3, to the question: how does the new management show up in practice? Let us start in Canada.

LE SOLEIL

The two cities of French speaking Canada that non-Canadians have all heard of are Montreal and Quebec City. They are very different cities. The larger, Montreal, is rather cosmopolitan. Sure it is French speaking, but there are English speaking residential quarters and in any case you could live there for 20 years without bothering to learn French. All sorts of things are effectively 'bilingualized'; like bookshops, where all the French titles are on one floor and all the English titles are on the next. Montreal is also only about a 45 minute drive from the US border; it is not uncommon for Montrealers to have second homes, businesses, or at least a fiscal presence in the United States.

Quebec City, on the other hand, is very French. The old town is a concentration of monuments, statues, inscriptions and historic buildings. It is also the capital of Quebec Province and so is the seat of the provincial parliament. It is only a three-hour rail trip from Montreal, but it seems like a trip back to France – probably France round about the 17th century. *Le Soleil* is a broadsheet, French language of course, newspaper published in Quebec City.

There is no leftwing versus rightwing distinction among newspapers in French Canada. The key distinction is rather that between sovereigntist as opposed to federalist. Sovereigntist means supporting the idea that Quebec Province should become an independent entity; federalist means supporting the *status quo* whereby Quebec is one of the ten provinces of a federally united Canada. *Le Soleil* is federalist.

But the challenges facing *Le Soleil* are business management ones rather than issues of political alignment. The newspaper industry is under siege in several ways:

I   Advertising revenues decline whenever there is a recession.

I   Circulation, though not necessarily readership, seems to have a built-in tendency to decline unless bolstered and revamped.

I   There is increasing competition from visual as opposed to written media.

I   The Internet may be another rival, or it may be harnessed.

I   Owners of newspapers increasingly see them as 'a business like any other', and are less concerned than they once were to make concessions to craft workers (printers) or to talented professionals (journalists) that might exempt them from the rigours of managerial control.

So how has *Le Soleil* responded?

In 1995 the company relocated its printing operation to a separate site, updated it to Web press, and started to run the printing as a separate business. That is to say, it only takes four days a week to print *Le Soleil* so the rest of the week the press can be used for revenue generating outside jobs.

The sales team responsible for selling the paper's advertising space used to be on a remuneration package that was 80 per cent salary and 20 per cent commission. In a deal that instructively took 18 months to negotiate these salespeople are now on 100 per cent commission; this bring them into line with advert space salespeople for radio and television stations (and also with those of the rival paper *Le Journal de Quebec*). Also the salespeople no longer have geographic areas, just lists of clients. As a member of the management team reported with satisfaction: 'It has raised revenue. They are working harder. Now they are in the office at 6 pm instead of leaving at 4.30.'

There has been downsizing too. From 420 employees down to 252 as of 1999, though this does not include some 40 working in the now separate printing unit. A little part of the downsizing was achieved by closing down the purchasing department, leaving line managers to handle their own procurement. The total wage bill had been C $24 million in 1993, but was down to C $16 million by 1999. This was partly the result of computerization and a simplification of some procedures as well as reflecting the downsizing. The paper also moved from a property which it owned to a newer, rented property, whose maintenance was provided by the landlord; this in turn enabled them to shed a few maintenance employees.

But this is not simply a story of denominator management. The former erosion of circulation was reversed, because the acquisition of the web press raised the quality of print and publication. Advertising revenue increased. The print unit generated some revenue as well as providing a service. What is more *Le Soleil* established a Web site, something only two newspapers in French Canada had at the time. The Web site stored lots of back material – book reviews, theatre reviews, reviews of cars, and so on – but as well as this the paper hoped to sell things like cinema tickets via its Web site, using its network of newspaper delivery boys to deliver them.

AN ENGLISH LAW FIRM

Moving from Quebec City to the English Midlands we would like to look next at a firm of solicitors, working principally in the commercial law area. A mildly angled question about possible 'changes in the industry' at the start of the interview evoked the response: 'Massive! It's a trade now, not a profession.'

This response is made more remarkable by the fact that the partner concerned was not someone on the verge of retirement but a solicitor who had only qualified 12 years earlier. There seemed to be three main themes.

Focus

The first theme is focus or specialization. The firm was largely concerned with commercial law but that in turn breaks down into:

▌ corporate;

▌ commercial;

▌ employment;

▌ tax;

▌ property;

▌ litigation.

Everyone in the firm specializes in a particular area. It was also made clear that there were specialisms within these areas listed above. So that if one takes, for example, corporate law, this would include:

▌ MBOs (management buy-outs);

▌ MBIs (management buy-ins);

▌ aviation;

▌ construction;

▌ other particular industries.

It was suggested that the days of 'the one man band', the single solicitor practising alone, were numbered. Such practices would be restricted to conveyancing (buying and selling of houses), occasional business sales/acquisitions, marital cases, work in the lower level magistrates' court, and 'wills at £50 a time'. The 'one man band' practice might not even have the financial and organizational muscle to put in the IT and other systems necessary to qualify for criminal work on legal aid.

One indication of the plight of the sole practitioners is that they are the biggest claimants on the Solicitors Indemnity Fund. They are more vulnerable because they are 'spreading themselves thin', trying to cover a variety of things in an age of specialization, bucking the trend to focus. At the other end of the scale the big London firms, known in the trade as The Golden Five, are expanding, going cross-border, and have 'billion pound clients'.

Another consequence of specialization is that training is endless. There is a lot of change in law, it is difficult to keep up with it, which in turn drives the specialization. All this contrasts with 'the old days' when it was a case of 'once you're qualified, that's it'.

Competition

Unsurprisingly, the competition has hotted up. US law firms have established in London, setting 'unheard of' salaries and fuelling the talent war. The London firms are reaching out into the provinces and grabbing the more lucrative assignments. Indeed, in an industry which is heavily tiered by size, location, and market presence, each tier is reaching down to take something from the tier below, saving the protection offered by specialization discussed in the previous section. Or to put it another way, the bigger firms are leaning on the smaller – buying them, cherry-picking their best people, and stealing their clients.

Competition is also being offered by some of the accountancy firms who are setting up associated law firms, usually under different 'brand names', and head-hunting qualified solicitors to staff them from a variety of sources. Though it seems unlikely that law firms and accountancy practices will actually merge to form business service conglomerates, this is only because the accountancy practices are so much larger.

There is a new internal competitiveness in the firms. Traditionally remuneration has been according to the 'lock-step' model. Its essence was that eventually one was made an equity partner and henceforth received X per cent of the profits; thereafter one advanced for some 20 years or so in terms of seniority based small proportionate increments. This has now (sometimes) been replaced by a more performance related remuneration system, which favours the aggressive 30 and 40 somethings at the expense of the old and wise. The change de-couples age from earning power, prefers merit to tradition.

There is also competition among the newly qualified for jobs in law firms. The vast expansion of higher education in the UK in the 1990s means that entry barriers have been lowered. This has meant that the profession has passed from being front-end loaded (getting sponsored at the start is crucial) to being rear-end loaded (getting a job when you are qualified is the challenge). In this situation of oversupply there are actually unemployed, qualified solicitors at the start of the 21st century, something that would have been inconceivable in the period of _les trentes glorieuses_. Given this oversupply, selection for some starting jobs tends to proceed in terms of extras. Intellectual ability, subject knowledge, and formal qualification, that is, are taken for granted: selection is in terms of additional (presumptive) indicators of personality, achievement, and market awareness.

Indeed it is one of the vagaries of the managerial age that cleverness alone is never enough. To put it another way, if your only strength is that you are bright (and good at passing exams) that you lack social skills, are not a team player, and are an IT illiterate, there is nowhere you can go.

Clients and their expectations

From a solicitor's point of view, clients are just not what they used to be. They have all sorts of crazy expectations, including:

▌ They want you to give them a quote up front, and stick to it.

▌ They are disloyal; they may hire you for this but not for that; they may hire you this time but not next time.

▌ In commercial law they do not come to you; you have to go to them in the sense of knowing their business and putting what the law says into a context meaningful to them.

▌ They may even seek a 'no win, no fee' deal!

But perhaps the underlying issue is that no one will take your word for anything, just because you are 'the professional', and are licensed to practice. To be of value to the client, the professional has to become proactively engaged. Once the solicitor told the client 'what the law had to say', spelled out the options dispassionately, *sine ira et studio*, but left the choice to the client. No more. Clients want you to tell them what to do, to recommend, to enter the world of their concerns and to direct them. The practice of law in contemporary Britain is a study in the end of tradition.

KVIKKER BESTANDIG – 'EVER ENERGIZING'

Now some manufacturing. The world's largest producer of chewing gum is of course Chicago based Wrigley. The second largest is the US pharmacy company, Warner Lambert. But in third place is a Danish company, Dandy, with its corporate office and largest facilities in the provincial town of Veijle on the east facing coast of Jutland.

It is a family firm, founded in 1915 by a husband and wife team, making boiled sweets (hard candy). By the 1920s they had gone into chewing gum. The company slogan, *kvikker bestandig*, means something like 'ever energizing'. It nicely suggests (at least to Danish speakers!) the pleasingly beneficial effects of the products.

It is a pity that I cannot bring the Dandy story up to date from my visit late in 1997 because there will have been developments since then. But even with this shortcoming it is an instructive story, and I would like to pick out one or two aspects.

The shaping of product development

It is a commonplace in parts of the confectionery industry that it is driven by 'kiddy power'. That is to say, a lot of the purchases are made by children or by adults for children. But also in the 1990s there has been a growing concern with health and healthiness in the West, which offers product development opportunities as well as restrictions on some existing products. This second consideration, the possibility of developing health related produce, has been recognized by Dandy, who segment their product range in terms of two dimensions – fun versus functional, adult versus child consumers, as shown in Figure 4.1.

There's another interesting twist: confectionery makers are often faced with the problem of whether or not to engage in own label manufacture, that is whether or not to make products to be sold by a retailer under the retailer's name rather than the manufacturer's brand name. This is a tricky question. If you refuse, you lose sales; if you do it, you undermine the exclusivity of your own brand and the price premium it may command (see Figure 4.2).

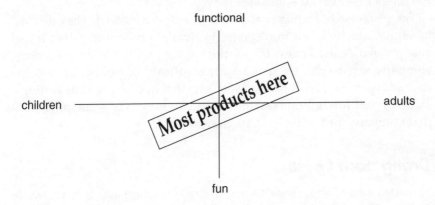

Example: bubble gum.

Dental hygiene plaque prevention products cluster in the top right hand segment, and of course products for children in the bottom left.

Figure 4.1

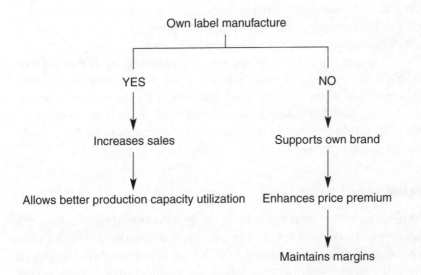

Figure 4.2

It is often the case that manufacturers whom one would think are too upmarket to compromise for the sake of sales volume do in fact engage in own label manufacture, fearing that if they do not do it for the retailer concerned someone else will.

The response of Dandy to this impasse is pretty smart. They do own label manufacture, not in response to retailer power but rather to get *quid pro quo* deals. That is to say they will provide a food processing company or maybe even a pharmaceuticals company in another country with own label products for sale in that country, thus getting a share of that foreign market, and in return they take something from that company and sell it in Denmark.

Drang nach Osten

The idea of a *Drang nach Osten*, a drive to the east, is a theme in German history and it reached its high point with the Nazi invasion of Russia in 1941. With the fall of European communism in the 1989–91 period there has been a less sensational but no less real commercial re-enactment of the drive to the east. Germany has been a leader in this, but not to the exclusion of companies in other countries. Dandy has been an initiator.

In 1989 Dandy entered the Polish market, and did well there until it was wrong-footed by Wrigley who came in with a sugar-free product that found greater favour. Dandy turned next to Russia, starting by buying up television advertising time and using it to create demand and brand awareness. This was followed by establishing a packaging plant in Novgorod and achieving worthwhile sales.

This Russian initiative was seen very positively by the company. The plant in Novgorod was staffed with well-educated, quality employees. The plant was regarded favourably by the local mayor as a provider of local tax revenue as well as well-remunerated employment. The establishment of local manufacture, as opposed to simply packaging, was envisaged.

Employment relations

Dandy was seen very positively in the local community. A premium employer in a smallish town, a family owned company with a paternalist image ('if you have been here a long time, you will be looked after'), it receives lots of unsolicited job applications. The company has no need to advertise for anything except skilled or specialist posts.

It has very attractive premises and facilities, though this is pretty much the norm in Denmark. It has an employees' suggestion scheme. A leisure club with lots of keep fit activities is available to the whole family, with recreation course teachers to help the young. An annual Veijle run, a regular Dandy family day (fun activities plus a factory visit), is all part of the scene.

But there were some innovations in employee relations. One was that a works agreement had traded longer hours for more flexibility. This is not a bad deal for employees who:

▌ keep their jobs;

▌ keep their wage level;

▌ work fewer hours.

But the flexibility requirement – working longer hours at short notice when needed – is disruptive of family and social life for employees. It also reduced overtime working (what would have been overtime is covered by the new flexibility) and therefore overtime wage premiums. The arrangement does not reduce production costs for the company, but it has two main effects: it reduces inventory, and the cost of holding it; and enhances the company's ability to respond to fluctuations in demand.

The opening of the packaging plant in Russia led to some reduction of employment in Veijle; the proposed establishment of production in Russia would have the same result, being in effect an 'off-shore' operation as well as a logistically rational way of servicing the Russian market.

Back at Veijle there had been some instances of skilled workers who were no longer needed; in some cases they opted for unskilled posts, so they stayed with the company, but at lower hourly rates. A new pay system had also been introduced that included a performance-related element, but part of the deal was that not all employees could be in the top slot for the performance element so that overall the wage average was pushed down a little.

The possibility that the company might become non-union was also mentioned. Now this seemed to me surprising in the Scandinavian context. Denmark and Sweden have some of the highest trade union membership rates in the world, usually cited as 70 or 80 something per cent (there are differences as between data sources, and over time): by trade union rate is meant the proportion of those who are eligible to join a trade union who actually do so. When I expressed mild surprise, I was told matter-of-factly that it had already happened at *Jyllandsposten*, a national daily newspaper in Denmark, marketed incidentally under a rather egalitarian slogan, a Danish version of the desire of many in the United States to identify themselves as 'average Americans'.

It might be helpful to end this vignette of Dandy on a corrective note, to show that the forces of turbo-capitalism have not yet made everywhere exactly like everywhere else. While being shown round the factory it was explained that production workers do quality checks at all stages and fill in forms which are passed to a central quality control bank for analysis, and that the process enables quality performance to be attributed to individual workers. They used to have a bonus for workers who hit 100 per cent quality, paid for every hour that this top rating was achieved. Then pretty much everyone hit these high standards, so the bonus was withdrawn. But quality did not suffer as a consequence!

In the spirit of the exercise of 'putting down bore holes' in a mix of organizations and countries to see what we come up with, we will look at one more organization, this time in the United States. The step after that will be to look across these cases for commonalities that may catch the essence of the new management.

SOUTH DAKOTA WHEAT GROWERS (SDWG)

SDWG is a farm cooperative in the US upper mid-West, operating in 24 communities in the Dakotas. It handles some 99 million bushels of grain a year. It did US $30 million of business in 2000. In the recent past it doubled turnover/output by moving from small to large grains: from wheat, etc, to soya and corn. It is owned by some 5,000 farmer stockholders to whom dividends are paid.

Knowledge industry?

It probably sounds a little bit pretentious to call SDWG a 'knowledge industry' because that phrase tends to connote research intensive and high tech business, Silicon Valley not the prairies of the upper mid-West. But consider the fact that SDWG is not making anything, it is helping farmers to produce and sell by:

▌ providing consultancy services;

▌ agronomy inputs;

▌ application services;

▌ market know-how, including hedging;

▌ handling the interface with the railroads.

It may not be rocket science, but this is a multi-part knowledge based service operation.

Traditional farmers?

A farm cooperative tends to evoke notions of community solidarity and mutual assistance as a counterpoise to rural isolation and the external forces of impersonal business. This is not absent in SDWG, yet the farmer members have a rather utilitarian involvement and certainly enjoy some commercial options.

It does not cost the farmer members anything to join SDWG. They can choose to sell their produce to:

▌ SDWG;

▌ rival cooperatives;

▌ independent grain dealers.

What will tie them into SDWG is the quality of services and the cooperative's ability to manage the market interface for them and get them good prices.

The farmers, it was gently suggested, are becoming less loyal. And those farmers are becoming fewer in number and bigger in their scale of operation. But SDWG can manage the market for them, and they sell direct to Cargill, the mighty food processing multinational.

The utilitarian orientation is caught in the payment options which the farmers can exercise when they deliver to SDWG:

▌ They can be paid straight away.

▌ They can defer payment for tax reasons.

▌ They can deliver to SDWG and choose what price to accept over a finite period with SDWG posting prices daily as the market changes (though in exercising this option the farmers sometimes end up getting less than under 'option one' when there is a downturn in the market).

In short, joining SWDG is a sound business decision, not the organizational expression of community solidarity.

Consolidation

Chapter 2 cited farming and farm produce merchandizing as examples of consolidation or concentration. All this is very clear in the testimony of SDWG:

▌ Farmers are getting fewer and bigger.

▌ The same is happening with agricultural cooperatives.

▌ There is also integration between producers and buyers where, for example, virtually all poultry raised in the United States is contracted to packers or food processing companies, so is some 85 per cent of hogs, and the same process will occur with beef, but more slowly. The essence of this integration is that producers are both grouped together and linked with buyers.

But there is also consolidation at the level of facilities, that is, elevators. SDWG have closed some elevators, and will close more. The General Manager remarked: 'I don't like it, but it has to happen' (on grounds of economic rationality of course).

In April 2001 there were 20 elevators, but the emphasis was on big new ones that can load a 110-car train in 15 hours. European readers might like to know that these trains are usually one and a quarter miles long! The 15-hour loading schedule allows the locomotive to stay in place while the train is loaded; in 'the old days' the locomotive could be taken away for days while loading was completed. Then after loading it is a three-day rail trip to the West Coast, a day to unload, and three days back for more fun.

SDWG have added three of these shuttle-loaders, that is elevator systems that can do the 15-hour job. Two are new, and one is the result of upgrading an existing facility. These three handle half the value of all the produce shipped by this farm cooperative.

BPG

In the early 21st century no organization is complete without a dose of business process re-engineering. As the General Manager put it: 'We operated 18 companies under one name, instead of one company with 18 locations. This was not efficient, we used to compete with each other, we couldn't have consistency, we needed to do all processes the same.'

Specifically SDWG:

▌ Integrated three administrative echelons within the organization.

▌ Consolidated IT and accounting systems.

▌ Realigned jobs.

▌ Reduced admin staff by 30 per cent.

Perhaps the most interesting thing about SDWG and the industry it serves is the line of causation. It all starts with the railroads' desire for greater efficiency in terms of schedules, staff rostering, stock utilization, and the simplification of their own business processes (the railroads demand electronic invoicing, for example). So it goes as shown in Figure 4.3.

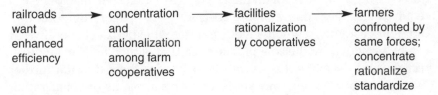

Figure 4.3

So the industry is being transformed by the need of the Union Pacific and Burlington railroads to load 110-car trains in 15 hours.

WHAT HAVE WE GOT?

We have looked at four very different organizations in different industries and in different countries. At a common sense level they have not got anything in common. Nonetheless we want to ask, do they, taken together, suggest any commonalities?

Relativizing the product

Although only one of these organizations, Dandy, is a manufacturing company, we would like to suggest that they all in a way relativize the product. Let us start with *Le Soleil*.

It is a story of a successful turnaround, in an industry that faces recognized problems – competition from other media, declining circulation, fluctuating advertising revenues, and so on. But how is this turnaround achieved?

The answer has to be by a mix of sensible business moves and denominator management, plus an innovative response to the Internet. And this is enough to yield a success story. But note that none of this is about *Le Soleil* itself. There is no suggestion that the newspaper was rendered either more attractive or more saleable in editorial or journalistic terms. That it became a better paper *per se*. The only change to the paper is the improvement in printing and colour reproduction that resulted from getting a web press. The turnaround called for business and management skills. You did not need to be a newspaper person or a media person although the CEO was.

If we take the English law firm clearly there is no product in the conventional sense, it is a knowledge industry. And in this debate knowledge and products are usually counterposed. What is more the law firm story shows the intensification of knowledge. This organization is doing well by recognizing the range of areas where expertise is required and then 'piling on the specialists'! It is the recognition that different customer segments require different expertise, beyond what can be provided by the sole practitioner, that is the key. The law firm recruits and develops the specialists, upgrades them through further increments of training, and keeps them by a results-oriented rather than a traditional remuneration system.

The agricultural cooperative, SDWG, takes the story further. This time there are producers, the farmers, but their produce is worth nothing unless they can get it to market and they cannot do this on their own. The likes of Cargill do not want to buy from a bunch of cranky farmers strung out across the Great Plains, they want to buy from concentrated intermediaries like SDWG who speak their language.

So SDWG and entities like it are vital in this value chain that spreads across several organizations from farmer to consumer. But what they have which is vital is know-how. They know how to manage the market, the hedging, the logistics, the interface with transporters and end users. Its strength is in the intangibles not in the producing.

Dandy which does actually manufacture is a nice test case. The product development is smart. And the perception of demand shift and market segmentation that underlies this product development is clever. But the actual product is not a great challenge. Remember the quality premium payable to individual shop floor employees was withdrawn because everyone hit 100 per cent.

The challenge is to do it cheaper. This Dandy also achieved by a mixture of employment contract changes (performance-related pay, flexibility, skill grade reclassification, and so on) and off-shore packaging and production.

There is a general moral here. This is that _Technik_, in the German sense of the engineering knowledge and craft skill impacting on production, is being relativized, put into place, made less critical. Computer control is replacing craft skill. Off-shore manufacture is replacing high wage Western manufacture. Shallow manufacture, as described in Chapter 2, is replacing deep manufacture. More of it can be programmed, less of it is discretionary. And because it is programmable it is less susceptible to differentiation, so cost and efficiency goals take over.

The product is not unimportant, but its importance is being relativized by the importance of other things. The ones we have discussed here are the grasp of business reality, knowledge, specialization, know-how, and network management.

Looking back to see the road ahead

To see more of what is in the four organizations whose stories we have told, it is probably helpful to look back. If one looks back at the period of easy growth after the Second World War, _les trentes glorieuses_ again, a number of things are clear:

▌ Production was central in that period, you could sell all you could make.

▌ Product development came from within, from the research resources of the company rather than from market impulse.

▌ The rising prosperity of the period tended to insulate companies from the environment.

▌ The past was shaping the corporate present, and would be projected into the future.

▌ There was no particular virtue in change.

▌ And there was no particular reason to drive hard bargains with suppliers or employees, the pressure on profit margins did not warrant it.

With the end of *les trentes glorieuses* all these considerations have been reversed, and it shows in our four organizations.

Tradition

Our four organizations all show a departure from tradition. The organizational past no longer shapes the present, never mind the future. It is most obvious in the English law firm: the practice of law is no longer considered a profession; the sole practitioner (what British people think of when they speak of 'a solicitor') is doomed; there is continuing training, what the French would call *formation permanente*; and clients won't take their legal advisers' word for anything, won't allow them to be dispassionate, and want them to make a specific recommendation in all cases. The practice of law has passed from being a gentlemanly business reminiscent of *les trentes glorieuses* to being a hot bed of competition where accountancy firms try to plunder the law firms' best people, and every tier is trying to invade everyone else's markets, grab their clients, and snatch their business. Lock-step, the system of remuneration that favoured the long-serving and senior has gone in many practices.

But it is not only in the law firm. The story of *Le Soleil* makes it clear that a newspaper is 'a business like any other', and if you get to turn around a newspaper it is business skill not editorial or journalistic *élan* that will be required. The agricultural cooperative SDWG shows the involvement of its members to be a utilitarian rather than a community solidarity phenomenon. SDWG closes elevators to the dismay of local communities, but doubles turnover. But what struck me most as a UK citizen who once lived in Scandinavia was the matter of fact suggestion at Dandy that it might become a non-union company. It is probably silly but when I heard this I thought of the joke in Bill Bryson's entertaining book *Neither Here Nor There* about his youthful travels in Continental Europe: 'How do you start a revolution in Sweden? You take your library books back late!' and a new version occurred to me: 'How do you know the revolution has come? They're recruiting for flexi-hour, performance-related jobs in non-union plants in Denmark!'

Workforce change

To take up this last point, workforce change is another *leitmotiv* that runs across three of the four organizations. *Le Soleil*, Dandy, SDWG are all de-manning. The English law firm is in fact growing organically, and thus protecting itself somewhat against corporate predators, but it is also benefiting from an oversupply of law graduates making it a buyer's market.

At the same time the conditions of service are getting tougher all the time. The advertising space sellers at *Le Soleil* are in the office until 6 pm, and it is all commission and no base salaries. The Dandy workers have kept their hours limit and their pay, but have to work overtime and unsocial hours on demand. Worst of all the solicitors in the English law firm affirm that you have to do everything fast; when the client wants it; at the weekend if necessary.

A little later I visited a second law firm in England where the same general ethos prevailed. A chance remark by a senior partner was evocative in this matter: 'It used to be the case that when you wrote a client a letter you could put the file away for three days at least' (meaning that a minimum of three days was required for the receipt of the letter and the client's response). But now it happens by e-mail, and 10 minutes later the ball is back in your court and you have to take action again.

COMPETITION AND THE EXTERNAL IMPULSE

Perhaps the most interesting thing that links these companies is that they are all responding to things in the external environment, both threats and opportunities. This is not at first sight obvious because at the same time they are all desperately proactive. None of these managements is just 'minding the store'. They are all taking decisions, solving problems, getting things done, and instituting change.

It may be a paradox but much of this activity comes from identifying change in the environment, and then doing something about it: responding to it, neutralizing it, seizing it, using it, doing all manner of things because of it.

Consider the English law firm:

▌ It is responding to:
  – the greater complexity of the law with more focus and specialization.

- the speed of change in the law with more retraining.
- the competition from other players in the field by growing organically itself.

▌ It has adopted meritocratic remuneration which will help it to keep the people it wants to keep in the face of widespread poaching.

▌ It has responded to perceived client needs for positive recommendations not dispassionate listing of options.

▌ It has responded to perceived client needs for fast response in place of traditional gentlemanly hours.

▌ It has taken advantage of the oversupply of law graduates to add qualities and competencies to the profile of the 'new-hire' lawyer.

This is some list. This is growth plus quality plus focus plus speed plus meritocracy. No wonder the partner I interviewed felt the profession he had joined had changed out of all recognition.

Le Soleil has perceived these threats to the industry and responded to them. It has upgraded its printing to match the competition. In structuring the remuneration of advertising salesmen it has taken not the (newspaper) industry norm but the wider media norm, exemplified by radio and television stations. It has cut costs and workforce in response to outside pressure. But it has also sought to enhance revenue by:

▌ Raising circulation.

▌ Raising advertising income.

▌ Making money out of unused printing capacity.

▌ Seizing opportunities offered by the Internet and crossing them with the physical distribution system it already has in place.

Dandy has identified public concern with health and developed products to meet it. It has seen a change in the socio-economic environment of Scandinavia which has made a range of employment practice changes possible – performance-related pay, rolling up overtime premiums, flexible hours, in some cases reclassification of employees downwards, abolishing the quality bonus – all of which would have been unthinkable in, say, the 1980s when I briefly lived in the region. It has recognized the opportunity created by the fall of European communism. First, to establish markets in Poland and then more securely in Russia. And second to engage in effect in off-shore manufacture in Russia, taking advantage both of lower wage rates and the high quality of applicants for factory employment.

But the apogee is probably the agricultural cooperative, SDWG. It has:

▌ Seen the need to rationalize (elevator) facilities, even when it runs counter to community traditions.

▌ Recognized that agricultural science has outrun (many) farmers, and responded, such as to create a market for agro-consultancy services; and for agronomy products.

▌ Seen that smaller farmers, who frequently have non-farm jobs, cannot always do what has to be done on their farms at the right time, and so provided them with 'application services' for a fee.

▌ Rightly perceived the trend to integration, to grouping of producers and the linking of them to food processing companies, a development that favours the intermediary with network management skills.

▌ Shown the ability to plug into the 'big picture' of fluctuating national market prices and hedging.

▌ Seen what the railroad companies want, and started giving it to them.

If you squeeze these cases they have something to say about competition. This is that we are inclined to see competition in a way that is arguably too narrow.

How do we conceive competition? In terms of other people (organizations, companies) doing the same things we are doing (making the same products, offering the same services, serving the same market segment) and maybe doing it better. Nothing wrong with this conception, it is the front line of what it is all about. But it is not the whole story.

Enhanced competition, which is the causal mainspring running through this book, does not only derive from the presence of savvy competitors in your market. In a more diffuse way it derives from changes in the wider operating environment. So if, for example:

I The socio-political climate changes, facilitating changes in employment arrangements.

I European communism collapses.

I Something called the Internet gets invented, and subscribers to it increase with geometric rapidity.

I There are unprecedented increases in the complexity and the role of change in the thing your organization deals in.

I Other organizations in the economic value-chain of which you are a part revise their expectations and objectives.

Then all this and more besides will 'hot up' the competitive environment, posing problems, invitations to rethink, along with the classic threats and opportunities of the SWOT exercise.

This more diffuse understanding of enhanced competition is probably the most valuable thing that can be taken from these four organizations whose operations we have looked at in some detail.

REFLECTIONS ON THE NEW MANAGEMENT

The relativization of the product that was discussed earlier has a further implication. This is that as core product considerations go onto the back boiler, and general management, strategic, and business issues come to the fore, then whatever it is that you do in business there are more people who could do it in your place than there used to be. Do not think that because you happen to be, say, CEO of a newspaper, only people from newspapers or media could possibly fill your position.

To put it another way, depressing product/industry and boosting business/management has the effect of decompartmentalizing the business world. Everyone is a potential rival for everyone else. The competition is thus feeding off itself, energized by the move from the particular to the general.

But this same trend also constitutes an opportunity. When the credentials are cast in terms of the managerial and general rather than in terms of the industry-specific then there are more qualified candidates. What we have called the managerial consensus is driving mobility, the movement of managers between companies. This increase in intercompany mobility does not show up especially well in the United States and the UK where positive attitudes to mobility have long prevailed. But the change is clear in some of the Continental European countries where traditionally negative attitudes to intercompany mobility prevailed. We argued this case in the last chapter with regard to Holland and France.

In Holland intercompany mobility used to be frowned upon as signalling a lack of loyalty and stability, and the undesirable presence of arrogance and ambition. In France where the élite educational institutions, the *grandes écoles*, license executive greatness, mobility used to be impossible for those without the *grande école* diploma and unnecessary for those with it. As we have seen from a perusal of current executive job adverts mobility now appears both acceptable and demanded in these countries.

So far then we have argued that the new management:

▌ decompartmentalizes industry and business;

▌ is a threat to incumbents and an opportunity to all;

▌ is driving intercompany mobility in the West generally, in some instances in countries previously hostile to management careers that zigzagged between companies and industries.

Sandhurst and the wider world

Once I visited Sandhurst, the UK's officer training school, at the invitation of a former student. One of the messages I got from people who talked to me was that a virtue of the Sandhurst system is that anyone who has been shaped by it will understand the mindset of others who have trained there without knowing them personally. So that one 'Sandhurst person' will know instinctively the priorities and disposition of another, will know what to expect from him or her 'in the field'. This is not only important in building *esprit de corps* but also useful operationally. This state of affairs is coming to be replicated in business management.

The effect of the managerial consensus is that everyone is playing to the same tune. Both their thinking and behaviour are informed by the same awareness and objectives. This facilitates a certain calculable predictability in business. It has become easier to second guess the opposition; after all, they mostly know what you know, and want what you want. At the same time it makes it easier for 'them' to second guess you.

In other words, the managerial consensus has introduced a dimension of transparency – everyone playing by the same rules, understanding means–ends connections in the same way. It is an approach to a level playing field, at least in the West.

Different countries?

To the key question, is the managerial consensus reducing the differences at least between the Western countries, the answer must be yes, but it is never likely to remove the differences altogether. On the side of the persistence of national difference there are several arguments that it is fair to put.

First, the last quarter of the 20th century saw massive research and survey evidence attesting to those differences – of business system, business values, and differences of managerial behaviour and style. The most recent surveys that I know of, that I was involved in, continue to attest to these differences in values among cohorts of managers drawn from different Western countries (Lawrence, 1998; Lawrence and Edwards, 2000).

Second, these value differences, different ways of understanding the role of the manager, are usually taken to derive from differences in national character. Most people are comfortable with this idea of national character, even if it is difficult to define.

Third, however, going beyond national character or temperament, different countries as sovereign states have different laws, institutions, and systems which will tend to shape business activity as well as management recruitment and employee behaviour. Only France has *grandes écoles*, only England has Eton, and even within the EU some countries have industrial democracy legislation going back over half a century (Germany) while some have none whatsoever (the UK).

So the managerial consensus is unlikely to eliminate the differences between countries but together with globalization and the shrinking role of the state in Western countries discussed in Chapter 1 it is likely to reduce it.

One effect of this is that it is more difficult to leverage advantage supposedly deriving from the differences between countries. There are several reasons and they tend to overlap, but key issues are:

▌ The differences have been reduced or relativized, made less important.

▌ Knowledge of business-relevant national differences has become more widely dispersed; the transparency effect, permitting advantage imitation.

▌ Or differences conferring an advantage have been neutralized by some other development.

Consider the question, are the US companies distinguished from those in other Western countries by the efficiency of their management systems? The answer is probably yes, but any margin of superiority is not likely to be decisive, one does not speak any more of 'a management gap', in the United States's favour as one did for 30 years after the Second World War.

Or consider Japanese cars. Figure 4.4, using 1989 data, shows that both national ownership and national location of car plants has a dramatic impact on quality:

	Japanese plants in Japan	Japanese plants in the US	US plants	Japanese plants in Europe	EU plants
Faults per 100 parts	13.8	63.9	86.7	83.2	89.7

Source: Calori and Lawrence, 1991

Figure 4.4

A heap of other output data from the same source attested further to Japanese efficiency. But the interesting question is, have differences of this magnitude persisted? And the answer of course is that they have been much reduced, that Western car manufacturers in general have learned and implemented JIT (just in time) systems, lean manufacture, and have pressurized both design cooperation and price reductions out of their component suppliers. And as for quality circles, does anyone remember that they started in Japan?

There is another twist to the car story. As the manufacture becomes more programmable and systematized, the emphasis shifts to design and styling. But styling would generally be held to be a European strength rather than a Japanese strength.

Or consider vocational education. Even Western countries vary a lot in the quality of provision. For decades Germany has been vaunted as having the best vocational education in Europe if not in the world. But if everything gets made in Thailand or Mexico, will it help them? All right, it is not as black and white as this, Germany is likely to continue to dominate a number of mid-tech niche markets where its performance is driven by craft tradition and engineering design capability. But it is indicative that during the 1990s Mercedes established a plant in Alabama and BMW did the same in South Carolina, in part to benefit from lower US labour costs.

REQUISITE DIVERSITY

There is an argument to the effect that élites should meet the criterion of requisite diversity. That is to say, the members of the given élite should not be all the same – by provenance, by mindset, by the basis of their superiority. That from intra élite difference will come friction, challenge, alternatives and perhaps symbiosis and imagination and the impetus to change.

The argument is usually used at the level of national élites. It has been noted before, for example, that the national élite in France is all *grande école* educated: that the political, administrative, business, managerial, and intellectual élites all, largely, have this *grande école* background and mindset in common. It means that they all have the same strengths (are all clever in the same way) and the same blindspots! The French national élite fails to meet the requisite diversity standard.

This is not all bad. It gives France unity and cohesion at the top. France is at its best where politics and technology meet, where élite conceived big projects are driven through by the power of the state. But it has its downside – it freezes talent outside of the élite, it is a brake on mobility and social change. If a problem cannot be solved by an application of the élite's wisdom, how will it ever be solved?

The same argument on requisite diversity may be applied to the business and managerial élite, both within and across the Western countries. The effect of the managerial consensus is to increase its solidarity, sameness, predictability and transparency.

FROM ÉLITISM TO SPONSORED MERITOCRACY

This trend towards a more homogeneous managerial élite and mindset is being accompanied in some Western countries by a move from recruitment on the basis of élite credentials – social, traditional, or educational, to recruitment and advancement on the basis of merit. But it is the recruiting and promoting organization, of course, that defines merit. *Voilà* the sponsored meritocracy. It is in part being fuelled by an oversupply of college educated people in many Western countries, forcing employing organizations to discriminate further in terms of their own requirements rather than accepting an externally conferred label.

A management consultancy in Germany, for instance, told me that the company had widened its recruitment from just a few schools like INSEAD to some 30 or 40. It is a way of saying: 'We know what we want and we will choose!' and away from the premise that the labelling done (for us) by a small number of high prestige colleges is all we need.

At one of the UK retail banks the manager of a Service Centre, where customer needs are handled over the phone, responded to my question about whom managers picked and how by saying: 'It is a complete mix. There are a few from other banks. We've got an ex-teacher. Certainly people from retail backgrounds. We don't recruit 18-year-olds from school.'

The last two points are particularly telling. Retail backgrounds means having people with customer-care skills and experience; not taking them straight from school means general educational attainment is not enough and will not be the filter. This last bit is particularly revealing in that the UK high street banks have a long history previously of taking people straight from school at 16 with 'O' levels (later GCSEs).

At a different level and on another occasion I had the opportunity to ask the MD of a steel plant in Sweden about graduate recruitment and careers. His reply distinguished between the old and the new systems:

OLD: take graduates into R&D, later move them out to production and marketing.

NEW: take graduates into specific jobs; but expect to move them within the organization quite quickly.

It is the same ethic. Hire people just because they have degrees in the right subject (= external labelling, drawing from an élite outside the company) and see what becomes of them – not any more! Instead the company will pick, on specifics, for specifics, and advance by performance (= sponsored meritocracy).

One of the most indicative signs of this move away from élitism has in fact been in France. From the late 1990s one has seen companies proclaiming that they will reserve some of their management traineeships for people who are not *grande école* graduates. It is a minority movement so far, but again it is signalling a recognition that the pre-labelled élite candidate may not be all the company wants.

None of these examples or the comments on them are meant as criticism. There is a compelling logic about companies rejecting externally labelled élites, at whatever level, and picking on the basis of what they think they need. The argument is rather that the two developments – consensus and meritocracy – will reinforce each other in practice. So that: if a management consensus is developing; and companies reject the external élite sources; they will probably all be picking in terms of much the same internally generated criteria; which will reduce diversity, and promote homogeneity.

SUMMARY

To sum up, the gains of the managerial consensus are:

▌ efficiency and cost reduction;

▌ strategic awareness;

▌ recognition of external threats and opportunities;

▌ proactivity.

We have tried to exemplify this in a positive way in our four deliberately diverse cases.

The downside is that this managerial consensus, reinforced by a move from élitism to sponsored meritocracy, is producing a swathe of managers across the West marked by:

▌ homogeneity;

▌ conformity;

▌ lack of requisite variety.

In turn this leads to:

▌ predictability;

▌ transparency;

▌ calculability (all reading from the same script).

The premium on being creatively different, and having the ability to reconfigure, has never been greater.

5

Companies respond to more demanding customers

The one thing that is universally asserted in all companies and industries is that customers are less loyal and more demanding than in the past. They are less likely to buy from you because your company is 'a household name', because you are their company's long-term supplier, because their parents patronized your company, because your company is 'the obvious choice' or simply because they used to.

The expression that is typically used is that customers increasingly have a 'shop around' mentality. This phenomenon is easier to recognize when the customer is the general public, ordinary people making choices and switches by whim or rationality, looking for the lowest prices at the petrol station, the lowest charges at the bank, the best trade-in deal, the lowest mortgage interest rate, the longest deferred payment period at the furniture store or white goods supplier.

But the phenomenon is there in industry-to-industry, business-to-business relations as well. Banks and business consultancies, agricultural cooperatives and civil engineering companies, law firms and telecomms service providers, all report switching by institutional or business customers.

One of the most interesting instances of customer activity bordering on the 'shopping around' I came across in researching for this book was in cancer charities. It goes like this:

▌ Donors want to make dedicated gifts, in support of research on particular cancers.

▌ Cancer (research) charities proliferate to meet this need.

▌ Donations rise in the 1990s boom.

▌ The desire of donors to make dedicated gifts is reinforced by information available on the Internet.

▌ Cancer charities respond by focusing on particular cancers, ones where research will get you furthest fastest.

▌ And they work hard to convince the public that the part of its research which is *general* biological research really will impact on key types of cancer.

The 'shopping around' is part of the explanation of the importance of brands, emphasized in Chapter 1. In a world of increasing competition and fickle customers branding is a way of trying to neutralize both trends, of attracting customers to particular providers of products or services. Hence the mad scramble to brand, to invest with distinctive and recognizable identity anything that is remotely 'brandable'.

Companies have also responded in kind to the 'shop-around' customer choice mentality with inducements that are calculable and have a cash value. So we have seen the proliferation of loyalty cards, all sorts of schemes that involve the accumulation of points for repeated purchases of a provider's goods and services eventuating in getting something free – simple buy five and get one free offers, frequent flyer schemes offered by airlines and airline alliances, and so on.

Sometimes there is a slightly blurred quality to this operation. If we take, for example, house building in the UK there is a fairly widespread acceptance of high price new houses by buyers, because of the confidence invested in house price inflation by buyers. So you do not mind so much paying a lot for your new house, the higher the starting price the more it will rise over time. Yet house builders have to compete on something, so they tend to keep the headline price high and/or uniform, and compete on extras – fitted kitchens, free white goods, carpets, and even offer additional features, say conservatories, at a low cost but separate from the headline price.

This phenomenon is exacerbated when the house builder is experiencing difficulty selling the last five houses on a development. You must NEVER sell the last house for less than the first house, it would undermine the steadily-appreciating-asset ethic. So your only alternative as builder to mothballing the last units for six months is to unload them deftly with hidden extras.

But there is more to the corporate response than branding and loyalty cards. For manufacturing companies, of course, there is a drive to raise quality, that in the West has been in train since the 1980s. But adding service to product has become more critical.

ADDING SERVICE TO PRODUCT

Just about every manufacturing company we have encountered in the last two or three years whose customers are other manufacturing companies speaks of 'getting closer' to its customers. This is also sometimes expressed as 'working back up the customer's decision chain'. In practice this usually means doing design work for customers, in part on spec, and bearing some of the development costs. There is also a move in the direction of 'supply and fit' or 'supply and install' deals with industrial customers, rather than just delivering what they ordered and leaving them to get on with it. The UK and Swedish steel companies in the study also speak of getting to know their customers' business better in the expectation of being able to suggest new applications for various types of steel. On the same theme Corus, the name assumed by the joint entity after the merger of British Steel and Hoogovens of the Netherlands, spoke of going downstream and acquiring stockists, to control service levels to end users and to actually do more for these end users, more cutting and shaping to tie in customers. Giving service a quite literal meaning, a machine tool manufacturer in the United States spoke of keeping machine tools in-house and doing in effect sub-contract work on them for industrial customers who would previously have bought the machines and done the work themselves. The CEO was also very strong on the issue of knowing the customers' business; this included knowing exactly what the customer buying a machine tool wanted it for, making sure the customer made the right choice, and even collaborating with machine-buying customers to help these customers raise their productivity.

A similar development in any customer industry facing environmental exigencies is cooperation from suppliers to help the customer achieve compliance with environmental regulations or, more generally, to improve environmental performance. An example would be the Swedish chemicals company EKA, acquired by AKZO of the Netherlands in the 1990s but largely autonomous (AKZO at the time of the acquisition had no rival product). EKA's core business is making two whitening agents, that is, two chemicals, used in paper making that help to make the paper white. EKA also design, and have made, the equipment needed to use these bleaching agents in pulp mills. Part of EKA's range of competitive advantage is assisting customers in meeting rising environmental standards. Also, and this is rather more common, EKA sought to consolidate the relationship with customers through service and maintenance contracts.

Another recurrent theme in this case of adding service to product concerns lead times. A lead time is the time it takes to make something from the time a firm order is placed. These lead times are being shortened. As one of the UK furniture makers put it: 'No one accepts four to six week delivery any more. Now we deliver in the week.'

In the summer of 2001 Marks & Spencer in the UK was reported to be concerned with lead times in its children's wear range, wanting to improve on the normal 21 weeks. By joining with one of its long-standing suppliers, Desmond & Sons of Northern Ireland, it would bring together designers, researchers and a range of specialists from both companies, reducing duplication. The Marks & Spencer head of children's wear, Michèle Jobling claimed: 'With this new system we should be able to go from concept to garment in 8–12 weeks. And we will sharpen that up, to 4–6 weeks for T-shirts. (*Guardian*, 30 August, 2001).

Surrounding the speeded-up delivery there are typically a range of other trends or developments, including:

▌ Companies are increasingly manufacturing to order rather than for stock.

▌ Customers are able to input orders electronically.

▌ Customers may even be able to look into a supplier's operation electronically, access information on volume, throughput and schedules, and decide on the viability of their order.

▌ Suppliers may also invoice customers electronically, as with SDWG (discussed in Chapter 4) and the railroads that ship its produce.

A nice example of a product competing as much on service as on product quality is offered by Scania (GB) Ltd, the UK presence (sales/service/marketing) of the Swedish truck manufacturer. Scania's market share in the UK had risen from 10 per cent in 1992 to 20 per cent in 1997, but perhaps more significantly the company quadrupled its service revenue in the course of the 1990s. The offering includes:

▌ A finance subsidiary financing vehicle purchases running at £240 million by 1998.

▌ The development of truck rental (periods of up to a year) as an adjunct to contract hire (over a year) with more than 1,000 trucks on rental at the end of the 1990s.

▌ The progressive introduction of satellite tracking of individual trucks that will yield single truck databases facilitating maintenance/service and better control of costs.

This list is of particular importance as truck operators come to think in terms of lifetime costs rather than in terms of acquisition costs. The databases will help Scania to understand customer needs better in a period where moves from single to double truck-driving shifts is anticipated, or even 24 hour/7 day usage.

The line between adding service to product and substituting service for product is not always clear. Probably the most famous case of the latter version at the start of the 21st century involves IBM. At the risk of simplification, IBM compensated for falling mainframe sales by developing its service division, now known as IBM Global Services, primarily an outsourcing operation. As a summer 2001 article in *Fortune* puts it: 'The Group (IBM Global Services) does everything from running a customer's IT department to consulting on legacy system upgrades to building custom supply chain management applications.' (*Fortune*, 27 August, 2001, 52).

It is projected that Global Services will furnish 40 per cent of IBM's revenue for 2002. The key question is whether this Global Services division's massive growth has reached the high point or whether it is still on a growth trajectory. The division is already the world's largest provider of IT services, by 2000 revenues.

We want to move on from this discussion of product enhanced by service to service enhancement itself.

ADDING SERVICE TO SERVICE

Sometimes it is even the case that once upon a time there was no service!

In 1989 the water companies in England and Wales were privatized, giving them a new concern for customers and service. The newly appointed CEO of one of these overlapped with his predecessor from the local authority days, and asked him 'Who are our largest customers?' No one, it emerged, knew. Warming to the theme of customer abuse this CEO told me that in 'the old days' the water company:

▌ Tried to make you pay whatever the meter said, never mind if there was a leak.

▌ If you thought there was a leak, made you prove this to the authority's satisfaction before it would take responsibility for it.

▌ Had a system whereby alleged leaks could only be reported in writing.

At a less basic level, quality of information offered to customers is a recurrent theme. The UK builders merchant Ridgeons, for example, emphasized staff knowledge and training and the product information service. Interestingly, Ridgeons also claimed to be the first company in the industry to hire out tools and equipment, giving customers an alternative to purchase that has since become commonplace.

Nor is this service enhancement limited to the private sector. One of the UK universities visited, for instance, spoke of setting up a centralized student administration and pastoral care facility. This provides students with a 'one-stop' facility, and all at one place rather than having much of this administration decentralized into the various subject departments.

Sometimes of course enhanced service is computer based. Menards is a chain of DIY stores in the upper mid-West of the United States.

These stores are equipped with computers for customers to use in planning the construction of garages, fencing, decks and so on. Even if you do not actually want to build a garage it is fun to play at it on the computer, which will offer you a choice of designs, dimensions, and materials, and at the end will print you out a parts list (all in-store and in stock) together with a total price in turn broken down into components.

United States owned Mercer Management Consulting in Germany offer another manifestation of service enhancement. Part of this is bundling; like the UK university cited above Mercer seek to offer the client 'one stop' consultancy services; though the client may well want a variety of services the trend is to want to deal with only one provider, with that providing organization managing any sub-contracting interfaces for the client. Mercer also stress that there is a trend to longer-term involvement with clients, typically in the form of moving from strategy and analysis, the traditional high-level service offered by consultancies to corporate clients, to implementation. This idea that consultancy recommendations have to be implemented for or more often with the client is also echoed at Accenture (former Andersen Consulting demerged from Arthur Andersen).

Mercer Consulting again made some interesting points about changing trends in payment by clients, with this becoming rather more contingent, along the lines of no win no fee in litigation. Specifically Mercer mentioned that: you only get the fee when it starts to happen! If the client only makes 80 per cent of the savings your recommendations promised, you only get 80 per cent of the fee.

Mercer also mentioned, albeit as a minority trend, taking an equity stake in client companies rather than a fee. Running through these examples is the theme of doing more for the client, in whatever way the client wants it done.

Yet service enhancement is perhaps most compelling when it is discretionary rather than programmable. Buzz, the KLM owned low cost airline that commenced its operation out of Stanstead airport at the start of 2000, suggested that it wanted to be differentiated in customers' perceptions by dealing effectively with a situation when something goes wrong, admitting however that this might lead to a tension between empowerment and consistency.

Airlines generally are a good industry for observing this drive to enhance service. All the conditions are right, namely:

▌ overcapacity;

▌ being a cyclical industry;

▌ thin margins;

▌ having expensive depreciating assets (aeroplanes);

▌ the necessity to gain slots – even with the aircraft you cannot make money without slots.

A slot is the right to use a given airway at a given time. Without slots you cannot launch and land aircraft. Slots are naturally limited by sky space and the capacity and configuration of airports. While in the United States slots are a freely traded commodity, in Europe the market is fettered by the intrusion of national governments and by various regulatory authorities. Nonetheless, to give an idea of the pivotal value of a slot, unofficially a prime time slot at London Heathrow was worth around £10,000,000 in spring 2001.

To make it worse the service that airlines want to offer is constrained by all sorts of entities over which they have limited control – the types of aircraft available, air traffic control systems, airports, governments, and even the cost of aviation fuel (all an airline can do is forward buy if they think the oil price is rising).

This sameness of product and lack of control over key facilities poses a challenge for service enhancement, but it is one well recognized in the industry. I recall a talk by an SAS spokesman at a conference in Stockholm in 1990 arguing that competition had moved from the sky to the ground, especially with regard to business travellers, with check-in at leading hotels in the key Scandinavian cities, limousine service between airports and hotels, and so on, a lot of this having since become common in the industry for premium fare passengers. In the same vein airlines like to vie with each other in the provision of executive lounges for first and business class travellers, boasting of the munificence of the lounges and the abundance of IT provision for harassed business travellers. The introduction by BA in the spring of 2001 of sleeper seats on selected flights for premium fare passengers is another example. Alternatively the service enhancement may be logistical in nature, in the sense of the power of the hub and the scheduling of connecting flights. In the spring of 2001 industry watchers were confronted with the novel fact that Air France was back in profit. This is ascribed primarily to the redesign of Paris Charles de Gaulle airport. This is not an architectural redesign, though there have been some improvements in ground access and in-terminal mobility, but logistical redesign which has improved the interface between short-haul feeder flights and higher revenue long-haul ones, making the most of the capacity. Charles de Gaulle and therefore Air France also benefit from the fact that the airport is not yet full, unlike London Heathrow and Frankfurt and to a lesser extent Amsterdam Schipol.

In the West the airline that is arguably most different is Virgin Atlantic, which started service in 1984 with flight VA1 from London Gatwick to Newark, New Jersey. If Virgin were not so big one might describe it as a niche operation. In fact it is niche in the sense of cherry-picking routes to fly, pretty much all long-haul routes: 75 per cent North Atlantic, 25 per cent rest of the world.

Apart from the cherry-picking and successfully hacking their way into London Heathrow where the yield is 15 per cent higher than at Gatwick, Virgin have enhanced service by rearranging the price-class categories. So that Virgin upper class is described as business class price for first class service, and includes:

I 'Drive-through' check-in at Heathrow, only seven minutes at the airport.

I An in-flight beauty therapist.

I Flatbeds, 7 degrees off the horizontal, that you can sleep on.

I The 'freedom menu' – you can have anything you like from the menu at any time during the flight.

Then there is Premium Economy, described as a mid-class, between normal economy and business class, something that might appeal to money conscious business travellers during a recession. Virgin have also introduced hotel check-in for economy passengers, giving them 'an extra half day on the beach' at some destinations, and aim to do this at Gatwick.

In a more general way Virgin has managed to create a youth/fun image; it is popular with young people, and a first choice airline for the Japanese.

A simple case of service enhancement concerns delivery. Wherever companies have to deliver something, that delivery operation tends to be seen as a chance to show quality of service, and may be adapted or supplemented in a way that would tie in customers. I found this particularly true of US companies in the rural mid-West, where repeatedly I heard the *dictum*: 'We have our own trucks. We don't outsource delivery.'

Take, for example, Pizza Corner in Valley City, North Dakota. It began as a pizza restaurant just off Main Street which then led to meeting local demand for a part-baked pizza that could be finished at home. Now the company is delivering in five or more states, gently pushing out the perimeters over time, its typical customer a bar or tavern that wants to be able to offer customers a good (reheated) pizza. Talking to one of the brothers who own the company there was a general emphasis on consistent delivery service, need for good equipment, no truck breakdowns and dependable drivers.

Against this general concern with service there are two specific things the company does which it says distinguishes it from competitors. First, it manages stock for its customers, delivering on a two-week cycle. That is to say, the customer does not have to order, Pizza Corner does not deliver a fixed amount, but delivers whatever is needed to top up the stock to last another two weeks. A simple thing, but helpful for those at the receiving end. To put this the other way round, as you go down the value chain there is an observable tendency for each link to demand more from the preceding link and that 'more' is offered in the form of taking out some complexity, making it simple for you.

To complete the Pizza Corner story the second thing is that the company's handmade pizzas are vacuum-wrapped. Handmade is not generally superior to machine made, except that handmade have a better ridge on the circumference which stops the toppings flowing out during heating. But vacuum-wrapped confers a distinct advantage in preserving flavour and freshness. The competition's products are loose-wrapped which means the pizzas will take in the smell of the freezer and admit frost or ice.

Next let's look at Harms Oil Company, among the top 50 oil wholesalers in the United States, with anticipated sales for 2001 of 175 million gallons. Harms Oil is pushing customers to let them manage stock, something that confers a two-way benefit. Harms Oil, with its 100 trucks and own drivers, wants to avoid a situation where everyone orders at short notice when they hear of a price rise, and deliveries cannot be easily met. *En passant* it was mentioned that farmers do not meet the reliable demand criterion, tending to order and consume in two quick bursts a year. So like Pizza Corner, Harms Oil likes to take care of the ordering and delivery, keeping customers topped up rather than delivering a fixed amount, using

GPS technology. But the next move will be putting probes in customer tanks, so Harms will know when to fill. This will facilitate greater anticipation by Harms who can watch the price on behalf of their customers and fill full when oil is cheap and put in enough to keep the customer going when the price rises.

Another example, of a more composite nature, is HRS Food service, a food wholesaler founded in 1949 with bases in Rapid City and Aberdeen, South Dakota. HRS tells the same story: own trucks, own drivers, even own repair shop and mechanics: drivers expected and rewarded for 'going the extra mile' for customers, and so on.

But there are other elements of the service tie-in. The HRS customers are institutions – schools, hospitals, prisons, hotels, and so forth. New legislation requires every food-serving institution to have someone on the staff who has done the serve safe food course, so HRS offers a training course for it. Furthermore HRS:

I Provides food service equipment.

I Designs kitchens for institutional customers.

I Provides salespeople with laptops, as in the Falcon Brewing case mentioned in Chapter 1, leading to instant deals and order inputting; the laptop has the complete customer history programmed in.

I Makes sure that the salespeople can also give instant nutritional information.

I Has installed computers for some customers, so that the customers can order electronically.

I Offers customers Internet ordering if they prefer this.

I Has chemical and beverage specialists who sell and service the drinks machines.

I Can also handle dishwashing and laundry for institutions.

Together with reliable delivery this is a nice range of service tie-ins for a food wholesaler servicing institutional customers. Moving away from the theme of delivery we would like to round off this discussion of service enhancement with two more examples, chosen for their idiosyncrasy, one UK, the other in the United States.

Long winter on the Prairies

Hub Music and Vending is an amusement machine company. It buys the machines and does deals with location operators. It puts the machines into arcades and taverns, and employs technicians who service the machines and collect the takings.

But Hub Music and Vending is in South Dakota, one of the few US states to legalize the video lottery. The state introduced it in 1989, that is to say the bill was debated and passed in that year and the state's share of the profits (after some 65 per cent of the spend has been returned to the players) was set at 22.5 per cent. The process of (re)enactment was repeated in 1992, 1996 and 2000, with the share of the state's take rising inexorably. In 2001 this share reached 50 per cent. The video lottery take is now the second largest source of state income after sales tax (South Dakota has no income tax). On hearing this story I was reminded of a conversation I once had with a hospital administrator in west Texas, whom I had quizzed about the problem of retaining senior medical staff, who replied: 'You can't depend on their hypocrisy but you can usually depend on their greed.'

Now the company in question is doing fine, but it is difficult to expand since:

▌ It cannot operate out of state (and only a few states like Oregon, Louisiana, Montana have legalized video lottery, with West Virginia as a definite maybe).

▌ There is loads of competition in-state.

▌ There is a saturation in-state.

▌ In any case the locations at which the video lottery machines may be installed are limited by law – they cannot be put on street corners or in shopping malls.

▌ In addition, there is an understandable reluctance to engage in growth by acquisition in case the abolitionist lobby gains the upper hand.

▌ And if you allow location-owners to cut sharper deals where they pay less, competitors will do the same to protect market share.

So what is left for customer retention and market share enlargement? SERVICE. All the usual things were mentioned: having honest and decent staff, offering prompt service, an inclination to oblige location owners by installing at their request a larger range of amusement machines, updating the equipment for them, and so on. But the one I had not heard before was organizing pool and darts leagues to draw people into the taverns and promote machine use. All the location owner has to do is to guarantee that the punters will come in one night a week starting in October – a not overly ambitious goal for the small town upper mid-West. Hub music does the rest: organizes the show, keeps the statistics, does the promotion, organizes the parties. As one of my US business interviewees said to me: 'Any idea is a good idea.'

Living for ever

The health club industry has grown rapidly in the UK in the last few years. The proportion of the population who are members has risen, not to US levels, but industry watchers do not expect rates to go that high anyway. There is already speculation about how soon rates will peak. So in this maturing part of the leisure industry some segmentation is already apparent, for instance between the groups shown in Figure 5.1.

Against this background the general manager of one of the club chains I interviewed was serving an older and better-off clientele, attractive as a customer group in various ways. Clients were:

Working class muscle builders	v	Middle class fitness devotees
Time rich customer, for example retired or semi-retired	v	Time poor customers, for example 20 + /30 something, in the City
Provision for adult sub-groups	v	Family clubs
High-fee image-enhancing	v	Affordable fitness

Figure 5.1

▌ loyal to the chain, static;

▌ not price sensitive;

▌ in many cases time rich;

▌ mildly averse to change (this is good news because it means you do not have to put time and money into bringing about change).

The service offering matched this customer group. Club membership was held at a level that enabled staff to know 90 per cent of regular users by name; the audio-theatres (VDU screens) above the exercise bikes and other equipment were turned off to encourage adjacent machine users to talk to each other; social and cultural events were organized by individual clubs, and so on. In other words modest steps were being made in the direction of the London club rather than the model of Saturday night at Grand Ole Oprey.

Additionally, the company claimed to be the first chain to do cholesterol testing. Then it had gone on to devise a system that would crunch the data from medical history, whether or not the individual smoked, information about cholesterol, blood pressure, body mass index and a few other things that were too sophisticated for me to get my mind round, that allows you to compute the individual's biological age. Furthermore this biological age may differ from the customer's chronological age. We will call this difference the x factor.

Now there may in practice be a few losers, a few tested club members where biological age will be higher than their actual age. But mostly this is going to be a good news scenario. After all only 5 to 7 per cent of the population exercise regularly. So the club members are a self-selected minority concerned with fitness and actually doing something to promote it. The interviewee himself was '11 years younger' than his actual age according to the computation. Even better, the x factor can be improved over time, so there is always something to shoot for. So if at 53 you are only 47, you could aim to be only 50 when you are 60.

Almost as good as playing the South Dakota video lottery.

MULTI-CHANNEL

Another response to more demanding customers is to give them options when it comes to enjoying the goods or services in question. Indeed we have amassed several examples already, for instance the willingness of builders merchants to sell or hire equipment; of machine tool companies to sell the tools or alternatively to act as sub-contractor and do the work for what would otherwise have been the equipment purchaser; of Saab to lease you a truck, let you have it on contract hire, or even sell it; of companies that allow you to order their goods or services in a variety of ways.

This multi-channel phenomenon is probably most common in financial services with telephone banking, Internet banking, and the paperless administration of insurance claims. Indeed the generic form of the multi-channel is in the form of 'clicks and mortar', a phrase I first heard from the then (1999) CEO of Blackwell's, the UK book chain, who was offering telephone and Internet ordering in addition to its chain of bookshops.

No doubt these alternative ways of accessing goods and services are a benefit to customers, or at least to sub-groups of customers. At the same time these multi-channel arrangements are not always one way in terms of the benefits conferred. Retail banks, for instance, would love to be able to close the branches and make customers manage their accounts via call centres; already 'the back office' has been ripped out of most branches and the administration centralized, with customer calls to the branch typically re-routed automatically to call centres. Airlines would also love it if all passengers were to book over the Internet, so the airlines could cut those travel agents out of the loop – the UK low cost carrier easyJet is an interesting case of this development. To get the best fares you need to book well in advance. But the call centre will not accept bookings for more than three months ahead. To book further ahead you have to do it over the Internet. The former easyJet ticketing office at Luton airport is now personless, but there is a computer on the counter.

In retail operations it is probably fair to say that the jury is still out on the benefit of Internet sales. The case for, in terms of customer choice and convenience, has been made many times. Talking to a mix of UK retailers, however, I have found that some treat it as a defensive move. You have to offer sales via the Internet, or Web-fulfilment, because X per cent (it is always a small number) want it and will go to a rival if you do not offer this facility. One retailer went as far as the 'I wish it had never been invented' routine, suggesting the money spent on Web-fulfilment would have been better spent on opening new stores.

Nonetheless the 'clicks and mortar' phenomenon is at least in part driven by customer expectations, as a part of the provider response that is the theme of this chapter.

ADDING CUSTOMER GROUPS

The generation of new customer groups is particularly interesting in the present climate because companies are caught between two forces. On the one hand, this is the age of focus, core business, 'stick to the knitting', and leveraging core competence. This does not favour diversification at all, and it particularly disfavours unrelated diversification. But the heightened competition we see as the mainspring driving contemporary developments leads companies to go for MORE whenever possible. At the same time the more demanding, 'shop around' customer orientation that is the starting point for the present chapter pushes companies in the same direction, the need to increase turnover. After all, one will make less per head on demanding customers as these customers increasingly expect higher quality, better service, more back-up, more extras, faster model changes and more customization, all of which the companies have to provide at cost to themselves.

To these two opposing forces – stick to the knitting but try to increase revenue – a third consideration should be added. This is that many companies are operating in mature markets, as we argued in Chapter 1, so it is often difficult to increase market share. If you look at companies whose operations and development you are familiar with, you can see that these forces are impacting on many of them. These companies are not going for wild diversification, but neither are they inactive. They are pursuing a discriminating middle course, going for what I have identified as cognate customer groups (see Figure 5.2).

The essence of cognate customer groups is:

▌ A company identifies a new group that (can be convinced) it needs an existing product or service; though this new group will be differentiated from existing groups in some way. **Or:**

▌ The company looks at its core competence and asks if there is something a bit more they can do with it, which will bring another customer group within its ambit. **Or occasionally:**

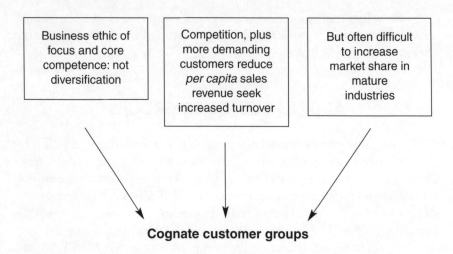

Figure 5.2

▌ The company takes something it has to do anyway, even if it is not the core activity, and expands it horizontally to embrace new customer groups.

As an example of the first version consider the UK pub. OK, it is a long time since the pub was a male preserve, but we have now come a long way from the stage when it was 'all right for women to go to pubs' (implicitly, if accompanied by men) to a time when women are customers in their own right, and often initiators when they go with male partners, that is, choosing when and where to go.

Two related things have driven this development. First, the broad change from traditional pubs to pub–restaurant chains or at least to pubs offering food has changed the 'going to the pub' experience for married women. While for women it used to mean boredom loyally endured while husband talked to male cronies and drank draught beer, it now means having a meal out with male partner.

Second, and this is key for women visiting pubs independently rather than in the company of men, is the development outlined in Chapter 2 where in 1989 the then Monopolies and Mergers Commission promulgated the Beer Orders requiring breweries to divest many of the pubs they owned (vertical de-integration) in the interests of stimulating competition. This meant that the pubs ceased to be a downstream extension of manufacturing (brewing) and became a service/retail entity in their own right. The divestment by the brewers, still in train in 2001 with the sale of the Whitbread pub estate, brought lots of new owners and operators into play, new operators who thought through or at least evolved strategies of market positioning, targeted segments, competitive advantage and branding.

One by-product of all this is that the term 'female-friendly' is now a standard term in the industry. And there is a loose consensus about what makes a pub female-friendly. At one end of the scale it is an ensemble of décor/hygiene/security factors (more attractive furnishings and décor, better toilets with well-lit and carpeted corridors leading to them, safer and better illuminated car parks, air management, smoke control and so on).

At the other end are some less tangible factors. There is survey evidence backed by successful pub designs that suggest women like pubs with big panoramic windows. It means you can see what you are getting into before it is too late. So if you look in and see a smoke filled bar peopled by septuagenarian males drinking pints of mild and puffing Woodbines, you can move on to somewhere more enticing.

Another development is the emergence of bars of a more continental (European) style. The Ha Ha Bars would be an example, cafés where there is also a coffee machine, where you don't have to drink beer, mineral water is also on offer, and the décor and layout are not traditionally maleist. The café-bar closes the gap between the pub and the café, and at the same time lowers the threshold for women.

Finally on this example, one of the pub chains with which I had contact, was pleased with the high number of women customers but also intrigued by it. In response the company carried out exit surveys, and the women customers mentioned all the practical things that management anticipated – lighting, safety, air management, etc – but the three factors mentioned most often, in ascending order, were:

▌ Panoramic windows, being able to see in first (as above).

▌ Panoramic windows again, being able to see out, not feeling contained, and able to be seen.

▌ Sexy barmen.

Surveys carried out by men no doubt.

Or consider Speedwing, a subsidiary of British Airways (put up for sale in 2002 in the wake of the post-11 September downturn) that offers systems and consultancy services to other airlines (and airports). Part of its operation is Speedwing Network Services, which involves taking data from client organizations and having it processed, in fact cross-border in India. It is about inputting data that requires human intervention. The client provides the data, Speedwing has it crunched in Bombay. It arises where there is no automated interface between systems and the interface has to be effected by human intervention.

Fine. And where do the cognate customer groups come from? From Speedway's realization that the same service can be offered to other industries, the common feature being the need to crunch data across non-automated systems. Speedwing is now doing it for pharmaceutical and insurance companies.

The distinction made earlier in this section between the three ways of evolving new customer groups is not always cut and dried, but some examples do fit very nicely. Consider the case of the UK company Crown Derby.

What Crown Derby is instantly famous for is its tableware – high quality, distinctive, high-end. It is something of a protected, upmarket niche. Yet by the same token it is a small and static market.

Competition is up. Rivals have gone cross-border to take advantage of lower labour costs (whereas all Crown Derby's production is in Derby, it is part of the magic). There has been huge investment in the Far East and especially in China in new ceramic businesses, and governments have supported this and bought the technology from Germany. These developments have led to huge overcapacity. Crown Derby may be above a lot of this, yet there is still this cauldron of competition bubbling away.

Perhaps more serious, however, is the big change in lifestyle, in the way people entertain, and in the way they eat. This trend is from the formal to the informal, from eating in the dining room to eating in the kitchen, from entertaining in the home to entertaining outside the home. Result: the demand is for simpler and chunkier tableware.

Weddings are good news of course for the likes of Crown Derby, because quality china finds its way onto the wedding gifts list as well as at the reception. But there are fewer weddings than in the past, and people are marrying later in life.

But tableware is only part of the business. Tableware is not the only manifestation of the talent of Derby designers and craftsmen. There is also giftware. The giftware arm is split between collectables and ornamental, the latter being decorative accessories purchased for visual appeal rather than for series completion. And giftware is going nicely, especially collectables, where there is a huge growth with people on all sorts of incomes and social statuses. There is a magnificent display in Crown Derby's lobby and factory shop. Interest is also fostered by all sorts of collectors' clubs, special offers, and magazines. In the United States alone the Crown Derby collectors' club has 17,000 members.

Moreover in the UK interest may well be driven by TV programmes about antiques. These have driven the price of antiques up. They draw attention to collecting as a hobby. And old brand names keep on coming up on the *Antiques Road Show*. This advertising would cost the industry a fortune if it had to pay for it, but it is all FREE.

A particularly good site for observing this phenomenon of the development of new customer groups is the UK water companies. Or to get it right, the Regional Water Authorities in England and Wales, that were privatized in 1989 (it did not happen in Scotland or in Northern Ireland).

These water companies are an interesting test case because they are beautifully trapped between two forces.

The first is the regulatory authority Offwat, which controls prices, sets investment targets, lumbers water companies with EU environmental and quality objectives, and generally bosses them around; there are reviews every few years; in the November 1999 review the companies were told to reduce their prices to end users by 10 per cent; even if the companies find a way of making extra money in UK it has to be short term because at the next review they risk having it taken away; 'so much for monopoly status'!

Second, the normal tactic of striving to increase market share is only marginally viable; if you are a Welsh water company it is scarcely viable to supply South East England; to be precise there is an access code in place whereby one company can use another's physical network to distribute water, but has to pay for it and it would only be worthwhile to supply a major industrial user.

These companies, then, have a motive *par excellence* for diversification. So what do they do?

Well, the first smart move is to get away from the regulator, which can be achieved by going cross-border. We made a passing reference in Chapter 1 to Anglian Water managing water supply in Buffalo, New York State. Aside from Buffalo at the start of 2000 Anglian also had initiatives and/or contracts in Wellington, New Zealand, in Chile, in the Czech Republic and in Australia.

Anglian has also entered the field of facilities management, for other UK water companies. That is to say doing the maintenance and rebuilding where required. Vivendi and Lyonnaise des Eaux in France are doing just the same, and doing it cross-border. In support of this initiative Anglian in the UK bought Morrisons, a Scottish construction company, in the summer of 2000. Car fleet management has become another Anglian venture: Anglian buys cars from manufacturers, leases them to its own employees (more cheaply than when it was done for them by a third party organization), and leases vehicles to other organizations.

To take one of the smaller companies as an example, Bristol Water has specialized in leakage management. This of course is something the water companies have to do for themselves anyway, and the expertise can be sold to foreign water companies – Malaysia was one example proferred by Bristol Water. In conjunction with another of the companies, Severn Trent, Bristol Water had a contract from the World Bank in Trinidad, where Severn Trent ran the water supply and Bristol Water did the checking, balancing, and leakage control.

Severn Trent itself, headquartered in Birmingham, has been strongly proactive. Some of its initiatives follow:

▌ Buying Biffa, an integrated waste management company; integrated means landfill, recycle, and waste disposal.

▌ Trying in 1996 to take over South West Water.

▌ All the water companies have laboratory facilities, of course, to do their own quality checks; Severn Trent has focused on the £80 billion market for laboratory analysis/environmental service in the United States, and has become the number one player in this market.

▌ Running operations in a variety of Western European countries (France is a no-go area) though in contrast to the French companies, without taking ownership of the assets.

▌ Endless water supply and water treatment and effluent handling assignments in the United States.

▌ Making a specialism of leakage problems, as has Bristol Water. Severn Trent developed with a contractor a proprietary product known as 'silent soldiers', which when installed show you where the leaks are; when you know where they are you put in pressure reducing valves to solve or at least reduce the problem.

This is only a quick look at three of the companies but there is a clear pattern. Additional customer groups are generated by:

▌ Doing what the company does at home, in other countries.

▌ Taking some part of the water operation, for example, leakage management or facilities management, and spreading it horizontally to other water providers, at home or abroad.

▌ Taking a competence, laboratory analysis, and broadening it to attract additional customers, at home or abroad.

▌ Occasional bits of related diversification, for example, Severn Trent's acquisition of Biffa.

▌ Taking a non-core operation needed in-house, for example, car leasing, and offering it to other organizations.

It is a very tight pattern, and this in an industry which has every incentive to be proactive in the search for additional revenues.

NOTHING LIKE A NICHE

The forces we have been considering, fiercer competition generally and more demanding customers, make niche product markets more attractive. We want to argue later that companies devoted to serving niche markets are not necessarily secure. There is a sense in which they are more vulnerable to corporate predators than is 'the average' company. Not only may they be sought (bought) by other niche players seeking to dominate the niche, they are also at the mercy of more generalist companies wanting to extend their product or service range, and these generalist companies are of course bigger. So that while we have seen Ford buy Aston Martin, we are never going to see Porsche buy General Motors. But this is not to say that the niche is not good business, for whoever owns the company that serves it.

In the context of the present discussion of corporate response to more demanding customers the niche-serving company has a number of advantages:

▮ By definition it is doing something that is a little bit special.

▮ So there should be fewer rivals able to do it.

▮ So even if the niche-serving company has fewer customers, there are fewer alternative providers of what they want.

▮ Hence (the company hopes) a measure of customer loyalty is enjoined.

This formula is jolly attractive in the age of the ever more demanding customer. To which may be added the conventional justification for the niche, that this something that is a bit special comes at a premium price, so margins rise in consequence. Again because the niche-serving company is doing something special, there are likely to be entry barriers, things which make it more difficult for others to invade its niche market by doing what it is doing. All sorts of things may constitute those entry barriers, including:

▮ Equipment set-up costs.

▮ Superior quality of product or service.

▮ Established relationships with customers, such that they are not likely to be tempted away by a 2 per cent discount from a rival.

▮ Know-how.

▮ Strategic perception – the niche-serving company has seen an opportunity that others have missed, and even if it can be cloned the company enjoys first-mover advantage.

Let us consider one or two examples:

A tale from the Yorkshire Dales

Once upon a time in the small Yorkshire Dales town of Masham there was a family brewery called Theakston, run by successive generations of the Theakston family. As noted earlier, brewing is an industry which has seen considerable consolidation in the UK, and in other countries, and Theakston's has been part of this process. In 1983 members of the Theakston family sold it to a regional brewer, who in turn sold it in 1987 to what was then Scottish & Newcastle (S&N), and later became Scottish Courage. At this time Theakston's in Masham was still being run by Paul Theakston, but he left in 1988 when S&N wanted him to take on a different job in the group. But tradition and continuity run deep in these parts and by the early 1990s Paul Theakston was resolved to see a brewery owned and operated by his family in Masham again.

The site next to the original Theakston's brewery, still going strong as an S&N brand, came onto the market. It was acquired and brewing started again in the autumn of 1992. This new enterprise is the Black Sheep Brewery, and a black sheep has become their emblem and brand. This story is relevant to a discussion of niche creation and protection, but an introductory note on what is different about UK beer will help to make sense of it.

In Continental Europe and the United States people mostly drink bottom brewed or bottom fermented beer, which is light in colour. The British call beer of this kind lager. Traditionally the British themselves, and the Irish, have drunk top brewed or top fermented beer, which is darker in colour. The very dark kind is called stout, and the medium dark kind, the majority, is called ale in the brewing industry and bitter by the general public – a pint of bitter is what you ask for when you go into a pub.

Now the British, open in all things to learning from other countries, started to develop a taste for lager some decades ago. In the 1970s a magic point was reached where lager consumption passed the consumption of bitter. This trend had the effect of wrong-footing the UK brewery industry somewhat; they were not used to making lager, indeed it is an open question whether there are any indigenous UK lager brands.

So all this lager that is consumed in the UK is mostly brewed under licence from Continental European brewers such as Heineken or Stella Artois (now Interbrew) or it is simply imported, as is the case with brands from more distant countries: the beer counter in a UK supermarket has brands from all round the world, nothing is too exotic for us, in stark contrast to beer displays in Continental European countries. Such is the UK enthusiasm for foreign lager that Denmark's Carlsberg has actually established a major brewery in Northampton to service the UK market.

All this choice in lager, this *embarrass de choix*, may lead to lager brands being heavily differentiated. There are up-market brands and downmarket brands, and supermarket own label versions and you never know who made (brewed) them; there are everyday brands and specialist brands; average strength (3–3.5 per cent alcohol) and strong brands (7–10 per cent alcohol). Meanwhile ale or bitter has been relegated; a drink for middle-aged or older people, invariably men – young people drink lager, women who drink beer are more likely to drink lager. Bitter is not usually available in restaurants that offer beer as a possible accompaniment to food: restaurants mostly serve bottled lager, the more upscale the restaurant the more upscale the brand. So bitter has been corralled. Figure 5.3 shows a two by two table on the two beer types crossed by status.

	Low end	High-end
Ale/bitter	Yes	
Lager	Yes, own label and other brands	Yes, exotic and quality foreign brands

Figure 5.3

If you refer to Figure 5.3, part of Paul Theakston's vision in recreating the family brewery in Masham was seeing an empty box in the top right-hand segment. This is where Black Sheep is.

OK, I have overstated a bit, Black Sheep brands are not without competitors, but Black Sheep was the first mover in the premium bottled ale segment at least. And Black Sheep has all the right credentials:

▌ It has family tradition.

▌ It is in the right place.

▌ Two-thirds of the output goes to pubs in a 70–80 mile radius of Masham.

▌ It has local contacts and networks.

▌ It is a nice old-fashioned brewery, with appeal to *aficionados*.

What is more it is a good story. It is as if the US Justice Department closed down Bill Gates, made him sell Microsoft to Hewlett Packard, and four years later Microsoft II turned up on the next block in Seattle.

I have told the story with the necessary unpacking to push home the idea of strategic perception. But know-how is probably a more conventional way of protecting a niche market.

Churning or qualifying

Those who do not understand IT and look at it from the outside see a static monolith. But those on the inside are all too conscious of the rate of change, with a succession of knowledge/skill sets passing across the corporate stage. I have talked to people in 2001 who speak of 'having started as a COBOL programmer' and recalling a time in the UK when 'it was IBM and ICL and that was about it', and they say such things like ex-Air Force pilots recalling the vagaries of the Spitfire. Those who could upgrade IBM mainframes had their (last) moment of glory preparing for Y2K. Now people want major integrated process systems, where everything interfaces with everything else. It is e-commerce skills that are in demand now, and the ability to develop e-strategies.

This kaleidoscope of skill need and techno-change is one reason why a lot of companies meet their IT personnel needs by 'buying in bodies' from contract recruiters. It is also the case that the need fluctuates over time – while all companies need an IT system and are usually staffed to operate it, they cannot easily cope with big projects, system changes, and new technologies.

For all these reasons contract recruiters, as they are called in the trade, organizations that have lots of IT people on their books and hire them out for a fee to companies that need them, have been flourishing since the 1970s. But there are a lot of these contract recruiters. They are at their best providing 150 staff for six months, or 200 on semi-permanent hire. They achieve economies of scale, are drawn to big operations, compete on price and have thin margins. Again because they compete on price they are often frustrated in their attempts to consolidate relationships with corporate clients over time. They get, say, three commissions in a row from a company, feel they are building a relationship with the HR manager, and then find someone else in the company has dumped them in favour of a marginally cheaper rival.

This is the background against which Opta Resources, a fast growing company in the south of England, should be viewed. Opta also hires IT staff to companies that need them, but deals in the top 10 per cent. That is to say Opta is providing staff who have managerial and interactive competence as well as technical skills, people who can effect change projects for corporate clients, who are engaged with the client's own permanent staff to effect change and then to manage knowledge transfer. For such people Opta can of course charge more than the contract recruiters. Opta has taken the trouble to find these top 10 per cent people and to 'qualify' them; that is to say, to assess their managerial competence and experience, to document their past assignments and the capability these will have conferred, and thus know the kind of higher order assignment for which such people would be suitable.

In theory you could get these top 10 per cent from the contract recruiters too. If you ask, they would give you 300 CVs (resumés) and you, the would-be client, would have to plough through these to try to figure out who the right people might be, and probably get it wrong, because the contract recruiters will not have qualified the people on their books in such a discriminating way. But Opta has.

What is more, since Opta management has the ability to qualify in the way we have described it can also conduct more meaningful dialogue with clients than can the typical contract recruiter. It is more likely to know, that is, what the corporate client 'really needs'; and particularly where the client is doing something big that is new to them it would not be new to Opta who can deploy its discretion and experience to the client's advantage.

This is a niche protected by know-how. Here is a more subtle one, in the United States. Computer Doctor is a franchised computer repair operation that had 120 stores in autumn 2000 and was planning to have nationwide coverage. The customers are a mix of: personal computer users; commercial customers, including a lot of shop chains wanting service for their electronic tills.

Computer Doctor was planned as a franchise operation from the start. In its recent expansion phase picking the franchisees was the key corporate task. Unlike Opta the franchisees do not have to be computer people, indeed 97 per cent of the franchisees are not. The franchisees don't do the repairs, they hire technicians to do it; but they are trained to know what, and how long it should take and what it should cost, so that they don't get ripped off by their technicians. They also pick up a lot of knowledge about computers by osmosis, without being technicians themselves.

In fact the demands made on the franchisees involve the following skills:

▍ financial capability;

▍ marketing;

▍ interpersonal;

▍ management.

Regarding the first of these Computer Doctor aim to sign up people with 'a three spot capability', that is, they have to be able to set up three stores or service points in a geographic area fairly quickly.

The franchisees are picked, primed, developed and got to the point of deciding by an elaborate information package into which a phased decision process has been built. Now what Computer Doctor are looking for is people who are at a midway point on the scale:

innovation ———————————————————— conformity

Sure the company wants franchisees who can operate within the system, but is also looking for some flair and vision for developing the outlets and growing the business. The response of (potential) franchisees to this package above, like: Do they master it? How quickly? Do they think through certain problematics, such as property acquisition? etc, give evidence of systems grasp, stability, and management ability, but the package is so structured that responses indicate flair and innovativeness as well.

OK, this may not quite qualify as a niche protected by know-how, but if picking the franchisees is the key and you have: rightly identified what qualities you need; and developed a system to select them; you are certainly away to a good start.

FROM A HELICOPTER

Let us round off the chapter by looking down on the ground covered.

The background is the intensification of competition. The foreground is the more demanding customer, whether business or personal. The response of companies in this situation has been the substance of this chapter.

The patterned responses we have identified are:

I adding service to product;

I adding service to service, or upgrading or enriching service if you prefer;

I constructing multi-channel availability of goods and services;

I generating cognate customer groups;

I privileging niche operations, which by definition enjoy some protection against growing competition;

I protecting niches in various ways, and we have given examples of less obvious and less tangible ways of doing this; we have also noted that the ordering/selling operation itself, especially between businesses, is becoming increasing routinized and computerized.

Because customers of all types are more demanding, customer satisfaction and retention is taken more seriously, but the approach to it is typically formalized and survey driven, and this development is reported by companies in both the United States and the UK.

There is also an observable decline of loyalty and traditional relationships. This is not just true of customers as 'ordinary people' buying consumer goods, but also of business-to-business relations; examples encountered include the decline of traditional relationships between business consultants and their corporate clients, between civil engineering consultancies and their institutional clients, between law firms and clients, and of course these relationships are often disrupted by manufacturers or retailers simplifying the structure of their suppliers by concentration and elimination. Sometimes this is done to get more price leverage on fewer suppliers, sometimes there are efficiency gains, sometimes it is simplification for simplicity's sake – always, however, it disrupts some previous, and often long-standing relationship.

We might put this last point in a different way. As companies have become more proactive, they have given less weight to traditional attachments. They come to value less per se people or organizations that have been customers or suppliers or business partners for maybe years. In the matter of customers in particular, companies more commonly expect to win and hold them on meritocratic grounds, and are more ready to shed those that contribute less to the bottom line rather than to retain them in a spirit of diffuse goodwill.

6

A crisis of human capital?

It is quite possible to argue that business organizations in the West face a crisis of human capital in the early 21st century. The bond between companies and employees has been weakened, and that has happened at a variety of levels in the organization. The relationship between companies and their professional and managerial staff has been increasingly 'marketized and monetized'. Across the organization flexibility has been bought at the expense of loyalty. The corporate citizen of yesteryear is on the way out, replaced by those with 'marketable skills' and merely conditional attachments to their employing organizations.

The malaise does not have a single cause. There are a variety of trends and factors involved. Many of them have been canvassed already, especially in Chapter 1 where some of them were lumped under the heading of denominator management. These trends do derive, largely, from enhanced competition in the business world. They can all be defended in terms of organizational or business rationality; they all serve a purpose and that purpose is clear. Our concern here is not to critique the business rationale but rather to:

▌ Explore the phenomenon more systematically.

▌ Flag up its implications for corporate culture and organizational loyalty.

▌ Put the phenomenon into context; show, that is, how it interacts with other contemporary developments.

▌ Raise the question, so what?

ELEMENTS OF A CRISIS

A schematic depiction of some of the key elements may be helpful (Figure 6.1); most of them have been mentioned in earlier chapters.

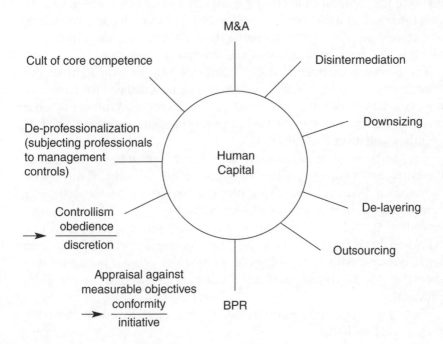

Figure 6.1

MERGERS AND ACQUISITIONS (M&As)

M&A blurs organizational identity. The more M&A we have, the more people there are who are not working for the organization they joined but they have not moved either! Nor is the change merely nominal. We know that many M&As do not work, do not deliver the gains that their initiators expected. One reason for this, of course, is that M&A seeks to merge two corporate cultures that are different, or to subject one of them to the dominance of the other.

M&A also creates at least initial uncertainty, however well the change is handled. For those with 'marketable' skills the temptation to move on is often irresistible – how much better to get a post with another company, probably a competitor, than be hanging around in the merged entity and seeing how bad it gets! Looking back over the last 10 years the most glowing accounts I have heard of mergers have come from CEOs (the ones that survived, to head up the merged entity) some time after the event.

Sometimes the realities of M&A are differently perceived at different levels in the company. One major company I visited in Sweden in 2001 was the result of a merger of four constituent Swedish companies, run as a purely Swedish entity for some time. Then it was taken over by a much larger, high-profile Norwegian company.

The Swedish managers at the corporate office made light of the four-company merger. As one of them put it: 'Of these four companies, one was more entrepreneurial, and had a bit of an impact when it merged. But the other two fitted in (with the initiating company) OK and they had a similar culture anyway.'

But the Swedish management were rather less enthusiastic about the Norwegian takeover (Swedes will be about as enthusiastic over a Norwegian takeover as US employees would be to the see their company bought by Canadians). One of the Swedes at corporate office confided: 'X (Norwegian company) was very influenced by its CEO, who had been there a long time. The Norwegians claim to be long term, but deal with many things on a day-to-day basis. They are more theoretical and good at marketing, but here in Sweden we are more practical.'

This is strong stuff! For anyone who knows Sweden there are powerful clues here:

very influenced by CEO	=	he is a rampant dictator
there a long time	=	washed up has-been
dealing on day-to-day basis	=	disorganized rabble
good at marketing	=	shiftless

On the other hand a trade union representative at the same company that I spoke to later reversed both judgements. Referring to the merger of the four Swedish companies he noted that the corporate office was on the site of X, one of the four, which used to compete with Y (another of the four) before the merger. There were, the trade union representative claimed:

> Jealousies over which managers from which of the four companies got what jobs in the merged entity. Workers from X were told not to say X in the local community but to refer to the company by the new name. The badges on their work clothes were changed to (new name). X had been the bigger of the two companies (represented in the local community; the other two were geographically removed) but one of the other merging companies seemed to appear all the time in the adverts after the merger.

Isn't it fascinating? The trade union rep is clearly affected by the loss of company X's identity after the merger, and its enjoined invisibility in the local community; whereas the Swedish corporate managers are unsentimental about the previous company identities – but then you only get to meet the ones who survived! On the other hand, they do care about being bossed around by the 'theoretical' Norwegians. There is more to come. The trade union rep had a positive view of the Norwegian takeover. While the Norwegian acquirer is a conglomerate it did already have interests in the relevant industry, which the union rep found reassuring. He also ascertained the Norwegian bid price at the time of the takeover, and again was reassured by the fact that it was reasonable – not the kind of offer that could only be justified to shareholders by some démarche of 'making the assets sweat', to use the phrase popularized by business journalists in the 1990s.

Sometimes even customers feel they are suffering from the blurring of corporate identity. The airline alliances discussed in Chapter 2, where alliances are quasi-mergers, are a case in point. Customers may 'sign up' for what they believe is, for instance, a journey with say KLM, which they like, and then find that some segment of the journey is with KLM's alliance partner NorthWest about which they feel less enthusiastic (Americans sometimes impishly refer to NorthWest as 'Northworst').

One thing, however, that one can always depend upon is that M&A will lead to downsizing, as with the Lloyds and TSB bank example given in Chapter 1.

DISINTERMEDIATION

In a strict sense disintermediation occurs when some organization is cut out of the loop, as when airlines exhort and/or pressurize people to book via telephone call centres or on the Internet, thereby eliminating travel agents (and their commission). It probably is not a large-scale phenomenon at the present, although it may grow with increasing resourcefulness, especially with regard to the use of the Internet.

Probably more important right now is the compression of operational linkages. Many an initiative in supply chain management, for example, involves streamlining if not actually cutting out medial organizations of the wholesaler kind. Result: fewer people do more, faster and more efficiently, but at the same time are more pressurized, while traditional practices are abandoned or traditional relationships disrupted, as we tried to show in the micro-discussions in Chapter 4 of four organizations taken from four different countries.

There is a broader consideration. In the old days, where diversification and vertical integration were fashionable, companies had sub-units that managed these interfaces, forwards and backwards in the chain, as well as simply outwards. In the disintermediating climate, these sub-units are marginalized. The most obvious example would be buying and selling sub-units especially in business-to-business operations, which have been progressively marginalized by centralized buying, Internet buying portals, simplification of the transaction process (salespeople with a lap top), electronic billing, and so on – with a lot of examples of these phenomena having been offered already. This is a diffuse phenomenon, where disintermediation verges on downsizing.

DOWNSIZING

We suggested earlier that downsizing is again both a dynamic and a diffuse phenomenon. That is to say it has 'progressed' in various ways – from blue-collar workers to supervisory and managerial grades, from manufacturing to other sectors, from private industry to the public sector. Above all it has progressed from something that is done as an emergency measure in bad times, recession or imminent company failure, to something which is always desirable as tending to make good results better by reducing the cost structure and by improving those telling ratios – the essence of denominator management. It is probably helpful to add one or two things to this general testimony. First, because downsizing has become so omnipresent it is bound to give rise to the belief that 'no one is safe'. This in turn will make loyalty to any employing organization more conditional. It makes it less likely that people will embrace organizational objectives, participate in corporate visions, or lend themselves to the persuasive purposes of charismatic corporate leaders.

Second, we need to distinguish between hard downsizing and soft downsizing. Hard downsizing is where there used to be 1,000 employees and the number is simply reduced to 600. Soft downsizing is where traditional employees, those who are full-time, permanent staff, and enjoy holiday, sickness, and pension entitlements, whose employment is protected by the labour law of the country concerned, are replaced by a more 'flexible', perhaps one should say a more dispensible, variant. Possibilities here include part-time employees, temporary workers, contract employees, people from agencies. The replacement of traditional employees by those more flexible alternatives does not necessarily occur on a one-to-one basis. Or to put it another way the hard and soft version may intermingle.

Third, staff downsizing will weaken organizational memory and undermine company know-how. The more company operations are staffed by people who do not have at least an expectation of long-term or permanent membership, who are not core staff, the less they will know of the organization's business, of its customers, and of course of its past. They will depend on short-term training rather than on longer-term socialization. They will depend more on systems than on discretion, where discretion must be guided by experience and a sympathetic familiarity with the organizational purpose. Remember The Main, the men's clothes shop that had survived the opening of the edge of town mall with its discount clothes retailers in Aberdeen, South Dakota. The Main cited as a key advantage its employment of older, more knowledgeable and experienced staff.

This whole question of the importance of organizational memory and the ability to exercise discretion should be seen in the context of macro-economic change in the West. With the move from manufacturing to services in all the Western economies there are quite simply more people in more companies having a customer interface than ever before – precisely at the time when the personnel changes that are part of denominator management undermine the quality of this interface.

Again the impairment of organizational memory and discretion is inimical to several of the responses that companies are making to heightened competition and more demanding customers which we canvassed in the last chapter. How many companies are responding?

▌ by adding service to product;

▌ by adding service to service;

▌ by developing cognate customer groups.

These responses are undoubtedly served by quality front-line staff as well as by supporting professional staff who have reason to believe that their interests and those of the companies they work for are the same.

DE-LAYERING

De-layering invariably enjoys 'a good press', since there are two good arguments that support it. First, taking out organizational layers means taking out ranks in the hierarchy. Thus de-layering embodies positive values of status equality, anti-hierarchy and anti-bureaucracy – a pretty good vote winner. Second, it also carries the charge of pushing decision making down closer to the point of action. This is better for efficiency and better for the customer who is thought to get a more realistic decision from someone in 'the front line' not some excerpt from the company rule book emanating from further up the hierarchy. Over the last two decades one only has to allude to 'the flat organization' to win audience sympathy and to occupy the moral high ground.

These are good arguments, but they do not tell the whole story. When organizational layers are taken out it tends to be supervisory and management grades which are affected. It is these grades, and particularly the supervisory grades, that are staffed with people of experience. The de-layered will tend to be the repository of what we have called the organizational memory. So their loss to a company when de-layering occurs may be disproportionate to their numbers.

It is possible to take the argument a little further – taking out supervisory grades leaves those below with less direction. This is usually treated as a plus; employees are empowered, get to do more, make more decisions and are freed from the dead weight of supervisors and managers second guessing them and checking up on them. Some truth in this, no doubt. But they may also suffer from lack of guidance and direction, and flounder a bit. It may also be the case that the outcome is foreseen at the time of de-layering and in consequence the more discretionary parts of the job are taken out, outsourced or moved sideways to some staff echelon. In other words de-layering may lead to a dumbing down at the work level below the layer that is taken out.

Finally de-layering increases spans of control, where the span of control is the number of people who report directly to any manager or supervisor. Bigger spans of control in turn mean more pressure for those on the receiving end of them, people spreading themselves thin, and a greater reliance on systems and rule of thumb means of control.

OUTSOURCING

As we suggested in Chapter 1, outsourcing, like downsizing, is dynamic and diffuse. It has changed over time, and tends to spread upwards and outwards across companies. Outsourcing does not just involve simple things such as catering and office cleaning anymore; we are now in an age when (many) companies do not do their own HRM, outsource IT, and sometimes license the complete operation to a consultancy company. Breweries often do not bottle their own beer, farmers do not sell their own crops, airlines do not do their own ground handling, and UK water companies sometimes speak of 'getting out of reservoirs'. It is becoming a question of 'what will they think of next?'

BPR – BUSINESS PROCESS RE-ENGINEERING

Like de-layering, BPR is usually sold on the basis of enlarging employee's jobs and discretion, so that it raises self-esteem and job satisfaction simultaneously. Again these are reasonable claims, but not the whole story. It is also the case that:

▌ BPR invariably leads to downsizing.

▌ The administrative streamlining is usually achieved by joining up bits of the process, so that what used to be done by two people sequentially is now handled by one person.

▌ More is therefore done by fewer people.

But there is a more diffuse consideration. There is always an 'evolved over time' dimension to culture: it is invariably presented in terms of shared meanings, common values, corporate folklore and company tradition, 'the way we do things round here' and all that.

The point is that BPR is the antithesis of all that. BPR is a tribute to the desirability of change, a monument to impermanence. It is saying that quite small things, these administrative processes within the organization that nobody ever thought were worth changing until the mid-1990s, things you just took for granted, may be turned inside out if there is a chance of improving cost efficiency or customer service (Hammer and Champy, 2001).

BPR is mostly small change, credible change, but often still disruptive. Small change may have a big impact if it lacks a big cause.

APPRAISAL

Regular appraisal is integral to the managerial consensus described in Chapter 3. The ideal type is:

▌ Appraisal conducted by the individual's line manager (this makes it real, not some ritual exercise by the personnel office).

▌ Appraising performance against measurable objectives (this measurability of the objectives makes the appraisal tangible and transparent).

▌ Having appraisal feed through into a bonus or performance-related element in remuneration (again, totally rational, and instantly comprehensible).

But appraisal also has the effect of 'downsizing' the human spirit. It does not leave it to the incumbent to translate the mission, interpret the situation and its needs, to act in the company's best interests: it tells the incumbent what to do. It opens up the possibility that the incumbent will be told in appraisal 'Sure, you transformed the contribution of your part of the organization! But you were told to do x, y and z, and you only score 6 out of 10 on these. You don't make the bonus this year'. In short performance against measurable objectives is prioritizing conformity over initiative.

CONTROLLISM

A measure of control has always been inseparable from management. Control, indeed is part of French mining engineer turned chief executive Henri Fayol's classic formulation of what management is all about (1916). So does it make sense to talk about controllism, the term suggesting a diffuse exaggeration of the control function? There is a case for this view, in that:

▌ There is more control than there used to be.

▌ Control applies to more people, for instance to professional people used to self-regulation by their professional conscience (but one can also find less august categories of employee newly subject to control).

▌ The operation of control has been facilitated by computerization; in consequence a lot of this control is impersonal, the result of computer control or computer based data compilation, rather than on the checking up by supervisors or line managers.

Consider for instance the British truck driver. Once upon a time these drivers were known as 'knights of the road', an expression of chivalry and skilful execution based in freedom (from supervision) and self-direction. There is even a sociological study from the 1960s (Hollowell, 1968) that argues that lorry driving was seen by its practitioners as vastly superior to factory work, the blue-collar norm at the time, precisely because of its freedom from control. Once you backed out of the depot and hit the road you were on your own, no foreman breathing down your neck, no one checking your output for the shift, no keeping pace with a moving assembly line.

Where are these 'knights of the road' now? Well, they are typically over-controlled, computer punching, non-diabetic (subject to mandatory health checks, like airline pilots) guys with social skills and customer interactive competence, not allowed by 'the computer in the cab' to change gear when they want to, sometimes expected not just to back the artic into the yard but to stock the shelves in the supermarket and be responsible for the produce display.

The new reality for at least UK lorry drivers often includes:

▌ A computer chip embedded in the truck tyres to monitor inflation (correct tyre pressure leads to fuel economies).

▌ An onboard computer that can receive simple messages from the control centre.

▌ Computer monitoring of stoptime (time spent not driving, typically unloading time) with automatic reporting of any stop of more than 15 minutes.

▌ Computer monitoring of the fuel efficient use of the gears, with automatic reporting of drivers who waste fuel, usually by staying too long in third gear.

In the UK 5,000 drivers left the industry in 1997. In the same year 1,500 new drivers qualified. We have deliberately picked an example from an ordinary blue-collar occupation, in contrast to the increasing controls and performance measurement to which school teachers, university teachers, and healthcare professionals are exposed, which have had publicity in recent years.

Such controls of course may also be employed at the level of the organizational unit, rather than with regard to individual employees as in our lorry driver example above. Controls of the organizational level kind have been commonplace in financial services in the UK for a quarter of a century. They are also common in the public sector (or ex-public sector!). The privatized water companies discussed in Chapter 5 are monitored against a variety of criteria, and all the data is published. Or consider the following example from the private sector – from car retailing.

By way of introduction it should be said that, in the UK at least, car retailing is not an industry marked by much mobility, especially at management level. It does not, that is to say, tend to attract managers horizontally from companies in different industries. So most of the managers are ex-salespeople who have 'grown up in the industry'.

The particular company we would like to cite has a medium-sized national dealership chain specializing in several up-market makes and brands. Each dealership is assessed every 3 months on 10 performance variables. This leads to:

▌ An overall score.

▌ The scores are published across the network, so every dealership knows how all the others are doing and there is intense competition for position in the league tables.

▌ If any of the dealerships gets an 'improvement needed' in any of the 10 categories there will have to be an action plan and follow-up.

Sometimes computer based controls are used on customers as well. One credit card company I visited explained that they do random checks at point of sale authorization. What the company is doing here is comparing the transaction for which authorization is being sought with the card-owner's profile, and checking for anomalies. A 73-year-old bachelor living in Yorkshire spending £400 in the lingerie department at Harrods is an anomaly that probably means a stolen card.

Now all this control is perfectly comprehensible, serves useful purposes and may well raise efficiency and benefit customers. But at the same time it is alienating. People feel better when they are trusted. How do you know when you are trusted? You know you are trusted when there are no controls. It is for this reason that we have included control alongside BPR and outsourcing and downsizing as tending to undermine organizational solidarity and corporate culture. What is more, the stronger the professional identity of those being controlled, the more resentment it breeds since 'the professions' typically embrace the idea of self-responsibility for determining the right course of action and executing it on an honour basis.

CORE COMPETENCE

The related ideas of core products, core business, and core competence have surfaced several times already. Core competence is a powerful as well as fashionable notion, it leads companies to get a lot of things right.

Yet from the present perspective, the threat to organizational solidarity, there is a downside. Put simply, one man's core competence is another's marginalization. However the core is conceived, not everyone is going to be part of it. Like George Orwell's pigs in *Animal Farm* some are going to be 'more [core] than others'.

If your part of the operation becomes 'non-core', whether as a result of strategic review or corporate response to environmental change, there are three likely possibilities:

▌ Your non-core entity is outsourced.

▌ This entity is seen as so non-core that it does not get done at all – you get fired!

▌ You are allowed to carry on serving the organization in this non-core role, but you become a second class citizen.

Now this is not an attack on the idea of core business and core competence. But it is an attempt to highlight a seldom mentioned downside, in the sense that none of the three options noted above is conducive to fostering organizational solidarity.

Implications

We have reviewed a set of trends and corporate responses, largely those identified in Chapter 1 as denominator management, not to assess their business rationality but to tease out their implications for organizational solidarity and corporate culture. Taken collectively these trends:

▌ Make it more difficult to identify with the company (especially M&A).

▌ Reduce security for employees at all levels.

▌ Sometimes entail involuntary curtailment of employment (downsizing).

▌ Sometimes change the organizational structure (de-layering, flattening the organization).

▌ May change administrative systems (BPR).

▌ In general oblige employees at all levels to cope with a high degree of change.

▌ Prioritize:
   – flexibility rather than loyalty;
   – obedience rather than discretion;
   – conformity rather than initiative.

▌ Drive performance by controls.

▌ Seek to recruit the (changing) human resources needed by paying the market price (or above).

This ensemble of trends and developments is also divisive, although no one has actually planned or plotted any of this. It is divisive in several ways:

▌ The old are more threatened than the young (old people hate change).

▌ Men are more threatened than women; women are arguably more adaptable, and are certainly preferred for a host of roles (interactive and customer contact) in the service sector.

▌ Those who lack 'marketable skills' are more anxious than those who have such skills.

It has been said before, but the paratypical victim of the trends discussed above is an older semi-skilled male worker, downsized out of manufacturing industry.

A solidarity organization

So far in this chapter we have talked easily about organizational solidarity and corporate culture, implicitly treating these as a *point de départ*, as an acknowledged reality being jeopardized by the developments outlined in the last few pages. Probably most of us can identify with the idea of organizational solidarity, feel we are experiencing it or at least that we have experienced it. Nonetheless it may be helpful to offer an example.

In the late 1980s I had a lot of contact with one of the UK's high street banks. Part of the contact was a research project that entailed shadowing a set of the bank's senior executives, sitting in on the meetings and being a party to all the discussions and encounters. Writing up the research it seemed to me that this bank enjoyed a high level of organizational solidarity in three ways.

First, at that time the bank practised an open and rather egalitarian recruitment. Most entrants to the bank, that is, were 16-year-old school leavers with 'O' level GCEs (what later became GCSEs). Not only were the bulk of staff in the bank's numerous branches recruited and qualified in this way, but so were the senior executives in my research project. Graduate recruits were a tiny minority. What is more, nothing else seemed to privilege any subset of entrants to the bank – not education, or region, or social class. Almost all started on the same terms, almost all progressed from the same starting line; at the bank's corporate office in London one heard more regional accents then upper-class ones.

Second, side by side with this egalitarian recruitment the bank at that time had a very long hierarchy – a lot of clerical work grades, more grades between clerical and managerial, numerous grades of branch manager, and more above and beyond. Now while this may sound unbearably élitist the practice was that almost everyone recruited at 16 aspired to some progress up the hierarchy, and practically everyone achieved this.

Third, these two features taken together – egalitarian recruitment and universal (if differential) advancement were the foundation of a tremendous organizational solidarity. Furthermore, there was undoubtedly a strong and easily identifiable corporate culture, of which senior people were very conscious, and when I attended training courses for young managers and even more junior people I found a lot of this culture had trickled down! Looking back, the key features of this culture seemed to be:

▌ It was polite, respectful, decent, and hierarchical.

▌ It was quite status conscious, yet classless, and able to use status in constructive ways – to mark the importance of events or initiatives, to authenticate communications, to protect individuals, to generate a quasi-automatic allocation of tasks.

▌ It was quite rule-driven, 'over-numerate' in the sense of decisions being more driven by numbers than by arguments, control centred yet liking those controls (feeling uncomfortable with anything that was open-ended, averse to the 'blank cheque' approach).

▌ It was genuinely cooperative, in the sense of a general buying into the culture and acceptance of procedures; on a lot of occasions I saw individuals who had the power to get their own way whatever preferring to play by the rules, cooperate with others, value the procedures.

▌ It was paternalistic (in a mildly bossy way); wanting staff to bank (only) with this bank, stay in credit, have the bank's own credit card 'forsaking all others', to have 'an appropriate' mortgage, and to live within their means; at the same time it seemed to generate a lot of loyalty and identification.

In particular I remember visiting a branch in a really run-down area in London where they had experienced three armed robberies; on one of these occasions counter staff had been threatened by a masked intruder armed with a full-length woodman's axe which he slammed into the counter 'to get attention'. None of the staff in this branch spoke about quitting, all of them spoke in anticipation of a long-term career, several of them referred to increments of training and expected promotions.

That was in 1986. Of this earlier model, almost nothing is left.

Homogeneous recruitment has gone. Universal advancement up the hierarchy has gone. Branches have been scaled down in the sense of the range of services, imposed routinization and taking out the more initiative based discretionary activity. Temps are in, there are more part-time staff, and both, of course, lack an investment of career expectation. But the key change is that much of the bank's operations have been shifted from branches to call centres.

Call centres have become the epiphenomenon of the new century. There is much to be said for them, much of it centring around the fact that they are amazingly cheap:

▌ They constitute an epic version of impersonal centralization.

▌ They enjoy economies of scale.

▌ They are staffed by (mostly) young people.

▌ The 'life expectancy' of call centre employees is about two years; so employers do not have to provide a career structure, with graded emoluments; and do not have to pay them a pension.

The prevailing climate is now one of:

▌ 'Learn your script' rather than exercise discretion.

▌ Expect high levels of centralization.

▌ Expect challenging targets: if you miss them one year, bad, if you miss them a second time, demotion.

▌ Accept that career prospects and the likelihood of advancement are now differentiated rather than universal, and do not of course apply to armies of temps and part-timers.

▌ Recognize that at the same time the organization has been flattened; fewer people take bigger decisions, and are likely to take them individually rather than in committee.

This before and after account is not meant as demonization. It is simply about noting significant change. The competitive forces which drive change of this kind are the starting point for this book. What is more, there is a country and industry specific cause, that is, one that applies generally to retail banking in the UK.

Back in 1984 what was then the Midland Bank (now HSBC) declared a policy of 'free banking if in credit', that is, the end of banking charges on current or checking accounts so long as they are not overdrawn. The other high street banks were forced to follow suit to protect market share. This was viable for banks given the interest rates that prevailed in the UK in the 1980s, which averaged out around 11 per cent. Insiders say it is viable down to 8 per cent. At the time of writing (September 2001) the base rate in the UK was 4¾ per cent.

The loss of solidarity in a changing world

So far we have explored the causes and constituents of the putative crisis of human capital, we have summarized their cumulative effect, and worked through a test case organization in terms of before and after snapshots. There is one more angle we want to consider in this chapter: it concerns the way in which a changing context sharpens the crisis we have depicted.

The emphasis in the discussion is on higher managerial and professional employees, not on blue-collar workers displaced by downsizing or outsourcing, however sad their plight. We would like to suggest that the decline of organizational solidarity and the weakening of corporate culture as we have known it in the past has a number of implications for management and professional employees of business corporations:

▮ Their loyalty is not likely to be unconditional.

▮ They will not 'give themselves' entirely to the employing organization; after all, it is not committed to them either absolutely or in the long term; who knows 'what tomorrow will bring?' – acquisition by a corporate predator, downsizing, de-statusing via the dynamic of core competence?

▮ In particular, higher level employees will want to 'keep something back', something they can sell to the next employing organization, probably a rival, if things take a turn for the worse.

▮ One manifestation of this is that they will not be inclined to allow their tacit knowledge to be made explicit, to be routinized and formalized – tacit knowledge is the product of your experience, intuition, and informal know-how; if the relationship is conditional tacit knowledge is something you want to keep to yourself, so that you do not make yourself dispensable and you have something to sell to the next employer.

▮ In such a conditional situation, CV/resumé building is more important then informal standing in the company; this distinction is pretty important; informal standing is boosted by giving your all and having internally visible achievements to show for it: CV building is about fashioning a kind of reality that will both look good on paper and play well at the next job interview.

That is the disposition to which the monetization and marketization of management talent leads. But we want to argue further that while the trend has been towards a conditional commitment between the organization and the employee, other changes have meant that the real corporate need has been in the opposite direction.

Consider that all sorts of developments have served to upgrade the expectations and demands made of managers and corporate professionals:

▌ The rise of offshore manufacturing has taken out a lot of routine operations; at most these have to be managed at arms' length rather than in-house.

▌ The rise of new technologies, especially telecomms/IT/ Internet/multimedia, have lead to a higher proportion of the corporate establishment being what used to be called 'science-based' industries.

▌ The de-layering at middle management level means that senior and general managers now constitute a higher proportion of the whole.

▌ Trends including outsourcing, the emphasis on core competence, and even BPR, imply an expansion of the role and contribution of professional service organizations – accountancy and law practices, consultancies of all kinds – all of which are staffed by highly qualified people, again people whose loyalty has been rendered problematic.

▌ The IT explosion has lead to a demand for (specialist) highly qualified staff.

▌ Growing salary inequality in the form of a widening gap between the remuneration of the qualified and the unqualified, between those with marketable skills and the others, between the outstanding and the average, drives mobility between companies for those in search of better remuneration: the trend (salary inequality) is palpably not a force for loyalty and stability. The cross-border mobility noted in Chapter 1 reinforces this trend: if you cannot get what you deserve at home there is bound to be an opportunity somewhere else.

IN SHORT

All these trends tend to: keep tacit knowledge tacit; undermine the idea of 'the learning organization' – after all, what can it really learn if no one is fully committed to it, and if its most talented members are 'here today and gone tomorrow', at least in spirit.

These last remarks about how a changing context renders the decline of organizational solidarity more poignant conclude 'the case for the prosecution'. In the next chapter we take up the questions:

▌ So what?

▌ Does it matter?

▌ What can companies do about it?

7

On solving the crisis

Is the problem outlined in the previous chapter one that can be solved?

Unless there are important changes in the business environment we have no reason to expect that the human capital crisis is going to be solved by 'roll back'. It would not be easy, that is to say, to undo or reverse the developments detailed in the last chapter thereby restoring organizational solidarity and the concomitant loyalty both ways. This is unlikely to happen across the board, whatever some individual organizations may do, because there is no constituency that has both the power and the incentive to make it happen.

Politicians may have an incentive in the sense that it would be nice if they could make it happen, but in a free market economy they do not have the power. Nor, for the most part, do they have the understanding of management or business processes. Shareholders have the power, at least in theory, although in practice it is difficult to exercise shareholder power unless it is very concentrated, and in any case shareholders do not have an incentive. Top management may or may not have an incentive; they may take the view expressed in the last chapter, or they may feel that trading loyalty and solidarity for flexibility and cost efficiency is a good deal, a price well paid (by others). But whichever way their judgement goes they will not always have the power to engage in what we might call restorative change, because however proactive and effective they may be they will be subject to the influence of the wider economy and to pressures from shareholders and the financial community.

RELATIVIZATION

If we cannot solve the problem by roll back, is there anything else worth doing? Well certainly it helps to put the issue in context, and to relativize it. Then we can have a go at finding answers for the intractable bits that are left.

There are at least three strands to this relativization. First, the crisis of human capital shrinks perceptibly when one separates the social problem from the management/organization problem.

Social problem

De-industrialization combined with some bits of the dominator management cocktail detailed in Chapter 1 is having a profound effect on blue-collar male workers. If they lose their jobs in the downsizing/outsourcing/off-shore manufacturing set of developments there are broadly three possibilities:

▌ After a period of unemployment they get re-hired in the service sector, at about 30 per cent less salary.

▌ If they ever get back into manufacturing, it will not be as core workers, and will not be on the same terms and conditions as when they left.

▌ If they are over 50 they may not work again.

With the benefit of hindsight we can see that manufacturing in the West did a marvellous job providing stable and reasonably remunerated employment for (mostly) semi-skilled male workers without 'marketable skills'. US political scientist Edward Luttwak once remarked that a family is a collection of human beings around a stable breadwinner (Luttwak, 1999). There may be an element of jocular cynicism in this judgement, but in 2001 most blue-collar male workers in the West would fail the reliable breadwinner test.

This occupational marginalization of (many) blue-collar males may well have a variety of undesirable effects including lowering self-esteem, undermining their traditional role as breadwinners and thereby impacting on family stability, and may even contribute to overt anti-social behaviours. It is also possible that in the middle term the problem will 'self-solve' though the generation of new blue-collar work roles that will compensate for the loss of jobs in manufacturing in the West. Possibilities might include:

▌ Further growth of 'physical distribution'.

▌ Growth of surface transportation; the shortage of truck drivers in both the United States and the UK has been noted already.

▌ Environmental projects that give rise to more on-site heavy labouring work.

▌ More projects generated by climate change that may generate more heavy outdoor work, sea defence and flood control projects, for example.

But probably the best hope is something we simply have not thought of, a socio-economic equivalent of colonizing the moon and making it safe for 'the women and children'. Whatever the fate of the blue-collar male, however, this is a social problem rather than an organizational problem. The organizational problem is rather at professional and managerial level, and we will come to it shortly.

Expectation and experience

First, however, there is another sense in which the crisis of human capital as formulated in the previous chapter may be more 'a moment in time' than something immutable. It is all about expectations. Happiness depends less on what one experiences than on how these experiences compare with one's hopes and expectations. The criminal expecting a five-year jail sentence may be ecstatic to get off with a £5,000 fine.

The reason why we can apprehend the downside of denominator management and the triumph of flexibility over loyalty is that many of us have something with which to compare this malaise: the recent past. For anyone who started work in the 1950s, 1960s, or 1970s (and for Continental Europe, and Japan the 1980s) today's organizational world is as different as was the period of the Great Depression of the 1930s. What is more this post-war generation shaped an organizational milieu and business culture that would perpetuate expectations of easy prosperity and benevolent employers.

But this post-war generation is incrementally disappearing from the scene, the recruits of the 1980s and 1990s are rising, and they have different expectations. In short, if you 'grow up' with M&A, downsizing and de-layering, outsourcing and BPR, these phenomena will cease to amaze and may also cease to alienate. So we do not really know what it will be like in 10 years' time, when the last of the old guard have passed out of the system, and the 'new guard' have come to maturity with different expectations.

Culture without stability

This in turn raises another question. All our conceptions of culture, including organizational culture, are based on presumptions of:

▌ continuity and stability;

▌ full organizational membership;

▌ reciprocal commitment.

All the things, that is, which are now in rather short supply. So reasoning from all the existing analyses of corporate culture, we see that culture being destroyed by the ferocity of change. But this may be wrong. Perhaps we can have positive organizational cultures that comprehend:

▌ impermanence;

▌ change;

▌ different levels of organizational membership – core members, temps, contract workers, outsourced former core members, part-timers, agency staff, and so on;

▌ endless mobility both ways across the organizational boundary, as one -time members become non-members and vice versa.

If a time comes when all these things – impermanence, change, variable membership, mobility – are seen as normal, because they are no longer new, because they are exhibited by a majority of employing organizations, because there are few people around any more who believe that the opposite represents normality, then perhaps culture without stability will be a reality.

Professional and managerial employees

If we put the social problem of displaced workers on one side, and ask what is the core problem for companies, it centres on their professional and managerial employees. The dissolution of traditional organizational culture and the predominance of flexibility over loyalty means that:

▌ Companies cannot be sure of keeping those they want to keep.

▌ Therefore they cannot be sure of 'capturing' the skill/knowledge/experience of these people.

▌ Companies cannot even count on employees' full commitment to the company while they are employed by it.

If this is the problem, are there any counters? What will involve people in an organization in the absence of a traditional two-way commitment? The answer is not going to be financial incentives. These are part of the problem rather than part of the solution. Money is not an answer precisely because it is a universal currency, it does not differentiate one company from another, it does not privilege one employer over another, it serves to neutralize corporate difference and to enhance the notion of the mercenary rather than that of the corporate citizen. So if not money, is there something else? There probably is, but it may be better to creep up on it sideways.

Getting your ticket stamped

In the early 1990s in Canada I was visiting companies and interviewing managers with the idea of a possible book on business and management in Canada. Often I asked managers a deliberately open-ended question: What do you have to do to have a successful career in management in Canada? One of the interviewees replied: 'Marketing, finance, production. They're the key functions. You need to get your ticket stamped in those.'

Not a radical idea, but it seemed a perfectly sensible one at the time. After all, there is a paradox about having a career in management, in that all the top jobs are by definition in general management, but you cannot start in general management. Instead you typically start in something specific, in a particular job or function like marketing, finance, production, or sales, personnel or HRM, design, engineering, R&D or PR. The paradox is to find a way into the general from the specific.

From this starting point the Canadian formulation above is very reasonable. Prepare for the general by doing several different specifics, get experience in a (manufacturing) company's main functional areas. After all, these three functions are very different in the demands they make and the experiences they confer. To take a simple aspect, marketing invokes a lot of looking outwards, finance involves looking upwards to senior management and shareholders, production a lot of looking downwards at elemental operations and the typically blue-collar workers who perform them.

These three functions imply different work patterns. For example production management is highly interactive. The day is spent talking with people, one to one, in meetings of various kinds, on the telephone, or as part of recurrent tours of the plant. There is contact with a range of superiors and subordinates, supervisors and worker representatives, as well as with colleagues from almost every other function, from design and from sales, from engineering and from HRM, from quality control and from purchasing (Lawrence, 1984). The need is for interactive skills, character, and above all energy. The pace is relentless but the buzz from the tumult of events and contingencies can be addictive.

Work in finance on the other hand involves a heavy element of self-direction. Sure, there is contact with others, there is consulting, discussing and reporting, and going to meetings. Yet a lot of the time people in finance are working in their own offices, heads down, concentrating on tasks that take hours rather than minutes, working to what are often self-imposed deadlines. There is also an element of compulsory objectivity about work in finance. Whereas for most management work, team work and collaboration is an overriding imperative, finance as a function is supposed to keep the score and do the calculations that enable objective appraisal and rational decision making, even if it makes you unpopular. This idea was engagingly formulated for me when I was chatting to a production manager at a German forklift truck factory who saw a colleague from finance approaching and commented to me that finance was referred to as the: 'Amt für Rache und Entlohnung!' (something like: the office for revenge and expropriation!).

Marketing is very different. It involves endless lateral and diagonal interaction with insiders in other functions or departments crossed with some kind of interaction with that part of the outside world that is made up of actual or potential customers. That outside interaction comes in a variety of forms, including:

▌ Face-to-face contact with customers.

▌ Vicarious contact with customers via the medium of market research data.

▌ Experimental contact with potential customers or merely the general public via interviews and surveys and focus groups.

▌ The 'imaging' of products or services.

Perhaps the clue is that marketing is difficult to define, but we can recognize when it is being done effectively.

In short, production, marketing and finance are very different areas of management work, they make different demands and confer different experience-values. So if you had this spread of experience, if you had performed even passably well in them, it would be a good *entré* for general management.

All that being the case, why does this 'getting your ticket stamped' idea sound so dreadfully dated?

THE AGE OF GENERAL MANAGEMENT

First of all, the 'get your ticket stamped' exhortation relates primarily to manufacturing industry. It is companies in manufacturing that have this array of functions or departments from R&D and/or design down the value chain to marketing/sales/distribution. But manufacturing simply no longer has the predominance in the West that it used to have. Increasingly in Western economies the tertiary sector (services) has come to represent a larger proportion of GDP than the secondary sector (manufacturing): the line was crossed first in the United States in the 1960s and last among the key Western economies in Germany in the 1990s.

The second argument is a bit more tendentious, not so easy to nail down in factual terms. Nonetheless I would like to suggest that what have come to be called 'the silos', the presumptively separate departments or functions like production and finance and so on, have been dismantled. Or to put it more modestly, 'silo thinking' in the sense of seeing the aims and interests of say R&D or of finance as an end in themselves, has receded. Talking about or even formally researching the tensions or differences of interest between these different functions and departments is not the hot issue it once was. Changed circumstances, in particular enhanced competition, have reduced silo autonomy and silo thinking. Team work and the idea of 'all working for the same company' may not have come naturally, but they have at any rate been induced by fiercer competition and fear of the consequences of corporate failure in a harsher business world.

Third, central to this ticket-stamping formula is the idea that production is central in manufacturing industry. This used to be true, but is now a bit questionable. While production has never been a high status area of management work, at least not in the Anglo-Saxon countries, it was always consequential. Producing goods, three dimensional artefacts, was what this company was there to do, even if managers in marketing had higher status and managers in finance were more likely to become board members while still in their 30s. Production was basic. Production managers would always claim that:

▌ They had more people (blue-collar workers) working for them than anyone else in other departments could claim.

▌ They were in charge of more of the company's assets (plant, equipment, machinery) than anyone else.

▌ Without their efforts sales would have nothing to sell and the 'bean-counters' would have nothing to count.

None of that is exactly untrue today, but it has all been relativized. Production has become too easy, it is the bit that pretty much everyone can get right, using the same robotic resources, computer controls, and the same business manoeuvres. Technical and electronic 'gearing up' has meant that production is done by fewer people (downsizing) and needs fewer supervisors (de-layering). Increasingly production is:

▌ Outsourced, often delegated to sub-contractors and suppliers.

▌ Outsourced cross-border, to achieve cost-efficiency gains.

▌ The victim of the emphasis on focus, leading to 'shallow manufacturing' as argued in Chapter 2.

To put it another way, a lot of companies have 'bottom-sliced' themselves. That basic activity, physical production, has:

▌ gone somewhere else;

▌ been simplified;

▌ been relativized.

It has been relativized in the sense that what comes before, design/R&D/imagination, and what comes after, marketing/sales/distribution, have become relatively more important.

Greater competition has shifted the focus out of the organization and onto customers, the idea that ran through Chapter 5. So a view of career development that is internally focused, is based on experience across several composite functions (ticket stamping), loses some of its salience and force. Outward orientation rather than internal focus rules.

Finally, enhanced competition and the accelerating rate of change have led to a greater need to rethink the purposes of the organization, more focus on competitive advantage, more trade-offs, in the sense of going for this rather than that in a situation where no one has the resources to do everything.

In short, more competition and faster change have led to greater strategic awareness. It looks something like Figure 7.1. In short, all the boxes in the figure have diminished the silos, and turned all managers into general managers.

Time	Response
The Golden Age 30 years after Second World War	No one thinks about strategy, they do not need to
Transition period 1980s for United States and UK, later for Continental Europe	Corporate leaders think about strategy; choices and trade-offs are now necessary
2000 plus	All managers think about strategy; strategic awareness percolates downwards.

Figure 7.1

THE EEL FACTOR

The emphasis has shifted. It is no longer about knowing what goes on in the various silos and being able to synthesize it when you get into general management. It is now much more about experiencing business processes, and learning from that exposure.

Because enhanced competition is driving change at an unprecedented rate, knowledge of change and involvement in it have become critical. It is about:

Exposure to change; Experience of change; Learning from change;

the EEL factor, that will enhance people's capability and promotability. It is also very stimulating if you are a participant, not a victim, and come to understand its purpose.

It will be helpful to break down the idea of business process change, not leave it as a blurred entity. There are several strands to it, although there is some overlap.

Ups and downs

First there is experience of business fluctuation, of changes in the fortunes of the company. It can be good news or bad news, but the experience is still valuable if you can understand the cause and recognize the effects. It can help you to a better understanding of how to cope well with disaster and how to exploit success.

We probably like the idea of exploiting success more than that of dealing with adversity. But consider how instructive the latter might be. Consider an example from the company history of British Airways. Around the third week of August 2001 the share price stood at £3.22 (and in the 12-month period to the end of October 2001 it had been as high as £4.70). But a few days after the terrorist attacks on New York and Washington on 11 September 2001 the share price hit a low of £1.13, which according to the business press put the market capitalization below the company's break-up value. Within days of the attack insurance costs had spiralled, security costs had risen, services had been cut and a first *tranche* of 7,000 redundancies had been announced.

At the same time there are possibilities to exploit the malaise into which the airline industry has been plunged. It may drive concentration in the industry in a way which was impossible before given government control and the sentiment attached to particular airlines as 'national carriers', ideas explored in Chapter 2 when the industry was reviewed as a test site for highlighting trends towards concentration. Now, sadly, a measure of concentration is likely to result from bankruptcy. Ansett of Australia went bankrupt before 11 September; Swissair was grounded for four days before being bailed out by a consortium of federal and cantonal aid strengthened by contributions from blue-chip companies like Nestlé (in fact Swissair was folded into its former shorthaul subsidiary, Crossair). In Europe Sabena of Belgium went bankrupt in November 2001 and other airlines look shaky, while in the United States there is speculation that US Airways will not survive, while in January 2002 American Airlines and Continental were posting losses.

But for key players, and British Airways is certainly one, there are opportunities too. The possibility of moves to eliminate industry capacity, to make tactical acquisitions, to get some cooperation with KLM past the EU regulatory authority (announced 1 November 2001) perhaps even to make a reality of the dream of anti-trust immunity for the alliance with American Airlines. Is there not a lot that insiders may learn in this time of industry crisis?

Or consider a more positive example. In the autumn of 2000 I had the chance to interview the UK Vice President of The Gap. While The Gap is a very familiar presence in the UK it is of course a US company with the corporate office at Harrison Street, San Francisco. At that time some 2,000 of Gap's 2,500 stores worldwide were in the United States, implying near saturation. Company policy had been to select the United Kingdom and Japan as key country-markets for (further) expansion.

So growth is the first theme. The UK workforce increased from 4,000 to 5,500 between February and September 2000. This is one of the very few companies in my sample of well over 100 that were actively increasing workforce size other than by M&A. At the time of the interview Gap were opening a new store in the UK every 18 working days.

Another theme here is managing a global brand. This is not an issue when most of the eggs are in one national basket supported by a bit of export but it becomes important as other national markets are developed. Managing a global brand means, among other things, new collections in stores, new adverts in shops, new displays in windows, and all of this happening identically and globally across Gap's ensemble of stores.

A wonderful position to be in you will think, even if it does not last for ever. Certainly, but also a learning experience and a range of challenges. The store growth poses problems of premises acquisition; staff recruitment, retention and training; and the issue of communicating effectively with growing staff numbers, spread over more sites.

Global brand management has to be simultaneous across all countries, which raises huge coordination issues. Unveiling new lines and collections simultaneously is important because:

▌ It supports the brand.

▌ It is a statement to customers about what the company stands for at any point in time.

▌ It gives more weight to sales/marketing campaigns.

▌ It offers economies of scale and scope.

▌ And not least because it enables cross-country performance comparisons.

All very comprehensible but it takes some managing. Having a global brand also raises in more acute form the question of uneven sales performance in different regions. Supposing a collection that is very successful in say Japan is less so in the UK: you cannot just take it off the shelves which would be to undermine the brand, but you need a safety valve. The chosen mechanism in this industry is usually factory outlets, very useful if:

▌ The company has over-bought.

▌ There is a slow-moving line.

▌ There is a need to dispose of 'seconds'.

Having this safety outlet has the further merit that it will encourage adventurous procurement in the first place.

The common thread that connects these two examples, British Airways and The Gap, is that whether it is good news or bad news it is change that has to be understood and exploited.

System change

Exposure to system change is another key dimension. At one end of the spectrum there are diffuse mega changes of the 'digitalizing the business' kind; at the other end more compact episodes of BPR. In between renewing and upgrading IT systems has become more common and more frequent, with more impact on operations.

Side by side with this are episodes of good old-fashioned organizational change, some of which has been touched on in earlier chapters. Probably the main organizational changes of the last 10 years are:

▌ Organizational flattening, taking out organizational layers, shortening hierarchies, pushing decision making downward, empowering (typically crossed with downsizing).

▌ The stronger ethic of accountability having worked against matrix structures, that is organizations having two cross-cutting dimensions, say product division versus geographic area, entailing double reporting lines for individual managers. There is a built-in dynamic towards greater organizational transparency and simplicity.

▌ The debate about whether priority should be given to local responsiveness or global efficiencies in companies operating internationally, the debate that says in effect shall we do it differently for

France because French customers have different needs and tastes, or shall we standardize it for Western Europe because it is more efficient? This debate is being progressively settled in favour of global efficiencies.

Changes of this kind are typical of the present time, and exposure to them is pretty much something everyone needs.

Internationalization

Not every manager works for an MNC (multi-national corporation) or for a company that has international operations.

First of all industries differ in their propensity to internationalize, even where in some cases these industries are peopled by very big organizations. Farming, for example, has not internationalized: you do not get many British wheat farmers who have land holdings on the French cereals belt to service the French market. Readers who find this example fanciful might pause and think how UK farming might have been helped by internationalization in the face of the BSE and foot and mouth crises. Or take retail banking. The industry is made up of enormous organizations, but even so cross-border expansion is hardly ever organic but by means of often rather shaky strategic alliances with banks in other countries – the alliance between Spain's Banco de Santander and Britain's Royal Bank of Scotland dating from the 1980s would be one of the few enduring alliances. Or consider car retailing: do British tourists see Reg Vardy or Sytner dealerships as they drive across France on holiday?

So not all industries have internationalized, at least not yet. A new wave of internationalization has also been unleashed by the privatization and deregulation of various activities in both Europe and the United States. In this connection we have already paid tribute to the international venturings of the UK water companies variously engaged in stopping leaks in the West Indies and in sewage disposal in the State of Mississippi. But the deregulation of public telecommunication across Europe is an even better example.

Take, for example, Holland, much of whose post-deregulation telecomms internationalization has been engagingly chronicled by Dutch telecomms engineer turned organizational anthropologist, Alfons van Marrewijk. The starting point is KPN (Koninlijke PTT Nederland, the Dutch equivalent of, say, BT in the UK). KPN was privatized in 1989 and introduced to the stock market in 1993. It initiated joint ventures in former Dutch colonies – in the Dutch Antilles, which failed, and in Indonesia, which succeeded. KPN was also an initiator and member of the pan-European strategic alliance Unisource (van Marrewijk, 1999).

Unisource was formed in 1992 and lasted until 1997 (when it fell apart!) and Dutch KPN was a key player. At the height of its development the alliance was known as AT&T-Unisource and consisted of five telecomms operators from five countries: Swiss Telecom, Swedish Telia, Dutch PTT, and Spanish Telefónica, as well as US company AT&T.

The fact that not all that much survived should not shroud the fact that these developments were new for the industry, and the experiences of alliance and joint venture wholly new for the companies cited with the probable exception of AT&T. In short, it was a powerful learning experience.

The joint venture with the Dutch Antilles foundered on postcolonial tensions reinforced by power inequalities and economic dependence on the part of the Antilles. However, the same potential problem with Indonesia was overcome, and van Marrewijk is very good at showing how the Indonesians juggled the situation in their favour, playing the cards they had, and neutralizing Dutch economic and technical superiority.

Something else that comes out of the study is that when it comes to cultural compatibility between professionals and managers from different countries, common sense is not necessarily a good guide. From the list of corporate players above, whom would you expect the Dutch to get on with best? In fact the answer is the Spanish (in spite of the Dutch having fought a war of independence against them in the 1568–1648 period). The Dutch managers admired the technical élan of the Telefónica engineers and were also impressed by Telefónica's grasp of internationalization; Telefónica were much further down this road having done it all already in Latin America.

On the other hand, the Dutch had high hopes for cooperation with the Swedes, and Swedish Telia was the first organization to join KPN in the alliance. Van Marrewijk says reassuringly that the Swedes seemed to be rather like the Dutch in terms of their scores on Dutch psychologist Geert Hofstede's cross-cultural study (Hofstede, 1980). At the first meeting of the two sides in Holland, the Swedish CEO endeared himself by asking for beer rather than milk at lunchtime, as an old friend might. But as the project developed the Dutch found that at the end of every discussion the Swedes would not commit on the spot, would always want to take it back to Sweden to consult and discuss some more (slowly), and would then come back with something different.

After Telia left Unisource the Dutch entered into rivalry with the US management from AT&T. After the Spanish left to concentrate on their more mature business interests in South America the Dutch really only got on well with the Swiss, largely it seems because the Swiss regarded themselves as relative beginners in telecomms deregulation and deferred to the Dutch.

The general point at issue here is that even large organizations involved in internationalization for the first time may be up against a row of operational and cultural problems, going beyond what can be solved by common sense. In short the EEL factor applies.

That claim is even more true of smaller companies in the early stages of internationalization. The enhanced competition and its causes explored in Chapter 1 have pushed internationalization down the size scale, so that now many SMEs (small and medium sized enterprises) are engaged in some form of internationalization going beyond simple exporting. This development is particularly true of Europe, as opposed to the United States. The sort of internationalization meant here covers cross-border M&A activity, strategic alliances, joint ventures, 'greenfield sites' in other countries for local production or service provision, and sometimes cross-border finance.

As part of a research group at University College Northampton, England, I explored the experiences of 20 or so mostly UK firms engaged in internationalization in the late 1990s (Lawrence, 1998, Chapter 6). The managers and business owners concerned obviously found it challenging and many of them encountered difficulties they had not anticipated – it was clearly a key learning experience.

One group of problems came from not knowing the laws, regulations, requirements, and institutions of foreign countries they entered. This seemed particularly acute for UK companies in Continental Europe when many of those European countries have stronger social legislation, mandatory employee representation or industrial democracy schemes, and in some cases higher average wage rates. A bit of this internationalization by the UK firms was in the form of cross-border acquisition, which the acquiring company expected to exploit by post-acquisition rationalization involving some de-manning. Several of the internationalizing companies found they simply could not lose employees, or could not afford to in compensation terms. The interviews the research group conducted were replete with remarks like:

> You've no idea how much it costs to make an accountant redundant in Belgium.

> We bought this company in France and then found it had something called a *comité d'entreprise* (a fairly mild employee representative committee).

> I can get a salesman for £35,000 in the UK; in Germany it is £65,000, and I have to buy him a BMW!

Falling foul of laws and institutions shaded into being caught out by differences of practice or expectation in other countries. One company that produced a range of food products had enjoyed considerable success in the UK, the key selling point being the freshness of these products which in consequence had a short shelf-life of around six days. The company hoped to replicate its success in Germany only to find that 30 days was considered short in Germany and 6 days was unheard of. As the British chairman put it: 'It is still part of German culture to store food for a comparatively long period. During and after the war years a whole generation of Germans learned the value of storing goods in cellars and this still has an influence on buying habits.'

This turned out to be only the most intractable of a range of problems centring on the rather different retail climate in Germany at that time with its proliferation of small down-town discount stores, logistical problems, and a relative absence of own-label products meaning that any non-German market entrant faced an enormous struggle to promote its goods in the face of established domestic suppliers.

There is a kind of predictable-to-unimaginable dimension running through these internationalization stories. Some of the issues could have been foreseen, some might have surfaced via market research or by hiring consultants, others are difficult to anticipate in the absence of experience. But the one thing that experience will teach you is that other countries will be different from your own, sometimes in ways you won't be able to foresee but which will nonetheless impact on your business. In short, expect difference.

This may seem a simple message, but the idea of difference between countries is easily obscured by the presence of universal products,

Coca-Cola and all that, transcountry youth and entertainment cultures, and instant communications. All this much talked about globalism is not so convincing when you try to take your business into another country.

We have pursued the issue of internationalization here for two reasons. First, it is not 'all history', not for all industries, not for all big companies, and certainly not for SMEs. The game is not over, there is a lot more of it to come. Second, it is an uncertain business. It does pose questions and raise problems, in strategic, operational, and cultural terms. The EEL factor applies.

Reconfiguration

By reconfiguration we mean the rewriting of industry rules by a company such that its operations and business are transformed. Sometimes such reconfiguration by corporate innovators will impact on an industry, such that it is 'never the same again'.

Grocery retailing, for example, was never the same again after the introduction of the self-service supermarket. Because it was so long ago and is so much a taken-for-granted part of our everyday world it is difficult to imagine what a big, and precocious, step it was at the time.

After Wal-Mart, the world's next largest grocery retailers, in descending order, are: Metro of Germany, Carrefour of France, and Ahold of the Netherlands. Ahold consists mainly of the Albert Heijn (the name of the founder in 1885) supermarket chain in Holland plus chains under local names in other countries, especially the United States and Brazil. The current Albert Heijn who ran the company 1962–97 recalls the self-service supermarket démarche in a biographical work (de Jager, 1998). It was worse for Albert Heijn than for others who made this transition since Albert Heijn had previously sold dry groceries rather than perishables (except for cheese) so going down the supermarket path also involved handling new merchandise.

Albert Heijn told me at a meeting late in 2000 how they opened their first supermarket in 1955, and it lost money. They opened more supermarkets, and they all lost money to start with. He recalled for me a top management meeting to discuss the crisis when someone had said: 'Down the street you have a successful grocery, a butcher, and a green-grocer; but the moment you put them together (ie, supermarket) it fails.'

Of course Ahold mastered the problem, with:

▌ operational analysis at store level;

▌ a drive to get sales up;

▌ cost cutting;

▌ quality raising initiatives.

And the company became the world's fourth largest grocery retailer. I have recalled the anguish and uncertainty experienced at the time just to show how daring and precocious it must have seemed to the prime movers at the time. This is what reconfiguration is like.

A more recent example, and moving back to the British Isles this time, is low cost airlines. Ryanair in Ireland from 1985 and later easyJet in the UK between them rewrote the rules of the industry and won. What differentiates them from the major airlines is a range of inter-locking factors:

▌ They have a single aircraft type (which reduces training and main-tenance costs).

▌ They offer short-haul only.

▌ This gives them better crew utilization (industry sources differ on whether they pay less than the major airlines).

▌ The aircraft run like buses, back and forth to the same destinations; so there is less that can go wrong, they do not have to buy things at foreign airports, and always 'spend the night at home'.

▌ They use secondary airports as a base, principally Stansted for Ryanair and Luton (plus Geneva as noted earlier) for easyJet.

▌ They fly to secondary airports, where there is a choice.

▌ They charge for all the extras, everything from a cup of coffee on.

▌ They are ticketless.

▌ They do not use travel agents; you book direct, phone or via the Internet.

▌ They are cheap.

On the theme of cheapness Ryanair caused a stir in the summer of 2001 by announcing that just prior to departure they would give away, like free, unsold seats. The rationale is that this does not cost them anything, they cannot store unsold seats for re-use, and the free travelling passenger only needs to buy a sandwich to make a contribution to gross margins!

Or consider an example from the car industry. Industry watchers sense that car manufacturers in the West want to withdraw from production, delegating more of the task to their component suppliers, pushing some of the responsibility for design and development back to these suppliers as well, and themselves functioning more as assembly plants. One also gets glimpses, however fanciful, of the car makers' ultimate desire to host assembly rather than actually do it. To maintain, that is, the assembly site to which suppliers would come not to deliver components but to fit them, leaving the manufacturer free to concentrate on design and marketing and perhaps on innovative customer finance packages as well.

All speculation and no data? Well consider this development. Canadian autoparts company Magna International, currently run by Belinda Stronach, the founder's daughter, has a factory in Graz, southern Austria. And guess what it does? It makes Mercedes SUVs (sports utility vehicles) and stationwagons under contract (Turrettini, 2002). In 2003 this same factory will produce Saabs. In 2004 it will make the BMW SUV as well.

If this becomes an industry model, when a components' supplier upgrades itself to subcontractor but does the whole job, it will be a powerful rewriting of the industry rules.

Involvement in companies that reconfigure often means exposure to visionary and charismatic business leaders. In the spirit of the last example, wouldn't you have liked to be part of the action when Herb Kelleher founded SouthWest to fly the Texas triangle (Dallas–Houston–San Antonio). Or how about a corporate office post at IBM when Lou Gerstner was turning it round? Or wouldn't you have liked to see Jack Welch transform GE? Wouldn't anyone?

We have pursued a speculative line of argument in this chapter. The starting point was the malaise, the crisis of human capital analysed and put up on the screen in the last chapter. We began by relativizing this somewhat. First, by separating the social problem (of semi-skilled male workers displaced by de-industrialization) from the management problem (of loss of organizational solidarity, 'monetization' of loyalty); second, by noting that we are (still) in an age of transition, but the time will (soon) come when no one will be able to remember the solidarity of the post-war years, the famous *trentes glorieuses*.

Next we suggested that it may be possible to conceive of an organizational culture and *esprit de corps* that comprehends change, instability, and a distinction between all employees and core members: this is not a prophesy, but at least it is an open question.

Next we had a critical look at the (not so) old adage for career success of getting your ticket stamped in a number of management functions, and suggested that both the predominance of manufacturing industry and the insularity of its silos had receded. The various forces at work here have created a situation where management generally is expected to be more generalist than specialist, in that:

▌ It is less 'silo-driven'.

▌ It is more strategically aware.

▌ It is more attuned to change.

Then we picked up the change idea more directly, arguing that exposure to change, experience of change, and learning from change, the EEL factor, is both a more important basis for career advancement than cross-silo experience, and that involvement in this business process change may provide the stimulus for involvement that once derived from diffuse organizational solidarity.

From here we had a closer look at the idea of business process change, and picked out four dimensions as key learning experiences:

▌ fluctuation, experience of the marked improvement or deterioration of a business;

▌ system change;

▌ internationalization;

▌ reconfiguration.

The final formulation would go something like this:

▋ Enhanced competition will mean more business change.

▋ Successful companies will change more than unsuccessful ones (this is not the same as 'all change is good'; it is more like, no good without change).

▋ Exposure to and involvement in constructive change will be its own reward for managers, perhaps replacing the corporate culture of yesteryear.

▋ If your company is 'changing right' it will be getting it right, and you don't need to change companies.

That is where we have got to. There are two postscripts.

Tacit knowledge

In the last chapter we suggested that the current lack of organizational solidarity would mean that managerial and professional employees would tend to want to 'keep something back', with which to appeal to the next employer. And the easiest thing to keep back are the bits of experience based, instinct-derived *savoir faire* often referred to as tacit knowledge.

We want to add here that while there is no sure fire counter to this, it is not an absolute obstacle either. There is a literature which seeks to address the issue of trying to formalize that which does not readily lend itself to being formalized, for instance Gamble and Blackwell's book on knowledge management (Gamble and Blackwell, 2001).

Also, an example from an organization very consciously engaged in this formalization may help. The example is from Mercer Management Consulting, which is US owned, but it was at their establishment in Munich, Germany that I was given some insight into Mercer's operations. What happens is that Mercer consultants write up the assignments they work on and assemble all the relevant documentation. This is sent to a central clearing house in Boston. The clearing house quality controls it and puts it into the required format, and it then goes into a database that can be accessed worldwide.

What is stored goes all the way from:

▌ a one-page summary;

▌ four-page core facts: timing, duration, staffing, etc;

▌ a large pack that includes final recommendations to the client;

▌ tools, how the calculations and so on were done;

▌ implementation guidelines;

▌ the final training pack.

The result is that when you get a customer enquiry, what might otherwise take three weeks takes a day.

Now it is unlikely that Mercer is alone among business consultants in doing this. My point is rather that this methodology, albeit adapted somewhat, does have an application outside of business service organizations.

Balance

The British Design Council in the run-up to the year 2000 made Millennium Product Awards to some 870 companies. All these companies thus share a technical élan and have recent and excellent innovations to their credit. The sample companies are, however, differentiated by business success, in that:

▌ 65 per cent of them are growing and developing;

▌ 15 per cent of them are doing no better than five years ago;

▌ 20 per cent of them are doing worse, or have gone out of business.

In a fascinating study Alison Myers and Javier Bajer of the Talent Foundation imaginatively tease out and contrast the characteristics of the successful and the unsuccessful (Myers and Bajer, 2001).

Now a key factor in explaining the success of the successful companies is their orientation to change. The successful companies planned for change, allowing time and other resources for handling it, whereas the unsuccessful companies admitted that they found change harder than the successful companies and did it more slowly. What is more the successful companies were much more likely to claim a variety of change-facilitating features including flexible job roles, flexible organization structures, responsive training, frequent assessment of strategy, open communication, rewards for flexibility and the encouragement of an improvement culture.

The Talent Foundation study represents an interesting and more specific confirmation of the arguments pursued in this chapter, namely that change is necessary for success, and that a positive involvement in this change by staff may become the nucleus of a new solidarity.

Finally, this study also argues that a feature of the successful companies is their balance. That is to say they are able to balance the demands of today with those of tomorrow, strike a balance between current operations and ongoing efficiency on the one hand with the conception and implementation of innovation on the other.

So that even in the brave new world tentatively depicted in this chapter, people will still be needed to mind the store.

SUMMARY

In this chapter we have put the crisis of human capital into perspective by:

▌ Distinguishing between the social problem and the managerial challenge.

▌ Noting that expectations determine experience, but expectations are changing.

▌ Looking critically at the old idea of 'getting your ticket stamped' in a variety of management functions.

▌ Noting that this view is rather dated now we are in the age of general management, that experience of change, the EEL factor, is now decisive.

8

Reviewing the unique business proposition

In this chapter we want to change tack and look at an ensemble of smaller and mostly newer companies in the UK and the United States. Some of these have come up already to illustrate various trends and ideas in earlier chapters. But the purpose here is more basic – we want to ask the question: What makes a viable business?

This 'war aim' is easier to pursue with smaller and newer companies. Consider that with large, established companies:

▌ It is easier to ask adaptive questions than basic questions; it is OK to ask how they are coping with, say, an ongoing economic slowdown than it is to ask what is their *raison d'être*.

▌ You cannot ask the CEO of General Motors, 'What is your unique business proposition?' (You would feel foolish doing so.)

▌ Even if you did ask, no one would be able to remember what Alfred P Sloan thought it was back in the 1920s.

▌ Big companies are not good at articulating their competitive advantages; this is in part because they are thought to be self-evident, and in part because they tend to be things that go with being 'an established player' in the industry, things like market leadership (if not market dominance), scale economies, maintenance of market entry barriers to deter rivals, the halo effect of corporate reputation.

Compared with this, smaller and newer companies offer a number of advantages, including:

▌ They are easy to get your mind around, however specialized their operations; you do not need the half-day lecture on corporate history, the range of product–service divisions, and the organizational complexities.

▌ Decision making is more concentrated; talking to one or two people will put you in the picture, you do not need to interview the top 20.

▌ There is more of what one might call 'decisional consciousness'; they do not do anything because they did it last year, because it is always done, because it is part of the corporate calendar; people running smaller companies are more aware of their decisions, good or bad.

▌ The organizational memory is intact, with companies if not young enough then at least small enough to remember why certain aims and purposes were adopted; after all, you cannot ask Ford, 'Why did you decide to make cars and not aeroplanes?' (This is not a stupid question, Ford in the Second World War held the record for aircraft production, turning out B24 Liberator bombers at 63-minute intervals at its Willow Run factory) but you can ask Opta Resources (see Chapter 5) why they decided to concentrate on the top 10 per cent of IT contract manpower.

These then are the considerations we have in mind for a focus here on such smaller and mostly newer businesses. Let us start with a basic issue, the idea of the unique business proposition.

UNIQUE BUSINESS PROPOSITION

It is rather a pity that the word unique gets into this formulation, since unique is an either/or word, whereas business propositions tend to exhibit varying degrees of originality. Let us start at the low end of the scale.

Imagine a smallish UK town that has three fish and chip shops. The entrepreneur who wants to open a fourth fish and chip shop can probably look forward, after 'a working-in' period, to a quarter share of the revenue enjoyed by the original three, unless he or she does something the others have not thought of. What is more, this possibility of differentiating one's way to a bigger market share is not very likely: fish and chip shops have been around a long time, there are not many new angles. Only a big change in the size or social composition of the 'smallish town' is likely to lead to a better business outcome. The fourth fish and chip shop is clearly not a unique business proposition.

But it is rather more difficult to illustrate the strong end of the scale, the genuinely unique. This is because if it really were unique, nobody would have thought of it yet. And if someone has thought of it, and there is an existing business that embodies the idea, then the chances are that it will have been cloned or that someone else/some other company will at least be doing something like it. In a literal sense then, uniqueness exists only at the point of conception and creation. Our concern in practice is with businesses that are more original and less imitative. Consider, for example, Triebold Paeleontology, a small US company launched in 1995, named after its founder. Triebold's business is digging up the skeletons of prehistoric animals, mostly in bits (it is quite good going to find 40 per cent of a single animal in one go), and assembling them to produce whole animals. These prehistoric finds are scattered around – Kansas, Montana, and particularly in the Bad Lands of South Dakota.

If not unique this is certainly original. The industry only emerged in the early 1990s, driven in part by *Jurassic Park* movies and Disney animations. Elements of its newness and originality include:

▌ Turning what was a hobby-interest of the founder into a commercially viable operation.

▌ Not only serving the existing museum market but creating new markets – corporations and private individuals as buyers.

▌ The fact that there is as yet light competition; companies in the industry are often differentiated by specializing in different types/groups of animals.

▌ A certain amount of sharing in the industry, in the sense of swapping bits to get whole animals.

▌ A certain amount of knowledge-sharing via seminars.

▌ Having growth significantly driven at the top of the value chain by discovering new prehistoric animals.

Triebold and similar operations do depend on scientific knowledge, but they are not what one conventionally understands by high tech, in contrast to Manhattan based company Searchspace, a subsidiary of the privately held Searchspace Group in London, profiled in an autumn 2001 edition of *Forbes* (Kellner, 2001).

Searchspace was launched in London in 1993 by four doctoral students at University College London's Intelligent Systems Laboratory. Originally they consulted for UK utilities companies and supermarkets, predicting electricity and product demand, but later concentrated on the development and application of pattern recognition software to expose money-laundering operations. Finding suspicious patterns is what it is all about; as CEO Konrad Feldman suggested by way of illustration: 'When you have cheques from different (bank) branches and they all get cashed in a single branch in a different country, you might be getting somewhere.'

At the time of writing, Searchspace employed 140 people, mostly software engineers, and expected 2001 revenues of US $20 million.

Or consider an example from US retailing, in this case selling brass musical instruments to high school bands. The market is served by two types of operation. On the one hand there are music megastores in big metropolitan areas. Because of the leverage they have with manufacturers/suppliers they are able to offer a good product range and keen prices. But not everyone lives in a big metropolitan area. Elsewhere there is a myriad of local music stores serving local communities. These stores are not especially cheap, and school bands are always operating on a budget that is less than they would like, but the stores are often the beneficiaries of local loyalty and offer a face-to-face service, important in the small-town United States.

How can you crack this duopoly and get into the brass instrument market? Answer: by catalogue and telephone ordering. There are some five big players in the catalogue business, and the one I know, Taylor Music, sends out its catalogue to some 19,000 schools across the United States and then takes orders over the phone, payment by credit card, delivery by US Mail or private carriers. It sounds easy, and it has been going for some time, but there are some nice twists:

▌ Taylor Music, the company in question, does not send its catalogues to schools in the big metropolitan areas, so it is not in competition with the music megastores, whose prices it could not beat.

▌ The company does not need to be located in a stylish (and expensive) place, and in fact operates out of Main Street in Aberdeen, South Dakota.

▌ It does target smaller communities that do not have a music store (or not a good one).

▌ For this company's target market being in a small town on the prairies is a plus, giving a down home image rather than big city glitz.

Not only has Taylor Music avoided competition with the big city rivals, but because of the scale of its operations it is cheaper than the local stores as well.

So far we have argued that while the word unique connotes an absolute unlikely to be attained in business creation, there is good reason to move away from the fish and chips model in the direction of greater originality, and we have offered examples from science based, IT, and old-fashioned domestic retailing. What we want to do next is to unpack further this idea of originality in business creation, and try to identify some of its possible ingredients.

Cost efficiencies

While the likes of Searchspace and Triebold Paeleontology are best seen as part of emerging industries, many new companies are entrants to established industries. For this latter, and larger, category superior cost efficiency may give them a degree of uniqueness that makes the difference. After all:

▌ Start-up companies are typically cost conscious in comparison to established industry players; and often they are doing it all on a shoestring which will accentuate the cost-conscious inclination.

▌ They do not have any of the extras, corporate luxuries or indulgences of established industry players.

▌ Whatever they do in the early days – make critical new appointments, buy equipment, add personnel, acquire premises, open new branches, and so on – they are doing it for the first time, which will make them more conscious and inclined to scrutiny.

Or to put it another way, while established companies sometimes make cost-efficiency gains by cutting the fat, newer companies have (yet) to put on any fat.

In Chapter 1 we discussed a UK house building company and its attempts to simplify the supply chain regarding the acquisition of cement, reducing the number of types and insisting that suppliers have a uniform price for all types based on past records of the mix of types supplied. Our purpose at that stage was to show how the cost-efficiency drives and BPR initiatives of one organization might unwittingly contribute to downsizing elsewhere, in this case among the salesforce at suppliers.

There is, however, another twist to the exemplary story of this company. A lot of its work was as a contractor to the bigger volume house builders, doing 'to the roof up' work (that is everything except the plumbing, electrical installation, kitchen fitting). The volume builders that are providing this work are only offering what they see as a 2–3 per cent margin. But our 'to the roof up' company is amazingly cost efficient in a rather slack industry. With its tight organization, its strengths of control, anticipation, and simplification, it has got costs down to a point where its margins in this subcontract work are more like 9–10 per cent.

This company is a particularly forceful example, but the cost-efficient entrant to an established industry is a quite general phenomenon. Cost efficiency increases margins.

Intimations of cheapness

For reasons explored and illustrated in the previous section smaller newer companies are often able to compete on price, and plenty do. This is a commonplace, but something more subtle that surfaced in several of the companies visited in the run-up to writing this book is the way that some of them, especially the more entrepreneurial ones, cultivated *an image* of cheapness.

This is not to say that they aim to deceive, but rather that they see being perceived as low priced by actual and potential customers as a competitive advantage. And these intimations of cheapness always have some substance, even if it is not the whole story. Two variations on the theme of cheapness seem to be: the company does do something at low cost for its customers, often choosing to offer some discount or to make some price concession that is unusual in the industry, thus embellishing its good value reputation. Or, the company starts out cheap, and when its reputation for cheapness is established, it becomes incrementally dearer.

One or two examples may help. A chain of music shops in the UK specialize in 'chart products', that is to say CDs of pop songs in the top 40. And the CDs really are cheap, at £2–3 below the average retail competition. The reason they could sell this cheap was that they were taking advantage of the strong pound at the start of 2001 and getting the product from Continental Europe where it was cheaper, not sourcing it themselves but buying it from importers. The company was also running a tight ship: while most of their stores are in high profile out of town or big city malls, the stores are also quite compact, they can be run by two sales employees, the rent is proportionately low, the company is careful to restrict itself to low cost self-advertisement.

So it really is cheap, and for comprehensible reasons to the credit of the business owner. But:

▌ Expansion (having more stores, the result of early success) put up overheads; so, while the top 40 chart products are still amazingly cheap, the shops now sell other CDs at a higher price sourced from UK wholesalers rather than from Continental Europe.

▌ There is some gentle manipulation of the top 40 in the sense that any title they cannot get cheap, for whatever reason, is replaced with something different but plausible which they can get cheap;

this sustains the image of 'really cheap chart products' while avoiding ruinous sourcing costs.

▌ The company has a compatible non-music product with high margins for which there is buoyant demand.

▌ CD is being superceded by DVD; but DVDs are more expensive anyway; so having established a reputation for cheapness with genuinely cheap CD chart products the company can gently slide into supplying more expensive DVDs.

Try another example. This is a UK pharmaceuticals wholesaler, supplying chemist shops with the things they sell. This wholesaler is cheap because: it deals in parallel imports; it sells generics.

These two may need a bit of unpacking. Parallel imports arise in this way. A company in country A makes a particular drug. It sells it to country B at a lower price than it sells into country C. The usual reason for this sales price differential is that country B is poorer than country C, the government has a smaller health care budget, and insists on lower prices, thus confronting the pharmaceuticals manufacturer in country A with the options: sell to us cheap, or do not sell to us at all. The twist is that the government, that is the health care authorities, of country C notice the differential and license imports from country B of produce sold to them cheap by the producer in country A. *Voilà*, parallel imports.

Generics are a little different. When pharmaceutical companies bring out a new product, which is tried and tested and licensed by the regulatory authorities of leading Western countries, the product is protected by patent for up to 20 years to enable the developing company to recoup the horrendous cost of development and clinical trials. But when this product comes off patent other companies will seek to replicate it, to produce a non-branded version of it to the same formula that will be sold at a lower price. These non-branded versions are called generics. A further twist to the story is that the generics are sometimes produced in developing countries with lower labour costs, further enhancing the cost advantage. India is the leading example (Tanzer, 2001).

If your stock in trade is parallel imports and generics, as with the wholesaler whose operations we are appraising, you are pretty much bound to be able to appeal to your customers, in this case single pharmacy stores and small chains, in cost terms. But there is more to come:

▌ The pharmaceutical wholesale industry is awash with what are called retro discounts – 2 per cent off if you pay on time, x per cent off if you order such and such a quantity, and so on. The wholesale company we are considering builds all these into the up-front net price; there are no fancy deals of the 'If you buy x of y you get a heap of z free' kind (this is the pharmaceutical equivalent of having only four kinds of cement, it is simple to calculate, easy to administer); so long as you pay within 30 days from the month end you get a price which is cheaper than that offered by main line wholesalers.

▌ Our company also offers discount on what are known in the trade as ZD (zero discount) lines – typically products requiring some special handling such as refrigeration – a nice touch this, does not cost much but it is eye-catching.

▌ The salespeople at our company are encouraged in fact to act as order-takers rather than hard sellers, and will even recommend to customers cheaper options supplied by others.

But this is not the whole story. Zenith, the company concerned, pride themselves on their service, even if there are some things offered by the much larger mainline wholesalers that Zenith cannot match. In the London area, Zenith's base, they deliver same day, using their own smart vehicles and uniformed drivers. Elsewhere they deliver next day using nationwide carriers. They offer a big range of produce; they are a one-stop shop. They make order-placing easy for customers, calling them at an agreed time each day; customers can also e-mail, free-fax or free-phone Zenith.

It may also be the case that Zenith have bucked an industry pattern in these customer ordering arrangements. For the mainline pharmaceutical wholesalers, some 98 per cent of the ordering is by e-mail, and the likes of Zenith cannot equal this, but they offer personal contact over the phone. Dispensing is a lonely business, especially if you are an individual in an independent small shop rather than employee of a nationwide chain. Dispensers like to chat, and Zenith recognize this. Picking the people who take the orders is a key issue for them, and they go for ex-dispensers rather than pharmaceuticals company salesmen (who may be inclined to pressurize customers). The response of order-takers is also expected to be efficient. As one of Zenith's owner-managers put it:

The person answering the phone is the critical interface. Here if you pick up the phone you must be able to take the order; don't tell the customer you need the product code first, or say you can't find their account. Our phones flash up who is calling; if they have a problem, we own it.

All this is worth something, and with generics and parallel imports you do not need to charge high prices. But as one of Zenith's managers explained: '... we offer service too; with quality of service you can protect your price.' A more diffuse variation on this theme, not necessarily limited to smaller or newer companies, is the gentle price manipulation of branded and non-branded goods offered side by side.

Branded goods typically command a high price with customers. Buyers are willing to pay because they know the manufacturer, probably perceive the manufacturer as prestigious or at least as reliable and offering a tried and tested product. And of course the manufacturer will have invested resources in developing and promoting the brand. At the same time retailers and wholesalers are also expected to pay a good price to the manufacturer for the privilege of selling or dealing in the brand, and their margins are correspondingly modest.

From the retailer/wholesaler standpoint, all this is reversed with non-branded (private label or own label) goods. They are cheaper to start with, retailer/wholesalers may commission their own source of supply, and may get further leverage by finding off-shore suppliers in low wage countries. So although the non-branded goods have to be sold at a discount compared with established brands the retailer/wholesaler margin may be better.

All this is generally recognized, but there is a further twist. This is that while branded goods command a higher price, there is easy comparability. You cannot fudge a Porsche 911 or a tin of Heinz baked beans; what is offered for sale is instantly identifiable, and if there are price differences buyers know they are comparing like with like.

It is this comparability that is lacking with non-branded goods. Buyers simply do not know if one retailer's private label is as good as that offered by another retailer, so there are no meaningful price comparisons. All the buyer can see is that the non-branded product is cheaper than the branded. This lack of comparability among non-branded alternatives makes it easier for retailers and wholesalers to improve their margins, since they are less likely to be compared with each other.

So far we have as ingredients of a good business proposition:

▌ superior cost efficiencies;

▌ getting vital supplies cheaper (chart products and wholesale pharmaceuticals in the last two examples offered);

▌ being price competitive;

▌ offering some price advantage to customers that fuels a reputation
for cheapness.

One barrier to price competitiveness for smaller and newer buyers
that is often cited, however, is their inability to buy in bulk, an advantage enjoyed by larger manufacturers or service providers. But not
only have we found particular exceptions to this piece of business folk
wisdom, as with Zenith above, but particularly in the United States we
have seen smaller companies joining to form buying consortia to get
some leverage on suppliers. The up-market men's clothes shop, The
Main, discussed in Chapter 2 did this; and so did the food wholesaler
HRS Food Service, discussed in Chapter 5 as an example of adding
service to service. Indeed the small-town United States offered us
rather more examples of relatively small companies dealing one to one
with suppliers, also considered in Chapter 5 as an example of
enhanced service.

Configuration

Sometimes it is configuration that is central to the successful business
idea. Configuration in the sense of identifying several things that
contribute and combining them into a working whole in such a way
that something distinctive is created. Consider as a nice low-tech, easy
to get hold of example the Dallas based company Retro, mentioned in
a different context earlier. Retro is in the compulsory gift business (in
the sense of gifts given by convention to people the giver does not
know well, such as gifts to business visitors or representatives of institutional customers), and its key product is stylish ballpoint pens in
appealing light aluminium containers. Sounds easy but there are some
nice touches here. One is to recognize that there is a difference
between gifts exchanged among friends and within families on the
one hand, and gifts that may be exchanged between people who do

not necessarily know each other at all well, may even be meeting for the first time. The gift-giving in this second case is driven by business convention and a desire by business hosts, sellers, suppliers or whatever to reinforce their image with customers in a pleasing way. When you have recognized the difference, the next trick is to serve this market in a distinctive way. The gifts have to carry a presumption of acceptability, since the receivers are not well known to the givers, and will vary by age, sex, and doubtless preference. What better than artifacts that are useful but may still be differentiated by style, and that are in a small way an accoutrement of one's occupational status.

Moving from the conception to the business, it is magnificently dispersed across country borders in that:

▐ Design and marketing are organized from Dallas, Texas.

▐ The mechanism (for the ball point pens) is sourced in Germany.

▐ Production takes place in Taiwan; although one of the product lines is styled and made in Italy.

▐ Sales and distribution are in the United States and Canada.

What we have described here is a rather ingenious configuration whose elements are: identifying a distinctive market segment, conceiving appropriate products, and then creating a value chain dispersed across several countries/regions, each conferring an advantage. It goes like this:

▐ management control in the United States (efficiency);

▐ mechanism from Germany (Technik, quality component);

▐ product import from Italy (style);

▐ manufacture in Taiwan (cost efficiency);

▐ sales in the United States (affluent market).

We have come a long way from the humble fish and chip shop.

Try as another illustration the furniture industry in Denmark. Again the product is nice and tangible and easy to understand, though the business thinking is subtle.

Denmark is a furniture country. There are some 600–800 furniture companies in Denmark. One cannot be precise about numbers over time because of both start-ups and acquisitions, though the industry exhibits a clear trend towards concentration, as always. Of these hundreds of companies only 10 are big with a turnover of over DK 250 million. A lot of the small companies make cash and carry products, with thin margins of course; they make industrial products, cabinets and so on, where they have to compete on price. A lot of them supply Ikeå: but when Ikeå sources cross-border, say in Poland, the Danish companies are in trouble. They also sell to the big retail chains, where bargaining power of course lies with the buyer not the seller. The market was also depressed for some years during the 1990s: downsizing means less desks!

So the question is, how could one possibly succeed in this overcrowded, often thin margin, concentrating business, where power has moved down the value chain into the hands of the buyers?

The company we are going to look at is Fritz Hansen in Allerød, suburban Copenhagen, based on my contacts with it in the late 1990s. To be up front, Fritz Hansen is not a new company, indeed it had its 125th anniversary in 1997, but it is small – kind of. With around 200 employees and only limited outsourcing/subcontracting, it is not bigger than most of the companies discussed here, but by the standards of the industry, it is quite big. This is important: it has options, it is not locked into the supply of Ikeå and does not compete on price.

The second thing is that Hansen has gone for particular product groups that take it away from the mass market, thin margin, price competition *genre*:

▌ conference furniture;

▌ dining area furniture;

▌ lounge and reception area furniture; this is especially corporate and organization reception area furnishing;

▌ office area furnishing, but not desking (desking is mass, thin margin, vulnerable to recession).

Only about 30 per cent of this is for domestic use in the sense of being destined for people's homes. With most of the products going into public, corporate and organizational space the emphasis moves from price to style, from cheap to quality. When you buy Fritz Hansen, you make a statement about organizational image and purpose. As the MD remarked: 'We make furniture for museums, to stand there for ever.'

To this we should add that having an attractive workplace, in terms of building design, environment, and outfitting is something of a Danish cult. Their bacon factories are as good as other countries' boutiques. In part this reflects the high average wage levels combined with weak salary differentiation, in the sense that the salary gaps between say doctor and nurse, pilot and air steward, editor and journalist, are smaller than they would be in the UK, France, or in the United States (Lawrence and Edwards, 2000, Chapter 10). So having a really attractive work environment is a plus, something that can be enjoyed by all, and unlike a bigger Anglo-Saxon style salary differential, the government will not tax it!

This all leads into a quality and style market, into what are called designer led companies. This is where Fritz Hansen is, in fact it is the biggest in the segment with a turnover of above DK 250 million.

Fritz Hansen does not actually have design in-house, designers are not its full-time employees on the company payroll. Designers are external, independent, and provide a fee based service; this is the set up of Fritz Hansen and it is normal for Denmark's designer led companies. And of course it functions as a virtuous circle. A company that is high profile attracts ambitious and talented designers.

A part of this high profile is that Fritz Hansen's design is not just regarded as good but also as distinctive. The design philosophy running through generations of products is functionalist and minimalist. There is also in this philosophy leading to style an element of harmony, though the idea is not easy to explain. In the Latin countries in matters of style, people have a relationship with individual items. In northern Europe and in Denmark and Sweden in particular the emphasis is on everything going together.

Now this minimalist/functionalist/harmony-style philosophy is Danish by inspiration but there is an appreciation of it that goes beyond Scandinavia. In other words, it is an international segment. Hansen has sales in Germany and Japan as well as being a leader in Denmark.

There is another twist. Most designer led companies are selling furniture under the designer's label. But Fritz Hansen is selling on its own name, it is branding itself, not branding the designer, and its standing has enabled it to reverse the industry norms. This corporate branding move is not only enhancing its image, but protecting its image. It would need a whole series of bad designs before it suffered, in the way that the Rolls-Royce brand would hold up even if a design team messed up a particular model. Hansen has protected itself against the rise and fall of the reputation of individual designers.

Finally, there is the matter of product quality. There is some outsourcing, for instance of wood cutting and aluminium components which are made in Sweden where wages are reckoned to be 30 per cent lower. But the finishing, the bringing together of end product all happens on one site, with a rather stable, tradition-minded workforce.

Now I do not mean to suggest that this company is perfect; at the time of my visit it did have problems matching output to (rising) orders. But what we have depicted is a rather effective configuration:

▌ Relative but not absolute size takes the company out of dependence on powerful retail chains.

▌ It is differentiated by:
  – design philosophy;
  – design creativity;
  – product quality.

▌ All this takes it into the high price, high end segments.

▌ It has a relationship with designers that is not programmable and this is self-sustaining.

▌ Its segment is international if not universal.

▌ It has inverted the industry norm by branding itself.

Any of these elements we have enumerated is worth something on its own. Put together they constitute market leadership. This is the power of configuration.

MEETING NEEDS

It is part of marketing folklore that all businesses providing goods and services are meeting needs. This simple (though controversial at the edges) declaration does not need to be reinforced here. Rather we can see one or two particular 'need creators' that may facilitate business creation and success, and we want to try to illuminate these a little. In doing this we are still with the theme of the 'unique business proposition', still trying to figure where this uniqueness or originality comes from.

Solving key problems

One *entré* appears to be the ability to solve a key problem. It goes something like this. There is a need, it may even by widely recognized, but there is some problem in the way of meeting the need. Thus the company that cracks the problem gets to meet the need. This is not quite an original idea, but usually 'the problem' is formulated in terms of science or technology or R&D endeavour – a sure fire cure for AIDS, a form of personal transport that is as flexible as the automobile but that does not use gas, and so on. What we would like to do is to give a business rather than a science version. In this connection, 'cracking the problem' is best seen as relative rather than absolute. With this caution one can see business ideas which are built around problem cracking.

If, for example, one wants to charge the highest fees for contracting out IT professionals one needs to be able to pick out the top 10 per cent, those with experience and management capability as well as technical skills. As we have seen (in Chapter 5) Opta Resources recognized this, and put effort and know-how into qualifying the top 10 per cent. This gives them access to a lucrative market, not price-sensitive and often with longer placements and more repeat-order business.

Or consider again Computer Doctor, the South Dakota based computer repair operation discussed earlier, that was conceived from the outset as a franchise operation. Picking the franchisees is key. Now it would be an overstatement to say of Computer Doctor 'they cracked it', but they have identified the basic (and contradictory) qualities needed and developed a procedure that simultaneously probes for both.

Another South Dakota company, Professional Mailing and Marketing, is in what might be called 'the substitute mail room business'. That is, it does (much of) what a US company's or other organization's mail room does for itself – and makes a profit out of it.

Just consider what a dicey operation this must be. To get the business one probably has to do it more cheaply for the corporate mail rooms than they can do it for themselves (I put it in this cautious way because some companies may be outsourcing just for the hell of it). Professional Mailing and Marketing is not a mail transporting operation, its contribution is putting material in envelopes and addressing them; the mail then goes via US Mail and Professional Mailing have to pay the Post Office like anyone else. So somehow or other there has to be a difference between rates paid by organizational customers and rates paid to US Mail, the difference being enough to cover the cost of the operation and generate a profit. That has got to be impossible, hasn't it?

Part of the answer of course derives from relative economies of scale. Professional Mailing and Marketing are not dealing in singleton 'Dear John' letters but in big batches – mail shots, advertising copy, subscription reminders, bank statements, alumni mailings for colleges, invoices and so on. All this material lends itself to mechanization and electronic automating – label printing, envelope stuffing, database accessing, electronic address list transfer and all that. Now those economy of scale advantages enjoyed by Professional Mailing and Marketing are relative: they will not be able to do it any cheaper than General Motors can do it for themselves but probably have the edge on the junior high school in Watertown, South Dakota.

But more important than the economies of scale argument is to understand the Post Office well enough to manage the interface with it. The Post Office, I was told in April 2001, used to have over 4,000 rates; then they changed the system(!). There is more national standardization now but dealing with the system is still far from being a walkover.

The trick in these dealings with the Post Office is to exploit their cheaper rates, typically for quantity going to the same zip code, and already batched up the way they like it. To do this you have to know the rates system. Then, as you are handling mail for different customers, there may be possibilities for cross-batching. So if you can co-mingle mail from different customers and get say 150 plus items for a five-digit zip code you get a reduction. Do this enough times on enough quantity and you build a profitable margin.

Guess the previous employment of Professional Mailing and Marketing's General Manager: he was a graduate employee (with a maths degree with a computer science minor) at the Post Office.

Try a last example of key problem cracking. In 2000 Wells Fargo Bank bought Aman Collection Service, a debt collecting agency in Aberdeen, South Dakota. Aman specialize in collecting from graduate and post-graduate students who have disappeared and not even started repaying their loans.

This, like Professional Mailing and Marketing's field, is another tricky business. Aman Collection Service does not have enforcement powers, only agencies of the United States government have that. When it finds the indebted students its options are to counsel them, point out the implications of non-repayment, urge lifestyle economies, show how the student only needs to make the first repayment at the standard rate to be 'in repayment' after which they can negotiate, and this works more often than it fails; two-thirds of the defaulters end up paying. But first you have to find them. This is the key problem.

The finding exercise is called 'skip-tracing' and it is for the most part done electronically – accessing records and databases, and sometimes buying data. And it came to pass that Aman Collection Service found that one of these data sources yielded a higher trace rate than the others. This data source came, indirectly, from records of the credit card transactions of a fast food chain with a home delivery service.

In the student debt collecting world, this is the secret of everlasting life.

Regulation drives business opportunity

It may be a paradox but regulation often creates uncertainty, scarcity, complexity or constraint, which in turn creates business opportunities for anyone who can hang in and find their way through it or around it.

Zenith, the London based pharmaceuticals wholesaler discussed earlier in this chapter, is a case in point. My two-sentence exposé of parallel imports, taking advantage of the fact that the same drugs may be sold at different prices in different countries because of government controls and varying health care budgets, probably makes it sound easy. It is not easy.

In the UK the Ministry of Health via the MCA (a subsidiary agency) issue licences for the importation of drugs from specified EU countries such as Spain and Italy whose governments have negotiated lower prices with pharmaceuticals manufacturers. The MCA do not make it easy for you to get this licence. All the would-be (foreign) suppliers have to be specified in advance; you have to have an assembly plant where you can repackage the imports and translate the labels and instructions into English. The MCA charge a fee for all this, and the process may take up to a year. And when you have done all that, I was told: 'The drug companies will find some cause to sue you; like you used their logo. This is just to slow things down!'

These parallel imports are a key part of Zenith's ability to thrive in this market. Wrestling with the MCA may not be fun, but this challenge is creating a business opportunity.

Or consider the South Dakota company Hub Music and Vending (Chapter 5) whose key business is the provision and service of video lottery machines. This is only profitable and attractive because just a handful of US states have legalized video lottery, and, even in those states it is still regulated in various ways, for instance in regard to the kind of location at which the machines can be sited, the number of machines at any one site, and of course the State government's right to a share of the takings. How nice for the State to have a revenue stream second only to sales tax in yield, and just for passing a law every four years.

Environmental legislation in the West is a fertile source of business opportunity, but let us stay for the moment with the upper mid-West of the United States, and look at garbage collection. In 1991 new guidelines came in restricting the number of landfill dumpsites, but Brown County, South Dakota had one.

This conferred a considerable advantage on existing Aberdeen based company Dependable Sanitation. It gave Dependable Sanitation a big catchment area, even by US standards, with 300-mile a day truck routes. Though of course it takes some business nerve (and investment) to exploit such opportunities, in the shape of bigger trucks, more handling equipment, and covering the cost of higher tipping fees as existing dumpsites are taken out. But without regulation, it would be too easy, and the industry would become overcrowded.

There is, however, another twist to the story, which is that different jurisdictions may have different levels of regulation. These differences may be exploited by enterprising businesses. In this case South Dakota's neighbour to the east, Minnesota, has banned landfills with effect from 2006, unless the waste has already been treated. Think what that is going to do for the catchment area of a company operating out of Brown County.

Regulation in the garbage industry also creates opportunities for specialization. Hospitals, for example, generate a lot of waste, some of it difficult to treat and dispose of, especially all the plastic waste. There is, of course, regulation here; this waste cannot just be dumped in landfills, but has to be burned in medical waste incinerators. In the 1980s Dependable Sanitation started a licensed medical waste incinerator, which at first was the only commercial one in South Dakota (some hospitals have their own). For a time Dependable Sanitation was handling the medical waste of the whole State, and taking some from hospitals in Minneapolis (about a five-hour drive, each way).

The moral is that wherever there is regulation it will let in the persistent few who have developed know-how, and keep the rest out. In garbage the next game will be computers, the garbage disposal challenge of the 21st century.

Time and space create needs

Finally we would like to suggest that time and space may be another identifiable creator of needs.

A number of service providing companies are cashing in on the time constraints of others. An example we have touched on earlier is (some) health/leisure clubs in the UK dedicated to the cash-rich, time-poor segment; in practice this means providing the facility just before and just after the working day, and making sure it is not cluttered up by children and families. Aman Collection Service, discussed in this chapter, is a case in point; the colleges on whose behalf it traces loan-defaulting graduates could if they chose do this for themselves. And the customers of Professional Mailing and Marketing could handle all their mailing, if they had taken the trouble to master the Post Office's 4,000 rates. These challenges after all are 'not rocket science', but they do require application over time. Here lies the opportunity, in that one organization's time constraint is another's business opening.

Another twist is that as the passage of time takes us through boom and slump, the kaleidoscope of opportunities changes. It has, for example, become a black reality in the autumn of 2001 that the events of 11 September have created opportunities in security provision and consultancy. A less gruesome instance was offered again by Professional Mailing and Marketing, claiming in April 2001 they had added 70 new customers in a month as an incipient recession drove cost cutting and downsizing.

It may be less obvious, but it also works for space. There is a Cyber Café on Barrington, the principal thoroughfare in Halifax, in Eastern Canada. A totally unremarkable fact you may think, an electronic equivalent of fish and chips. But when I visited it in 1999 I was told the next nearest Internet café was in Montreal. The journey time by train between the two cities is 19½ hours (it takes three hours to fly). When you know this, a Cyber Café on Barrington begins to look a good prospect. To which one may reasonably add some population features of Halifax, again conditioned by location and US distance. First,

Halifax is a student town, with six universities including the famous Dalhousie (the province of Nova Scotia has 11). Second, there are military service personnel in Halifax. As a cab-driver jauntily put it, half of the Canadian navy that is not on the Pacific Coast is operating out of Halifax! Both students and military personnel are known heavy users of Internet cafés, being young, familiar with the technology, and away from home with a need to communicate with parents, partners, and peer groups.

SUMMARY

In this chapter we have focused mostly on smaller and newer companies to try to get closer to the essence of business creation and success.

Taking the idea of the unique business proposition as a starting point, we tried to take it apart and show from where this uniqueness, or at least effective originality came. In this connection we suggested superior cost efficiencies, price competitiveness, promoting a value-for-money reputation, and above all having a resourceful and constructive configuration where all the elements count but the total effect is greater than the sum of the parts.

Then we extended the notion of unique business proposition to embrace the idea of satisfying needs, and further suggested that some of the companies we have researched suggest that advantage and opportunity may be offered by cracking key problems, and exploiting the limitation imposed by time, space, and official regulation.

In Chapter 9 we want to pursue the goal of wresting understanding from smaller companies by demonstrating how successful ones often exhibit a range of competitive advantage that surrounds the unique business proposition.

9

Competitive advantage

Staying with this idea of wresting insight from smaller and newer business, but changing the emphasis, we want to look at the issue of competitive advantage. Chapter 8 focused on the unique business proposition, modifying the idea a bit. That is to say, the approach was unitary, even if identified by a number of different springboards or even different elements, imaginatively combined.

Here we want instead to emphasize the range of competitive advantages enjoyed by some companies. The view is that a successful company needs both a viable business idea and a nexus of competitive advantage. The more successful companies we looked at were distinguished by both. Having a number or range of competitive advantages offers a corresponding range of gains, including the following:

▌ It is more likely that the company concerned will have the edge over the competition.

▌ It may indeed keep the competition out.

▌ It makes the company more distinctive.

▌ And therefore more difficult to clone.

▌ And there may be a subtle interaction between these advantages, for instance with the Danish office furniture company cited in Chapter 8, between having a slate of talented designers and having propagated the corporate brand.

▌ It renders a company less vulnerable; if something changes to its disadvantage, well, it still has other strengths to exploit.

On this last point of the protection afforded by a range of advantages, consider a fanciful but topical (November 2001) example, this time from the big corporate world.

The big three US automobile manufacturers get nearly all their profits from pick-up trucks, SUVs (sports utility vehicles) and mini-vans. They are US strengths which have not been neutralized by foreign competition, at least not yet, in the way that saloon cars have. Plus of course that the United States is a great market for just these kinds of vehicle given its size, the importance of the agricultural economy, and the fact that, as the Europeans see it, US drivers have the benefit of more or less free gasoline.

Background. When Bill Ford sacked Jacques Nasser in October 2001 and took on the top job himself, he brought with him something of a nice guy image and a reputation for environmental concern. One expression of the latter is the Ford Motor Company's US $5 million donation to National Audubon Society in February 2001. National Audubon is engaged in what *Forbes Global* calls 'a very public fight to save the spotted owl at the expense of timber jobs' (Burke and Meredith, 2001).

Ford customers in logging areas are protesting. A dealership in Libby, Montana, declared a 15 per cent fall in pick-up sales from February to September 2001. A Dodge dealer (selling a rival GM model) bought newspaper space in Great Falls, Montana, to advertise the Audubon grant and grab business from Ford. There are similar reactions in Oregon and elsewhere. Indeed this kind of action has become common in the last few years where rival sections protested against the Clinton administration's creation of National Parks to the detriment of farming, logging, and mining interests. A letter in a later edition of *Forbes Global* writing jocularly suggests that it is the Ford pick-up driver rather than the spotted owl that is the endangered species.

OK, this one is a bit fanciful. The spotted owl versus the Ford pick-up is not going to become a national issue, after all, people will not care that much about it in Southern Connecticut. But just imagine if it did become a national issue! Just as well Ford's competitive advantage is not restricted to the pick-up.

This chapter though is not about Ford or other major corporates, but about smaller companies which exhibit a variety of competitive advantages. Let us try to illustrate this. We will start off-shore.

Out on the oil rig

Marine Tech, founded in 1993, is primarily a marine electrical out-fitter, doing work on-shore and off-shore, both the planning and installation. Its principal customer for this work is the oil industry, and Marine Tech undertakes work across a wide area, including the Middle East and the United States, as well as for the UK oil fields (the company is based in north-east England, in a traditional ship-building area).

Since its inception it has grown both organically and by acquisition and also has an in-house unit that does mechanical work, and which has a different set of clients, as well as a business unit that handles provision and preparation of cables for the electrical outfitting work. The company's overall turnover for 2000 was around £90 million. This company has a range of competitive advantages, including the antecedents of its founders.

It was started by four partners, all of whom had been working until then in larger and more established firms in the same industry. So they are insiders, with experience and know-how.

But more than this, they have a critique of the industry as it was in the mid-1990s, an industry marked by:

▌ An old boy network, with deals done (commissions/contracts awarded) on the golf course.

▌ Fat engineering consultancy reports (and fees to match).

▌ A tendency towards over-engineering (for which the client pays).

And all this at a time when larger clients were becoming more cost conscious, and the oil industry was bringing in a cost-reduction programme known by its stirring initials as CRIME.

Against this background the founders began with a broad business plan. They expected to undercut the industry norms, by being leaner and; going for simple solutions.

Then over time they put together the group of companies or business units noted above, all of which are run as profit centres. This assembling of competences going from design to installation, electrical to mechanical, organizing supply and doing post-construction service, on-shore and off-shore, marks them out, gives them access to a variety of customers and commissions.

This multi-competence is reinforced by a few specialisms, such as:

▮ Hazardous zoning work, where electrical equipment has to be protected in areas where if it sparked it might ignite something – for instance they are doing underpass work in Scotland, where oil and petrol get drained off into an underground area where there is also electrical power – a lot of electrical outfitters cannot handle this hazardous zoning work.

▮ Verficiation work – Lloyds (insurers) of London have rules to which vessels have to be built, and there are different classes of vessel for insurance purposes; Marine Tech can do the verification work for such classifications.

▮ Assignments in extreme climates.

Now none of this, neither the multi-competence nor the various specialisms, put Marine Tech in a class of one. Most large, established firms can do all of this. But having all of this is unusual for a company that is still relatively new, small, and cheap. This small company with big company image, know-how, and capability, is a recurring theme among the more successful start-ups.

All this multi-competence is given a further thrust by the way Marine Tech get business. Because they started small and were new in the marketplace a lot of their early commissions were small. But by making a good job of them they attracted larger commissions from the same customers. This strong strand of repeat order business is a plus in two ways. It reduces promotional costs, (much of) the business comes to you, something that is well recognized. Also, you move faster down the learning curve of the organizations for whom you are working, get to know their business better, understand their structures and operating needs, all of which helps you to do a better job.

A simple story might illustrate the last point. A client company has two projects going on, literally side by side, each of the projects divided into modules. Marine Tech's role was supplying all the equipment. But the fork-lift truck drivers on site, not Marine Tech's employees of course, had difficulty unloading the delivery trucks and allocating the equipment to the right part of each project. Marine Tech responded by colour coding the cables by project/module. This reduced truck unloading time from two hours to a half an hour.

Indeed Marine Tech's culture was awash in stories of this kind: going the extra mile, bailing out customers, saving customers from the occasional shortcomings of their suppliers, helping suppliers to get it right, and so on. One of their claims was that they would take production managers and quality controllers from suppliers along with them for contract-winning meetings with customer organizations.

In short there was a lot of attention to detail in the client's interest – checking the quality procedures of suppliers or inspecting what they provide before using it; asking customers in what order they would like stuff delivered; after the colour coding initiative mentioned above, offering the colour coding service to clients, and so on. In general taking over the clients problems, no matter who caused them.

This ethos seemed to be underpinned by a rather matey internal culture, with the emphasis on:

▌ a close team;

▌ fun work culture;

▌ a relaxed, informal atmosphere.

One little manifestation is that they do their training on-site, after hours, and do not pay for it. And they will often have representatives from supplier companies in to support the training sessions, and then they go off – bowling. The culture is also pretty macho, all jeans and baseball caps and heavy swearing, as is the norm in the industry.

The company can operate cheaply. Going for simple solutions where possible, giving clients answers when you can, and not milking them. A cheapness supported by transparency. As one of the owners put it: 'We are not frightened to show clients our spreadsheets.'

That is a fair list of competitive advantages, and the beauty of it is that some of them are qualitative, so more difficult to clone, and there is some subtle interaction between them, as with culture/solidarity/'up-frontness'/problem-ownership.

Back on shore

A nice company to put side by side with Marine Tech for illustrative purposes is ConServe, a building services company in South London that has been going for 12 years. Building services here means the design and installation of all the stuff you cannot see – boilers, pipes, plumbing, air conditioning, heating and again electrical outfitting – in various corporate and other public buildings.

Like the founders of Marine Tech the owner of ConServe had 20 years' experience in the industry and was a director of a larger, more established company in Scotland before founding his own. Both companies, Marine Tech and ConServe, identified skill shortages as a challenge, indeed for any business depending on construction/mechanic/craft skills these skills tend to be problematic in contemporary Britain. Marine Tech met the challenge simply by being the best payer in a mildly depressed area with a shipbuilding tradition. But ConServe is in London, where the skill and qualified manpower shortage has the status of a key problem that has to be cracked. ConServe's responses included:

I Good remuneration packages for qualified engineers, unusual for a small company (and somewhat unusual generally in the UK with its history of underpaying engineers).

I Proactive moves to sell both the industry and the company at a range of London schools, enabling ConServe to have a good number of apprentices (though there is a fall-out).

I Best of all, plugging in to the Australian and New Zealand community in London, using word of mouth recruitment (ConServe is 'world famous' in Earls Court!).

ConServe had also inverted another industry practice regarding manpower. Until the Thatcher period (1979–1990) in the UK, building firms would have everyone who did work for them on their payroll. Thatcher then encouraged all the subcontractors to become independent, but this led to non-payment of income tax and national insurance. This in turn produced a ruling from the Inland Revenue that if anyone worked for you even in a subcontracting capacity for more than seven days you, say ConServe, were responsible for their income tax payments. ConServe's innovation was to set up a subsidiary company to 'look after all these subcontractor types'.

Again like Marine Tech, ConServe merged with a civil engineering consultancy company, so that it could offer clients 'one-stop shopping' from design to build. This was particularly advantageous during the 1990s boom when clients wanted whatever they commissioned built fast to get it up and earning money to pay back the loan with which they financed it. And in consequence they 'wanted you to do everything', welcoming the streamlining coming from having design in-house.

Another twist was getting building contracts in some of the EU countries, trading off the greater flexibility of the UK workforce. This can be important for commercial clients in a hurry who do not want their project held up because 'the Dutch and the Germans will never work at the weekend'. ConServe was setting up another subsidiary to handle these Euroland projects, indeed the owner spoke of being interested in 'avenues leading off the main business'.

Finally ConServe was an early adopter in the IT area. The owner speaks of being 'fully automated' and having the latest CAD (computer aided design) in an industry that tends to be a bit shambolic in IT terms. As we saw with the contract house building company cited in Chapter 8 as a paragon of cost efficiency, IT support will put control up and cost down.

Again, we see a nice array of competitive advantage:

▌ The company has deep industry knowledge.

▌ It has cracked a key industry problem (skills/labour shortage) in London.

▌ It offers in-house design and consultancy.

▌ It has foreign contracts in an industry where only the big players are international.

▌ It is developing post-installation service.

▌ It has automation based cost efficiencies.

▌ At the same time there is the unpretentious attention to detail and attention to client needs that was so clear at Marine Tech, leading to repeat-order business with institutional clients.

Back on the prairies

In Chapter 8 we cited Taylor Music to try to express the idea of a company with a unique business proposition. The essence of it is that they are selling (principally) brass musical instruments to school bands and orchestras via mailed catalogues and telephone ordering. They are focusing their efforts on small town and rural areas, thus avoiding competition from the big city megastores. But because they are nationwide they achieve economies of scale and can compete with local stores on price. That is the business proposition, but they enjoy a further spectrum of competitive advantage:

▌ They will take used instruments from the customer in part-exchange, which lowers the price.

▌ They have their own in-house refurbishment facility for fixing the older stuff they take in part-exchange; own refurbishment is unusual in the industry.

▌ Because of refurbishment they can offer customers a choice between new or used (new or nearly new is the industry norm).

▌ Some of the old instruments they take in are beyond repair; they flatten some of them, literally reduce them to something two-dimensional, and sell them as wall ornaments.

▌ Because the business is catalogue and telephone based, location is irrelevant; they do not need to be on Rodeo Drive.

▌ Indeed as they target non-metropolitan areas their location is an advantage; Aberdeen, South Dakota sounds more like your local store town than LA would.

▌ The catalogues are serialized and have a seasonal theme; the September catalogue, for example, is aimed at beginners, with sale-or-return and hire purchase terms.

▌ The catalogues are a creative focus; Taylor Music do the design, art work, and photography in-house; only the printing is sub-contracted.

▌ When potential customers call in, there is no telephone menu!

Apart from the economies of scale, selling via catalogue and telephone ordering is very efficient. As one of the partners put it: 'Five minutes on the phone, an hour if they come into the store.'

This formula must do marvels for unit sales costs. What is more this kind of operation has become more viable with the passage of time: the growth of credit cards and instant validation means no waiting for cheques to come through the mail and then clear; highway improvement and the choice of carriers has made delivery easier, and so on.

Finally, Aberdeen is a pretty good place for an operation of this kind. There are a group of Middle West states, including Minnesota, the Dakotas, and Iowa, that have the highest average educational attainment in the United States, so the context is right. And Aberdeen itself is a college town (home to Northern State University) with an educated workforce.

Put that set of advantages together with the original business proposition and you have something that is likely to work. It also will not be easy for anyone to do it very much better.

Another of these South Dakota companies, Aman Collection Service, was also cited in Chapter 8 as a company that had at the core of its business proposition the fact that to an effective degree it had cracked a key problem, skip-tracing, that is locating in this case loan-defaulting graduate students. Like Taylor Music it benefits from being located in a low cost area with a well-educated workforce. Like Taylor Music again it does not need to be in a location that is either posh or populous, because its skip-tracing is done electronically and its counselling and persuading is done down the telephone lines.

But again that is not the whole story:

▪ Although small, Aman Collection Service has been working on student loan repayments over three decades.

▪ It pools the good ideas from its best performers; easy to say, but how many big companies are able to negate the impersonality and cynicism that often go with size to make this happen?

▪ The high level of software-automation serves to hold down employee numbers.

▪ It also serves as an entry barrier; there are competitors, but not lots of them and not in South Dakota.

▌ The modus operandi, phones and computers, means that the company can go for non-local customers, and have been good at getting business in other areas of the United States, in a small way at first, and being supported by recommendations from mid-West clients.

But if one stands back a little, this is not such a bad business to be in. Sure, it is rather sad to think that 15 per cent of those who have had loans at college do not (at first) repay; that it is not uncommon for someone leaving college with a higher degree to have a debt of US $50–60,000. But two-thirds of the defaulters end up paying. This is not like trying to get money out of hire purchase defaulters; this is about persuading people on the way up that it is both right and in their own interests to pay.

The other engaging thing is that it is not about force, power, or the right to command; it is about establishing rapport down the phone line and influencing behaviour without recourse to any great sanction. In short, soft skills: difficult to codify, difficult to clone.

Over the counter

In Chapter 8 we outlined the operations of Zenith, a pharmaceuticals wholesaler, to illustrate the idea of a reputation for competitive prices as the essence of a business idea, but without telling the whole story. There is a progressive and dynamic connection between some of the competitive advantages as shown in Figure 9.1.

To the scenario illustrated in Figure 9.1 can be added the fact that there is a tangible entry barrier in the form of the time and cost of getting parallel imports approved by the health authority.

In short, there are a number of competitive advantages, and they fit together nicely.

Multum in parvo

There is something else which connects several of the successful smaller companies discussed in this chapter and in Chapter 8. This is that, while small, their success has been aided by their assuming some of the presence and capability of larger, established companies.

The first time I came across this phenomenon was when I was acting as one of the judges in a venture capital competition sponsored by US confectionery giant Mars. One of the contestants was dealing in

Parallel imports plus generics

↓

Potentially thicker margins

↓

Founders have industry experience, but as customers they
owned and ran a small chain of chemist shops in Greater London

↓

To concentrate on standalone chemist shops and small chains
(thus avoiding competition with suppliers to big, national chains)

↓

Dispensers in these shops not part of a big organization,
greater need for personal contact

↓

Zenith's emphasis is on telephone ordering, customers speak to a real
person, someone in fact that they speak to regularly, while the industry
norm is that 98 per cent of the orders are placed by e-mail

↓

In turn an emphasis on selecting the right kind of order-takers,
able to get it right but with social skills as well;
NOT pushy ex-pharmaceutical sales staff

↓

This last point made clear by readiness of order-takers to recommend
cheaper options from other suppliers, when appropriate

↓

Thicker margins allow Zenith to

↓

offer up-front discount, ie, lower prices,
as opposed to 'retro-discounts' normal in the industry

plus

some reduction on ZD (zero discount) lines
for which everyone else charges the full wholesale price

Figure 9.1

cadmium batteries, buying in big lots higher up the chain and on-selling small lots at a profitable margin to small business end users, such as model shops using the batteries to power, for instance, model planes. What the judges saw was a well-dressed articulate entrepreneur with a coherent business plan and an operation that was up and running and already making money, but lacking capital in the form of the prize money offered in the competition to fund expansion. This contestant was among the winners, and I was so intrigued by the simplicity and success of the operation that some time later I invited him to talk to undergraduates on a business creation course. His business had developed in the interim, but as this second meeting I learned that at the time of the competition he had been running the business with one assistant out of one room in a rented house in a run-down quarter of the dominant town in the area. But:

▮ The paperwork that the clients saw was immaculate.

▮ The price lists, delivery notes, invoices, calling cards, letter-headed paper and so on, all suggested an established business.

▮ All the ordering was by telephone (this was the pre-Internet era) so no one ever saw the modest premises.

▮ Whenever personal contact was necessary the entrepreneur visited clients on their premises.

This was not an exercise in wilful deception, but a considered effort to impress customers with the company's standing and efficiency, by letting them imagine a much larger and more established business.

There is little doubt that if you can stage manage the presence and paraphernalia of the larger, established company, it has a positive effect on business. But as we can see from some of the companies discussed here, it is not only about appearances. Consider Marine Tech, which by its organic and merger based growth put together a company that could do both electrical and mechanical work, supply cables, and do the consultancy in-house, together with a few other specialisms, such as hazardous zone work, that are usually the preserve of bigger and older companies. Or ConServe, which acquired a consultancy capability to support its construction and equipping activity, and set up off-shoots to handle subcontract labour and projects in Continental Europe. Or Zenith, small for what they do, licensed parallel imports and generics, offering a full product range to their pharmacy store customers (not just concentrating on a few cheap lines), and multiple ordering channels. In the London area all the deliveries were made by the company's own one-model new car fleet with uniformed drivers.

An interesting development in this connection is the emergence of a lot of companies whose business is in large part done electronically, supplemented by telephones, mail and physical delivery systems. Under the heading of 'done electronically' we are including here a lot of the order-taking, invoicing, data transmission, accessing of databases, record keeping, connecting with centralized markets, maintaining client profiles and tracking customer needs and even monitoring the lifecycle maintenance needs of equipment. When this trend, broadly IT developments, is crossed with an incremental shift in the West from manufacturing to services there are two effects that are relevant to the present discussion of small businesses getting ahead by simulating the appearance of big companies or by developing big company capabilities. The first is that for a lot of these new companies location is irrelevant. Both because of developments in telecomms and IT, and because of the nature of their business, a service rather than the production of three-dimensional artefacts, they can be put, or can arise, pretty much anywhere. Consider that:

I They do not need to be close to raw material sources.

I They often do not need to be physically close to customers.

I Even where customer proximity is an issue, it may be handled by some system of franchising.

The second effect is that these developments, the shift to service and growing IT capability, have also made irrelevant one of the basic features of the large company, big premises, in the sense of large manufacturing sites, and an imposing corporate office, somewhere credible. So at least on this one dimension of physical, architectural presence, there is no need any more for smaller companies to try 'to fake it', like my cadmium battery wholesaler from the 1980s.

Newer companies of this kind are very much in evidence among those cited in the upper mid-West of the United States. Professional Mailing and Marketing, for example, could be anywhere. What it takes from its clients (copy, mailing lists, data) it takes electronically; clearly it depends on regular trips to the Post Office, but the office concerned could as well be in Kansas City as in Aberdeen, South Dakota. Indicatively, in the spring of 2001 the company saw itself as picking up business generally as organizations sought to outsource and cut costs in the face of an economic slowdown, and in particular it targeted California, plagued at that time by power shortages. Or consider Aman Collection Service: it began locally, with business and institutional customers in the immediate area, but by 2001 it has been bought by Wells Fargo and is signing up out-of-state colleges. And why not? The skip-tracing is done on computers, the counselling and persuasion of indebted students is done by telephone.

Taylor Music does not depend on the Internet, its business is done by mail (catalogue) telephone (ordering) and truck (delivery) but even more than Professional Mailing and Marketing and Aman Collection, it is functioning nationally. It does not depend on its location, though it has turned its small town base into an image advantage, rendering it more acceptable to high schools in other small town locations, even if they are 2,000 miles away. Also, Computer Doctor could have been anywhere. It is expanding by franchise, and that could have been as well directed from Seattle or Atlanta. Triebold Paeleontology does not need to be in North Dakota: that is not where they dig up the bones.

In summary, the small UK and US companies in our little collection do give evidence of getting ahead by putting on a big company image and contriving the capabilities associated with more established companies. At the same time this is not the only pattern to emerge, so that the switch from manufacturing to service together with enhanced IT are also facilitating companies that are 'free floating' with regard to location and also free from the need for substantial premises.

A final reflection here is that manufacturing companies will become 'manufacturing companies' as the actual production increasingly goes cross-border. While most of the public discussion of the cross-border outsourcing of production is about companies that used to do it (somewhere) in the West but now do it, or some of it, in Eastern Europe or in developing countries, we can now identify stage two of this process, in the form of companies that never did do it in the West, that were set up *ab initio* to do the production in a lower wage area. One that has surfaced in this book is Retro, the compulsory gifts company in Dallas. It did not transfer manufacture from Texas to Taiwan, it always was in Taiwan, that was part of the *raison d'être*, it does not have 'to slim' or to mothball big plants – it never had them in the first place.

Notwithstanding its name, Retro may be the shape of things to come.

PRANCING PIGMIES?

Over the last 20 years, during which time competition has been progressively hotting up, there has been a lot of discussion about the need for established companies to adapt, change, innovate, exploit their innovations, and generally keep up with the times and the competition. Also running through this discussion is the suggestion that big established companies will often be slow to do these things, will find it difficult, have become sclerotic with age, and so on. This idea is nicely caught by the title of one of Rosabeth Moss Kanter's books: _When Giants Learn to Dance_ (2000), the idea being that these giants tend to be slow and clumsy but when they learn, the (new) world will be theirs.

On the other hand it is often said that smaller and newer companies do not suffer from this change resistant sclerosis. What is more, owners/entrepreneurs/spokesmen for these companies, talking about themselves, also often make the claim that it is the companies' size and/or newness that enables them to engage in fast footwork, nimble manoeuvres, adaptation to a changed environment, and so on.

We are raising this question in the present context of generally wresting insight from the smaller companies. So if big companies (giants), do find it hard to 'learn to dance', is it true that promising, or lively response shall we say, comes easily to the small companies?

Our sample, especially some of the companies in the upper mid-West of the United States, does offer examples of this adaptation, easy change, and companies reinventing themselves.

Consider Tri-WG Inc of Valley City, North Dakota – the small town location in a thinly populated area is relevant to the story (in late 2000 when the US census results were published it emerged that North Dakota was the only state in the Union where the population had actually gone down, slightly, since the previous census).

Tri-WG Inc makes rehabilitation equipment. But there have been recent changes in the structure of their market:

▌ mergers among hospitals;

▍ health care groups buying up hospitals, a prelude to cost-reduction initiatives;

▍ the Balanced Budget Act of 1997.

This last has had a diffuse effect on Tri-WG's business, in that it caused the moving of treatment from country areas to towns. It goes like this.

Before the 1997 Act being a physiotherapist was among the top five professions in the United States for return on your investment in education and training. But the 1997 Act has somewhat hamstrung the profession. This Act has impacted negatively on rural areas because it has limited reimbursements for routine treatments, and correspondingly increased reimbursements for high grade work, which has the effect of pushing people and resources into the towns. At the extreme it means that rural hospitals lose income and have to close; and in North Dakota there are several that have closed: 10 or more were on the verge of closing in spring 2001.

Prior to the 1997 Act Tri-WG Inc had dealers who took their produce and sold it alongside that of other manufacturers. But after 1997 the company found that as their products were among the best and therefore the dearest the dealers had difficulty selling them.

The response by Tri-WG was to cut out the wholesalers and to sell direct to end users. To achieve this:

▍ They advertise in trade publications.

▍ They have a presence at trade fairs.

▍ They use the Web.

▍ They engage in telemarketing.

But the key thing is that most rivals continue to use dealers. Tri-WG not only cut out the intermediary but are selling to end users at what used to be wholesale prices, and Tri-WG are the high-end producer.

This is pretty revolutionary stuff, which bucks the industry norm. There is also an odd side effect.

This is that now that Tri-WG have to do the selling themselves, directly and positively, albeit aided by a quality–price ratio advantage, they have cut back on new product development. In other words, putting energy into marketing the core product range deflects the company from product innovation.

We have told the story of Tri-WG because it is a good example of a smallish company very visibly re-adjusting to changed circumstances and by-passing the industry norms in the process. There may, however, be a more general message in the Tri-WG case, that is:

Downward pressure on prices
    →   resources devoted to marketing;
    →   simplification of the product range to compete effectively on a price-quality mix.

This shows the possible disfunctions of heightened competition, but at the same time it suggests a way to get ahead. If a company understands both parts of the equation – more resources applied to marketing, less resources available for new product development – and can buck the trend by doing both, wouldn't that be smart?

We introduced the South Dakota company Dependable Sanitation in Chapter 8 to illustrate the idea that government regulation opens up the possibility of a unique business proposition for any company that can develop the capability to discharge the task in conformity with the regulation. The more fluid and demanding the regulation, the greater the advantage conferred on any company that is able to cope with it.

We would like to go back to Dependable Sanitation, not to probe its unique business proposition further, but to demonstrate the smaller company ability to adapt. Dependable Sanitation has variously:

▮ Adapted to higher tipping fees as more stringent regulation took out many of the dumping sites.

▮ Adapted to longer truck routes, with 300 miles a day being common.

▮ Adapted to more and more sophisticated equipment, and, of course, to the need for bigger trucks.

▮ Accepted that the above entailed bigger capital expenditures.

▮ Responded (profitably) to increasing privatization of garbage disposal by the county authorities.

▌ 'Extended its repertoire' by being able to collect tyres and white goods, take lumber and handle contaminated soil.

▌ Entered the medical waste disposal segment for some years.

▌ Responded to more stringent air requirements, involving the analysis of emissions and residue from the stack where waste is burned.

▌ Taken on out-of-state hazardous waste disposal (South Dakota has no in-state capability).

▌ Responded to requirements to reduce the proportion of all waste that is burned.

To put the adaptation in more general terms, Dependable Sanitation has moved from a situation where the company 'took it away' and dumped or burned it, to one where it increasingly:

▌ reduces waste;

▌ recycles;

▌ reuses.

All this is being driven by regulation coming variously from the county, the Federal government, and from the EPA (Environmental Protection Agency). And of course one reason for the success of this company is that a lot of the other family firms could not meet these demands and exited the industry.

As a last case with some new twists we will take Harms Oil, the oil wholesaler among the top 50 for the United States reviewed in Chapter 5 as an example of adding service to service.

The owner started out working for Amoco. Then Amoco divested its wholesalers, he bought the one he now owns, but has become what he described as 'a multi-branded jobber' buying from all the major oil companies.

His first business is primarily the supply of oil as heating fuel. Then the utilities companies offered customers interest-free loans to connect to fuel efficient heating (gas). He pretty much lost this first business.

Next came sales into the construction industry, including highway contractors. But he came to depend too much on one big one, it folded, and he lost most of the business.

From here on the customer base is diversified to include:

▍ farmers;

▍ truck operators;

▍ contractors;

▍ businesses;

▍ gas stations;

▍ 'Mom and Pop' stores that have gas pumps.

These customer groups are not all equal in the sight of God or the auditor. Farmers order in a rush twice a year, but the 'Mom and Pop' stores look like being a niche one that can grow.

Now here is an interesting thing. While the growth and diversification has been going on Harms Oil has come to employ two CPAs (qualified accountants), an attorney, and an EPA specialist – these are all in-house, not on a retainer. This is interesting because it is sensible, it facilitates autonomy, enhanced capability, adaptation to environmental change, and the ability to take certain initiatives. It is also a little unusual. Entrepreneurs or owner-managers have an observable tendency to spend on tangibles – bricks and mortar, plant, equipment, rather than on intangibles – training, expertise, intellectual property, brand development, and so on (Lawrence, 1985).

To develop the 'Mom and Pop' niche Harms Oil is buying up these stores when they go bankrupt. Then the company looks for suitable people to take them over, and re-sells them. If they are sold on rather than leased the company does not get landed with the management responsibility; at the same time, since they are customers for gasoline Harms Oil supports them in various ways. The company's attorney and accountants give the 'Mom and Pop' owners seminars four times a year to keep them ahead and stay in business. Also, Harms Oil is using its buying power to get discounted foodstuffs from suppliers, that it passes on to the 'Mom and Pop' stores, thus giving them a leg-up. The owner likes to tell the proprietors of these stores: 'You don't have to beat Wal-Mart: just other Mom and Pop stores.'

SUMMARY

In this chapter we have taken up the idea that successful companies need a range of competitive advantages as well as a unique business proposition. And we have sought to illustrate this proposition from several smaller companies in the UK and the United States.

As an off-shoot of the premise we also examined the idea that smaller and newer companies get advantage from simulating or reproducing the character and capability of larger and more established companies. We found among our small companies some clear examples of the phenomenon in action, but also noted the convergence of two trends – manufacturing to service, and growing IT capability – that are leading to a wave of newer companies that are independent of location, do not for the most part need substantial premises, and are doing it all via computer, the Internet, and the telephone system.

Finally we took up the idea that smaller companies have a greater facility for adaptation and response to a changed environment, an idea firmly embedded in business folklore, but seldom put to the test. Again our set of smaller companies offered some interesting and positive examples.

After this episode of wresting insight and understanding from smaller companies we want in the following chapter to return to the world of the larger, established businesses and unpack what seems to be a poignant paradox: the power of individual managers is growing; and the presence of big companies is declining.

10

Paradox and trends

For more than 50 years voices have been raised to tell us how powerful companies are. Unpacking the mix of scholarly research and political rhetoric, three arguments support this contention of the vast power of the larger business corporation.

PRESUMPTIONS OF CORPORATE POWER

The first is size. Big corporations are very big indeed, by other organizational or non-corporate standards. Their revenues, employees, assets, market capitalization and often their wealth are all impressive. For decades commentators wanting to demonstrate the hugeness of mostly US corporations have alleged that their revenues sometimes exceed the GDP of the smaller European states.

The second argument is about the political influence exercised by the major corporations, in a variety of Western states. Corporations are often able to make political donations, direct subventions to political parties. They invariably perceive the need for political representation, and have the resources and *savoir faire* to effect this. Within the context of the nation state corporations invariably have an interest in fiscal policy and trade agreements as well as in more (country) specific issues such as environmentalism, welfare legislation, drug testing, health and safety legislation, labour law, the legal status and power of labour unions, and more besides. Sometimes corporations are courted by governments, as in the area of PPI (public–private initiatives) in contemporary Britain. Indeed, in an age when governments are concerned to do less rather than more, and are more exercised by their level of borrowing and by national indebtedness than was the case in the former golden age sketched in Chapter 1, these governments are progressively more inclined to turn to corporations for help in discharging what were formerly seen as the duties of the state.

There are cases where business corporations are pretty much told it is their duty to deploy their resources to support objectives the government wants to achieve. Researching in former communist East Germany in the 1990s, for instance, one came across cases where the government had clearly used a *noblesse oblige* argument on West German corporations to get them to invest in former East German SOEs (state-owned enterprises), to take them over, nurture them, or subcontract to them. Or to take a more recent example, when in the autumn of 2001 Swissair stopped flying for four days because it allegedly could not pay for the fuel, the consortium that baled it out included not only the federal and cantonal authorities but also such blue-chip companies as Nestlé.

At the community level these same corporations are clearly influential as payers of local taxes and providers of employment. And it is invariably easy to get them to do things for the local community, in the sense of donations, sponsorship, use of facilities and corporate resources. Even the most hard-hearted of companies that never donate to international good causes or national charities cannot resist the desire to show what good local citizens they are.

The third argument is about the international reach of the major corporations. Originally this argument drew attention to the fact that big companies, unlike national governments, often operated in a variety of countries. This operating was typically in the form of having manufacturing facilities in countries other than that of incorporation. With the passage of time it has become the case that this international reach has all sorts of implications, including:

▌ The ability to disperse the value chain cross-border, having different things done in different countries wherever it seems beneficial or desirable.

▌ This in turn has given rise to the dictum that labour is national whereas capital is international; so that in the event of strikes or workforce disruption companies can shift production between countries.

▌ Companies can use their presence in several countries to neutralize the wish of particular governments to tax and control.

▌ In particular this can be achieved for manufacturing companies by the mechanism of transfer pricing, the value attached to goods, usually components or partly manufactured items, transferred between different parts of the same company for book-keeping purposes; the device is used to raise the cost in high tax countries and to enhance corporate earnings in low tax countries.

Indeed to these considerations might be added the whole internationalization of finance. Not only have capital markets been internationalized, but we also have the treasury operations of multinational companies, borrowing and investing in different national markets often at the same time and exploiting the possibilities of arbitrage.

We have canvassed these arguments that support the idea of the power of corporations, not just because they have been urged by others but also because they seem convincing. Notwithstanding these entirely credible considerations we want to argue that in the early 21st century there are reasons to believe that corporations are experiencing a loss of influence. And the argument is about influence and identity rather than power, as we will try to make clear.

THE CORPORATION GOES OUT OF FOCUS

In part, it is about appearances. Many corporations simply do not have the strong identity, especially in the mind of the general public, that they used to enjoy. One reason for this is that M&A activity often blurs the identity of the formerly independent corporate units. It may even be the case that employees are quite emotionally affected by such changes, as we saw with the example of the Swedish company I visited in 2001 (discussed in Chapter 6).

Names change. Andersen Consulting became Accenture, Stella Artois became Interbrew, the UK academic publisher Macmillan became Palgrave, and in France BSN became Danone. Famous names even disappear. Who could have imagined US civil aviation without Pan American and TWA, or UK high street banking without Midland.

New names, crossed with changing business interests, sometimes cause confusion outside a narrow circle of industry specialists. To my shame I recall stumbling over the French company Vivendi in a telephone corporate awareness survey, and having to be prompted that Vivendi was the new name for the Compagnie Générale des Eaux, the venerable water company dating from the 1850s. Then all was clear, except that it wasn't. Although water still generates a significant part of Vivendi's income, CEO Jean-Marie Messier, who took over in 1996, was busy converting it into a media giant, with a presence in the United States as well as France (Cramley and Sancton, 2001), which was once touted as a potential rival for AOL Time Warner, Disney, Viacom, and News Corp (Leonard, 2001).

Indeed one might ask if we really know what some of these names connote. Try Philip Morris. Sure, cigarettes. The creator of Marlboro County. Yet via its ownership of Kraft General Foods Philip Morris belongs to the world's top six confectionery manufacturers; and as the one time owner of Miller Brewing it was the second largest brewer in the United States after Anheuser Busch.

There is a strong tendency for names to survive when they have value as brands, but not for reasons of corporate tradition or organizational continuity. French Perrier will always be Perrier, though it is owned by Swiss Nestlé. The Abbaye de Leffe beer, 6.6 per cent alcohol, is described on the label as 'the authentic Belgian abbey beer', in five languages. Now owned by Interbrew.

But perhaps the prize should go to the United States. Leinenkugel is a connoisseurs' lager. It comes from Chippawa Falls, Wisconsin, famous among serious beer drinkers. The advertising copy describes it as: 'A hearty lager from the Northwoods, brewed exclusively by the Leinenkugel family since 1864'. Sure, courtesy of Anheuser Busch (Budweiser).

MULTINATIONALISM AND MORE BESIDES

It has long been commonplace that the multinationalism of some companies tends to blur their national identity. They do such a good job of adapting in so many national contexts, they are not thought of as being, say, particularly Korean or particularly Austrian anymore. Philips would be a good European example. It is Dutch, with the corporate office traditionally located in the town of Einhoven; yet probably most British people would say it was Welsh if they had to make a guess.

Dilution and confusion of this kind is heightened, of course, by the explosion of off-shore manufacturing. And as the general public have become used to the idea that Western companies may have things made, quite reliably, in developing countries, the game has moved on with the frequent cross-border dispersal of the value chain. So that it is not simply production which is being outsourced to another country, but also conceivably design, major component supply, administrative processes, invoicing, data-processing, and even call centres.

Nor is it only national identity which is undermined in this way. The whole outsourcing operation tends to blur the boundaries of the organization. What exactly is the company if so much is being outsourced, subcontracted, handled by agencies or business partners? How real is a European airline whose ticketing is done in India, whose frequent flyer programme is administered from the West Indies, whose food comes from Gate Gourmet (a subsidiary of the former Swissair), that does not employ any ground handling staff even in its home country and switches passengers to other carriers in its strategic alliance group? How real is a Mercedes SUV, never mind how German, if it is made by a Canadian autoparts company in a factory in southern Austria?

Again, as we suggested in Chapter 6 discussing possible ingredients of a crisis of human capital, organizational membership has also become a bit problematic. How many people work for Company X? Well, it depends whom you want to count: the full-timers and the part-timers, core staff and peripherals, and what about the subcontractors and the people from the agency? Also this dilution of the concept of the workforce, this stratification of employees, impacts on what we have earlier termed organizational memory. There are fewer people who really belong to the company, and who have been there for a good while, so less people have a front-line involvement or experience based understanding of operations: all this puts the onus on induction programmes and organizational systems as alternatives to loyalty, experience, and discretion.

Another thread that is running through this diminution of company identity is the growing emergence of 'placeless and space-less' business operations. These tend to arise where service provision is conjoined with advances in telecomms and IT, and several cases in point have been considered in the two previous chapters. The companies concerned no longer have or need a substantial physical presence and their geographic location is either incidental or contrived.

INITIATIVE AND THE ENVIRONMENT

The key development that is serving to diminish companies is the shifting balance between initiative and the environment. Change in the environment is increasingly pre-empting corporate initiative. The change comes faster, it is more complex, competition has more sources, companies are increasingly thrown into a reactive mode, though one that is far from passive. Competition from inside and outside the industry, from home and abroad, and from substitutable provision, put a burden of change and reconfiguration upon companies. Always running hard to catch up would be an overstatement, but not without some basis.

This is how it often goes. Customers become more demanding, competitive pressures increase, shareholders clamour, cost cutting is in order. One company in the industry downsizes, and achieves a temporary cost advantage; competitors are forced to downsize too. Then a company in the industry engages in off-shore manufacture, achieves a cost advantage for a while until others follow suit. Next one of the competitors attacks administration costs with a BPR initiative and achieves a cost structure advantage until the competition does the same. Then the unexpected happens and firms in the industry collaborate to reduce their material and sourcing costs. They establish a joint Internet buying portal for routine, non-product differentiating consumables; for a moment, there is peace in the industry, while shockwaves from the latest initiative run through a host of industry suppliers who in turn enforce the rigours of downsizing and outsourcing. Then one company in the industry, disappointed by the brevity of the cost-advantage breathing space conferred by BPR, begins to outsource administration to a developing country, a *démarche* that cannot be ignored by competitors.

A pastiche? A contrived scenario? Yes, it is seldom as neat and regimented as the previous paragraph suggests, but it is still a recognizable dynamic.

It is considerations of this kind that have led us to posit the diminished stature of today's corporations. Next we would like to argue that though the stature of corporations is more questionable, the standing of their managers has risen, especially at the very top. People did not think CE, they thought Jack Welch.

There are three strands to the argument, the first of which very much centres on top managers. The successful CEO is more of a star than he or she used to be, not just in the United States but in the West generally. This development is entirely justifiable. After all, the job is much more challenging now, more demanding than it has ever been for reasons abundantly explored in previous chapters. This in turn has been reflected in an interest in business and in the achievements of top managers in a variety of Western countries that have not always regarded business success as the national priority. This revolution of the role of top managers has a number of tangible indicators:

▌ Dynamic salary inequality, where salaries at the very top are higher than they have ever been, and are more sharply differentiated from the remuneration enjoyed at lower levels.

▌ The managerial consensus outlined in Chapter 3 has meant a move towards a more unified market for executive talent cross-border, a point illustrated with a few high-profile examples in Chapter 1; in the UK a recent example (end 2001) is the appointment of ex-KPN Dutchman Ben Verwaayen as CEO of British Telecomms.

▌ The omnipresence of baleout deals; those on the way in to top posts put together a deal that means that come what may they will always be rich even if they are not famous.

Taking up this last point, the baleout deal or parachute package, the most sensational example in the UK in late 2001, concerned Marconi, whose share price declined from £12.50 to 13p in a year (*Guardian*, 2001). Lord Simpson, Chairman, left with £300,000 and enough pension contributions to push it over £1 million, and John Mayo, CEO, left with £600,000 – though it is said that he wants more! Another UK example that entertained the business scene through 2001 is that of Gerald Corbett, former head of Railtrack. He pocketed £1.4 million on being ousted from Railtrack, took a part-time job with Woolworth's getting them ready for demerger at £250,000 pa, took a further £500,000 for seeing this through, and is currently (January 2002) chairman of that company (*Guardian*, December 2001). Perhaps even more striking is the case of Swedish CEO of ABB, Percy Barnevik. It emerged that when he retired as CEO in 1996 he took a US $88 million pension. This, traditionally, is very un-Swedish, and led one Stockholm newspaper to compute that this payment would cover the salary of 7,967 Swedish nurses for a year (Tomlinson, 2002).

But this phenomenon of the baleout package has an interest that goes beyond the envy of the common man and the rancour of the shareholder. It is in an odd way recognizing the value of the species. After all when companies agree these packages for incoming leaders they do not know if the share price will follow the Marconi trajectory or that of Marks & Spencer (the best performing share on the London Stock Exchange in 2001). These deals are saying in effect that what we want the incoming person to achieve is so awesome the company will indemnify them against mega-failure from the start.

The second argument is that in a variety of ways companies have 'bottom-sliced' themselves. By a range of initiatives including off-shore manufacture, outsourcing, the differentiated workforce, de-manning, de-layering and empowerment, they have cut off and cast adrift some (lower or more peripheral) parts of the organization.

The effect on those who remain, especially on the managers, is to upgrade them. Thus a higher proportion of surviving managers are general managers than was the case before, a development worked out in Chapter 7 considering countervailing trends to the crisis of human capital. Whatever their organizational rank and job title surviving managers can claim at least metaphorical membership of the general management cadre given:

▌ The decline in silo thinking and behaviour, argued in Chapter 7.

▌ The presumption of greater strategic awareness.

▌ The actuality of their experience of change, denoted earlier as the EEL factor.

The third strand to the argument is more particularist. This is that there is an acute need for quality managers in some particular areas. One that has been canvassed earlier in the discussion of the company Opta Resources is the need for e-commerce skills. Another perhaps less obvious case is for site or project managers on turnkey or big installation projects. Consider that most of them are in the areas of energy and telecommunications, much of which used to be in the state sector, a factor that encouraged rather stable relations between the commissioning companies and their contractors. Thanks to privatization and deregulation and a growth in transparency and accountability, these relationships are now much more tense and competitive, site and project managers have greater commercial responsibility, they 'make more difference', so that the quest for good ones is more intense. Another example would be FMCG (fast moving consumer goods) brand managers. As suggested earlier (in Chapter 1) greater competition crossed with maturing and segmenting markets has put a premium on branding as a way of attaching present and future customers to particular company providers of goods and services. The effect of particular management capability needs of this kind have the understandable effect of raising the standing of management generally.

So far in this chapter we have sought to introduce and demonstrate a new trend, the paradox whereby the stature of corporations declines while the status of management rises. From here on the intention is to review in sequence a number of business trends that have been canvassed in earlier chapters. This is largely though not exclusively an exercise in restatement.

The springboard for all these trends and developments is enhanced competition and its diffuse effects. From that starting point we feel it is important to highlight the following issues.

Internationalization

This is both a cause and effect of heightened competition, but first we should say that the type and range of cross-border activity has increased immeasurably. Internationalization is no longer about exporting and the presence of a handful of MNCs (multinational companies) that have manufacturing plants in a few other, mostly Western countries as in *les trentes glorieuses* period after the Second World War. While these two phenomena – the rise of the MNC and the prevalence of exporting – have gained momentum, internationalization now assumes many additional forms including:

▌ off-shore manufacture;

▌ cross-border sourcing;

▌ cross-border provision or outsourcing of services;

▌ cross-border outsourcing of administrative processes;

▌ cross-border M&A activity;

▌ joint ventures (JVs) and strategic alliances with companies in other countries;

▌ the internationalization of capital markets;

▌ more generally, the international dispersal of the value chain.

Internationalization is an effect of heightened competition in two senses. First, as more companies find themselves in mature markets, sometimes saturated, and with declining demand or only replacement purchases, going into other countries offers the possibility of expansion, as well as spreading costs, particularly R&D and promotional costs, more widely. Second, heightened competition puts pressure on costs and prices in turn leading companies into off-shore manufacture and administrative process outsourcing.

This internationalization itself, however, accentuates competition because the opportunities and facilities for it are generally available. You may do it to them before they do it to you, but sooner or later they will do it to you as well! This cumulative internationalization is facilitated by the power of example, the development of *savoir faire* over time, as well as by developments in transportation, telecomms, and IT.

The 'do it to them before they do it to you' mindset also gives rise to international strategic war games where MNCs seek footholds in other countries, especially across the Triad (the United States, Japan, Western Europe) so that they always have the power of response as foreign competitors try to outflank them at home with price competition.

Markets and industries

Business focus and competition have progressively shifted from industries to markets. The key is not the provision of goods or services, but the relationship with customers/the market where you encounter competitors who want to beat you.

Furthermore, the rate of change and particularly of businesses that are reinventing themselves, together with technical change, and changes of industry structure, all mean that it is more difficult to see where the competition will come from. You are, say, AOL Time Warner and you think the international competition is News Corp and

Bertelsmann, and then you find you have a French water treatment company on your doorstep! Or again a Diageo drinks group executive has been quoted as saying that Diageo has come to realize that it competes with all drinks, not just alcohol, for 'stomach share'.

Branding

The brand has become an increasingly important weapon in the market based competition referred to in the previous section. Key developments have been:

▌ Massive corporate effort to strengthen brands.

▌ M&A activity, often driven by the desire to add to the portfolio of brands, as in the Perrier, Abbaye de Leffe, and Leinenkugel examples offered earlier in this chapter.

▌ Branding has also moved from products to services, with the struggle to brand being particularly acute with services marked by an intrinsic low differentiation.

▌ Moving the halo effect of some branded commodity so that, the company hopes, it embraces a different perhaps unrelated, commodity; the phenomenon is known as the nomad brand or the itinerant brand.

As we have seen when M&As occur, much may die, from corporate cultures to replicated functions. But brands have the best shot at immortality.

Rise of strategic consciousness

Competition and change have generated a diffuse need for strategic understanding. In stable and prosperous times, say, *les trentes glorieuses*, many companies do well by doing the same, by doing what they did before, doing what 'the industry' is doing. In such circumstances strategy may be viewed as a luxury while strategic misadventure does not carry the corporate death penalty.

No more; strategy with its choices and trade-offs, its concern with ends and with means to ends, is a must for all players. And most of the West has come to follow the US lead in cascading strategy down, creating strategic consciousness, unbuilding silos and instilling commercial awareness at all levels. Indeed participation in strategy development is now seen as one aspect of the learning organization.

Rise of general management

Competition and change again promote the importance of general management, an emphasis that is also driven by some negative developments of the de-layering, outsourcing, corporate 'bottom-slicing' kind already flagged up in this book. But the positive forces enhancing the status of the generalists are:

I   a commercial awareness that will dominate former silo-thinking;

I   understanding market dynamics;

I   strategic comprehension and proactivity.

But above all it is change experience, what in Chapter 7 was called the EEL factor, that is the prerequisite of general management.

Focus

This not the age of unrelated diversification and portfolio management: this is the age of focus. This ethos was succinctly encapsulated for me by the Dallas executive quoted in Chapter 1 whose view was: outsource everything you can, and what is left will be the core business.

There is probably an element of fashion in all this. Diversification had its day, and its turn may well come round again. But at the start of the 21st century the credo is back to basics, 'stick to the knitting', core business and core competence. It should be said too that this does seem appropriate. In a time of heightened competition, pressure on margins and pressure on costs, trying to do a core of interrelated things well is more likely to bring success than trying to do everything. So the current focus orientation:

I   Leads to widespread outsourcing.

I   It means that activities are passed backwards and forwards, up and down the value chain, for example, getting suppliers to make a design input and road hauliers to stack goods on the shelves.

▌ These in turn lead to shrinking the organization's boundaries.

▌ And the current focus orientation is partly responsible for the corporate 'bottom-slicing' already discussed.

▌ It also leads to a negative attitude to vertical integration; existing vertical integration links tend to be uncoupled.

▌ And on occasions to what we have called 'shallow manufacture'.

All of this is an amplification of a trend, not an iron law. There are exceptions. There are companies that are diversifying away from static or declining industries, as with the Philip Morris example cited earlier; and the example from the brewing industry – 10 years ago Whitbread and Bass Brewing (now Six Continents) were among the 'big six' UK brewers; now both have moved out of brewing and into hotels, food chains, pub-restaurant chains, and health clubs. Other companies have moved from products to systems, or like IBM are moving from products to service. And again in the UK we have seen how the regulatory authorities have driven the privatized water companies into some new activities to escape a no-growth domestic market and the keen eye of the regulator.

But these and others like them are exceptions, and one can usually see the particular reason for them. For the most part, Dallas rules.

CONCENTRATION

Concentration in the sense of M&A activity leading to more industries being dominated by fewer, larger players has been in train in the West since the 1980s and shows no sign of stopping. The reasons for this are clear: world overcapacity in many industries, mature markets, a response to heightened competition.

In the earlier discussion of concentration (Chapter 2) we noted several related phenomena:

▌ A tendency for clusters of industries, industries that is which are functionally or operationally related, to concentrate together.

▌ Counter concentration, where one industry concentrates defensively against concentration in another industry on which it depends. For example in the United States food processing companies have been merged, for instance General Foods plus Kraft plus Nabisco, to even the score with ever more powerful grocery retailers.

I Bi-polarization whereby concentration occurs at the top, resulting in the usual industry dominance by a few big players, small companies 'hang in' serving protected niche markets, and the medium-sized companies are progressively eliminated or assimilated.

Cost pressure

Pressure to reduce costs is omnipresent and inescapable. It no longer gets a company off the hook to say that they do not aim to sell on price but on say service or quality or Technik or innovation or design flair or total customer solutions or whatever. The response is fine, but you can still reduce your costs and improve your margins.

This in turn leads companies to engage in the variety of practices that we have bundled under the label of denominator management in Chapter 1. That companies do this is entirely comprehensible. Unfortunately, as we suggested at the start of this chapter the adoption of these measures tends to set up a chain reaction. One company in an industry does it, others are obliged to follow suit, the first mover advantage turns out to have been only temporary, and the result is group pain without corporate gain. Sadly no one seems to have found a way of reducing costs that cannot be easily replicated.

Managerial consensus

We have suggested that a managerial consensus has been emerging, an agreement on what management should be like and should do, stressing proactivity, systems, strategy, target setting, and controls. This managerial consensus overlaps with what is usually called managerialism. The consensus has erased much of the difference between the public and private sectors both with regard to their ethos and *modus operandi*. It has had the same effect on traditional differences between charitable or not-for-profit organizations and conventional business organizations. The managerial consensus has also tended to reduce the management style, qualities, and behaviour differences between the various countries of the West.

This is all largely positive, a reflection of the rise in management's status and in the general public's interest in business that occurred in a variety of Western countries during the 1980s and 1990s. There are arguably two downsides. One, which does not really concern us here, is that the dictates are sometimes applied inappropriately in non-business settings and are resented by, and demotivating for, professionals in, say, health care organizations or colleges of higher education. The other is that the consensus is prescriptive: it is not only raising standards but standardizing entrants to management, homogenizing the cadre. This reduction of the range of acceptable types and behaviours may have the negative consequence that Western management collectively fails what is called the requisite diversity test. That is to say, in any social organism a level of diversity is generally thought to be 'a good thing' in that it facilitates meaningful response to the variety of environmental challenge. There is also an argument to the effect that internal difference may be the source of creativity (as well as friction) and is thus to be welcomed (Lawrence, 1998).

Response to customers

There is a general agreement that customers of all kinds are more demanding now than they have ever been, and that companies therefore need to fashion a response, often in a context of mature markets and heightened competition. The 100+ companies we visited in the run-up to writing this book exhibited the following patterned responses:

▌ adding service to product;

▌ adding service to service;

▌ adding sales and distribution channels;

▌ generating cognate customer groups, new customer groups who might buy what existing groups buy already, or adaptation of facilities and output to appeal to new but related groups;

▌ exploiting niche markets, particularly if protected by qualitative (difficult to clone) _savoir faire_ entry barriers.

There is in fairness a possible qualification to the 'more demanding customer' thesis. This is to say that among personal customers for consumer products many are 'stressed out and time poor' typically because they work for organizations like the companies that are trying to sell them goods and services. This in turn will impact on their energy and predilection for 'shopping around'. With regard to business-to-business transactions the corporate purchasing function has been a leading candidate for downsizing so that surviving corporate buyers are less inclined to 'make a meal' of their purchasing decisions (how quaint that once upon a time 'knife and fork buyer', ie, don't place an order until they take you out for lunch, used to be a part of corporate folklore). One might put this qualification another way, and say that supply chain simplification has become a common way for companies to save themselves effort and money.

The crisis of human capital and the destabilization of corporate culture

Earlier we argued that a host of factors ranging from M&A to the constituents of denominator management have alienated human capital by preferring flexibility to loyalty. At the same time these factors have weakened corporate cultures by striking at solidarity and continuity.

This is undoubtedly an ongoing trend at the start of the 21st century. What is more, one can see companies responding to it in several ways:

▌ by offering more of the same; ie, money, as they pay above the market price for the talent they need;

▌ by compensating for the loss of organizational memory with systems and training;

▌ by trying to fabricate organizational cultures.

This crisis has every appearance of being a real issue, yet as we counter argue in Chapter 7 it may turn out to be 'a moment in time', albeit on an epochal scale. That is to say, consciousness of this malaise is the prerogative of those who experienced an earlier and perhaps kinder age. It is posited, and this is the counter trend, that the passage of time may see the emergence of organizational culture that does not have stability and continuity as prerequisites.

The environment outruns corporate initiative

A significant trend we feel is the idea that is canvassed at the start of this chapter: the idea that the rate of change in the external environment is setting the agenda for many corporations, that their lot is to fashion an effective response rather than to initiate. We worked through this idea in Chapter 4 where we reviewed the recent doings of four very different organizations – a French-Canadian newspaper, a Danish confectionery manufacturer, an English law firm, and a US farm cooperative – and noted that active and effective as they all were, every one a success story, they were in no small measure reacting to the imperatives and constraints of the outside environment. Returning to this theme at the start of this chapter we couched it in terms of a paradox: a decline in the consequentiality of corporations paralleled by a rise in the standing of (at least some) managers. The paradox is really quite explicable. The present environment makes unsupportable demands on corporations, demands for survival and performance in a hostile environment; this is recognized, and their standing drops. At the same time, managers are the only people who can save the corporations, who can do the near impossible, and they are valorized in consequence.

Power and the value chain

Finally, we would like to suggest that in mature economies power moves down the value chain. This idea has not been made explicit before, although it is lurking in some of the examples and business stories that have been offered. The essence of this is that every business entity seems to have the ability to 'dump' on the preceding link in the chain. So manufacturers get their suppliers to do the design for them, retailers dominate manufacturers, and consultants have their fees made conditional on the level of cost savings resulting from their recommendations. Just about every company visited in the preparation for this book was oppressing some other company in their business environment, or was eloquent in expressing the extent of their suffering at the hands of others. To an outsider, it looks like dog eat dog – and the mustard is free.

SUMMARY

In this chapter we have explored the paradox of waning corporate identity together with the enhanced standing of executives. Thereafter a selective restatement of the leading trends is offered including:

▌ Internationalization.

▌ The transition from industries to markets.

▌ The dynamics of branding.

▌ The diffuse rise of strategic consciousness, and the growing prominence of general management.

▌ Concentration and the implications of focus.

▌ The movement of power down the value chain.

In the next and last chapter we want to take a different tack and raise the question: what can be done with this bunch of ideas to get nearer to business success?

11

Ideas and actions

This last chapter is also partly an exercise in restatement and so overlaps a little with the previous chapter. But the purpose of this chapter is different: it is more practical.

First, it may be helpful to put it in context. This book was inspired by a desire to share the knowledge and understanding gained from my visits to companies and discussions with executives and business owners. Going to a lot of companies, but particularly trying to understand their strategies and strivings in a lot of different industries and spread over several countries, has been very stimulating. All this has given me ideas, enabled me to put things into patterns, perceive trends, sometimes to characterize their development over time, to posit some cause and effect relationships as well as to map the present and unpick its origins in the recent past.

But there is a shift of emphasis as noted above in this final chapter, namely from understanding to using. What follows is not highly prescriptive, and will not for the most part be in terms of a set of do's and don'ts. It is rather about synthesizing some of the ideas already canvassed and seeing what leverage they offer in dealing with the challenges of business, using them as diagnostics and as triggers for anticipation.

There are two diffuse propositions that underlie what follows:

If something is understood, there is a chance to shape it.
Every limitation offers an opportunity.

WHY ARE WE IN BUSINESS?

In Chapter 8 we deliberately illustrated the related ideas of the unique or at least original business proposition and the enjoyment of a range of competitive advantage, with lots of examples from smaller and newer companies. It is easier to identify originality and competitive advantage in smaller companies, not so much because of miniaturization but because the awareness is higher.

In larger established companies a lot of this is history, it is held to be self-evident, is unthinkingly embedded in the fact of existence and in ongoing routines. One ready indicator of this is that representatives of more established companies often respond to questions with 'what' rather than with 'how' or 'why' answers. With responses along the lines of 'We are the market leader in ...', 'Our product range encompasses ...', 'People come to us for ...'. These kind of responses implicitly fall back on the rationale that states, for example:

'This company was founded in 1869 by George Brown, whose portrait is in the Boardroom, and he must have had a unique business proposition at the time; and there must be competitive advantages or we would not still be here!'

But established companies should not really settle for this. It has got to be worth thinking and talking through these problematics, where the outcomes may vary from:

▌ Being able to identify strengths and advantages; this should be a spur to protecting and enhancing them.

▌ Being able to identify what they were; this surfaces the need for renewal.

▌ Not being able to think of any at all!

This last case is not frivolous. There are companies that are running on momentum rather than on driving force, and they may run for a good while on the fact that they are operationally viable, the systems are in place, and they have some market presence. But if the original _raison d'être_ has evaporated over time and there are no competitive advantages _vis-à-vis_ other industry players, then start working on it. These advantages are not God-given but the result of human ingenuity and resourcefulness.

ENVIRONMENTAL CHANGE PRE-EMPTS CORPORATE INITIATIVE

The pace of environmental change together with the overcapacity/ mature markets/enhanced competition explored at the beginning of the book all tend to take the initiative for change rather than the responsibility for dealing with change away from companies. This is not any kind of an absolute, but a shift in balance; it is one of those things that is more true now than it was 10 years ago. So that companies are increasingly running, not exactly to catch up but to get to the right place.

We sought to illustrate this phenomenon in Chapter 4 with examples of four very different organizations taken respectively from French-Canada, England, Denmark, and the upper mid-West of the United States. The striking thing is that these companies are all energetic, capable, and successful, but principally in response to environmental change. The world of the US agricultural cooperative, for instance, was being significantly shaped by the efficiency needs of the Union Pacific and Burlington railroads to have 110-car trains loaded in 15 hours. Again we reformulated this idea in Chapter 10 as part of the paradox of the declining influence of companies crossed with the rising powers of managers.

We are emphasizing the point that environmental change pre-empts corporate initiative because:

▌ It is in the logic of events, it is true, there is no reason to think it will go away any time soon.

▌ In a way, it is easy to miss it given the purposefulness of the managerial consensus; you look at, say, South Dakota Wheat Growers (SDWG) and you see a blaze of purposeful and effective action – but it is ultimately responsive.

▌ Everyone in business needs to take account of it, there are action
implications.

The first point is that there is a need to understand the trends and
general issues as never before. No industry is isolated from them, no
company is an island. Second, being customer focused, a phrase that
came in during the 1980s, has acquired new dimensions with the
passage of time. In business-to-business dealings this increasingly
means companies 'knowing customers' business', being able to 'work
up their decision chain', expressions we have heard from interviewees
in a variety of businesses – steel companies and law firms, machine
tools and trucking companies. Third, this customer focus, important
though it is, does not constitute the whole story. There is a need as
never before to know the industry and market – developments,
dynamics, initiatives, expectations. Whatever your business there is
bound to be some version of the Burlington and Union Pacific railroads. To put this point in the conventional language of organizational
learning, organizational boundary spanners have an enhanced
importance. That is to say, people whose organizational position
enables/requires them to look outwards are more critical then they
used to be. Traditionally 'boundary spanners' have been sales and
marketing people, and the HRM function in some senses; increasingly
it is coming to mean top management.

What it is all about is being able to see where it is going before it
goes there, being able to respond before 'they do it to you', being
ahead of the game. This in turn calls up the argument developed in
Chapters 3 and 4 concerning the managerial consensus, resting on the
replacement of élite recruitment with what we have called a sponsored meritocracy. If the initiative has passed from the companies to
the environment then the companies need an enhanced response
capability, which in turn has implications for the requisite variety rule.
Message: do not hire only those whose qualities fit the managerial
consensus, you may need a few oddballs.

DENOMINATOR MANAGEMENT: LIMITS AND IMPLICATIONS

Denominator management, in the sense of cost-cutting measures of
the downsizing/de-layering/BPR kind has been a recurrent mini-
theme of this book. It has to be taken seriously for several reasons:

▌ It is also in the logic of events; it is the understandable if not inevitable consequence of overcapacity/mature markets/enhanced competition.

▌ It is subject to the 'prisoner's dilemma' ethic; sooner or later in any industry some company will choose to go down this road for the (short-term) competitive advantage it will yield; other companies in the industry will be forced to follow suit, albeit unevenly and raggedly.

▌ It has serious consequences; it creates unemployment and/or insecure employment, workforce alienation, undermines organizational solidarity and corporate culture, and leads to ambivalent organizational commitment.

A possible indicator of the insecurity malaise in the UK may be found in the number of cases heard by employment tribunals, mostly initiated by employees or ex-employees who believe that they have experienced some unfairness. Applications for cases to be heard before these tribunals ran at 29,000 in 1988 but had reached 130,000 by 2000. This startling increase is perhaps more remarkable for having occurred in a period of weak and declining trade union power.

So what do you do about it? First, be cautious. The advantage it will confer is likely to be short term as other companies in the industry follow the lead. At the same time, they will not all do it at the same time, nor with equal degrees of efficiency and completeness, so there is a potential gain though it is not very calculable. To put this another way, measures of this kind tend to buy time rather than superiority. A more enduring competitiveness will have to come from something else, something that is more likely to be creative than defensive. Second, when you do it remember it will have consequences that go beyond cost saving: it will undermine everything from senior professional commitment to organizational memory and the quality of customer service. Be alive to this, mitigate the downside in so far as it is possible. Third, remember when everyone in the industry has done it, no one will have an advantage, all companies in the industry will be on a tighter rein, so before you are stampeded into it think about what the next game is going to be because there will surely be life after 'cutting the fat'. Finally, one might reflect on a possible paradox. This is that in manufacturing, changes in materials, product design, and production methods or processes often lead to real and sustainable advantages. Frequently these changes are incomprehensible to the layperson, and not really comprehensible to many in the companies actually concerned, outside of a scientific/technical 'hardcore'. Yet such developments often confer:

▋ worthwhile cost savings;

▋ product upgrade, giving a lead in the market;

▋ some product range transformation whereby the best can be offered at the price of the second best.

But the key thing is that because of their technical opacity such developments are easier to guard and more difficult for others to clone (more difficult, not impossible). I have on occasion been entranced by such developments, when I could just about understand them. At the UK company ICI, for instance, I was once told of a highly ingenious way of simplifying the process by which an intermediate substance was produced, essentially by collapsing stages in the process. And why did they risk telling this to an outsider? Because although I sort of understood it I could not go away and do it or tell anyone else how to do it – that was its beauty.

Whereas the cost-cutting initiatives of a business or organizational kind are all too transparent. OK, to actually engage in BPR rather than to have a grasp of the principles is not a five-minute job, it involves getting into the detail and administrative or technical minutiae, and the substance of it varies endlessly across organizational context and operation. But if you cannot do it on your own consultants will do it for you or coach you in how to do it. Or take supply chain management. Often it can be cracked with insider knowledge plus persistence, as in the example given in Chapter 1 of the building firm getting down to four types of cement with a single price. Where it entails logistical or other complexities beyond the capability of the initiating company, well there again, that is what consultants are there for.

Probably the trickiest one is outsourcing. As we suggested back in Chapter 1 outsourcing began with routine even pedestrian things – catering, security, office cleaning, stationery/printing, and so on. But things moved on. More integral things become the objects of outsourcing – IT, sometimes the more discretionary bits of HRM such as graduate trainee recruitment. It has now got to the stage where some consultancies are speaking of going for 'big bets' in the sense of major corporations which can be persuaded of the advantage of outsourcing **all** services – IT, HRM, finance, administration, and so on. Now that it is reaching this stage the operation is not so readily 'clonable' by all players in a given industry. The magnitude of the operation, not to mention the consultant's fee, the preparation required, the implementation and adjustment, call for a management sophistication that not all players will have.

Another manifestation, the cross-border outsourcing of manufacture to achieve a cost advantage, may also fall short of the readily 'clonable'. If a company is not that big, if its international activity is limited to exporting, it may lack the contacts, network, overseas presence and *savoir faire* to match more sophisticated companies in its industry in setting up off-shore manufacture, and thus will be handicapped in matching bigger companies' cost structure. And while none of these obstacles is insurmountable, everyone has to start somewhere, there is a learning curve to be gone down, and the late starter may never get up to the speed of competitors who started earlier.

But these mature manifestations of outsourcing seem to me to be the exceptions rather than the rule to the 'clonability' of cost-cutting measures. To put this in a more positive way one might say that the next game in denominator management will be some initiative that has the opacity of technical change such as to confer on its discovers a more durable advantage.

CULTURE AND CHANGE

A tension between culture and change has been suggested, on the grounds that culture is the product of stability and continuity. And there is growing recognition that corporate culture has been weakened by change generally and especially by change in its cost-reducing, denominator management form. All this has tended to buy flexibility at the expense of loyalty, adaptability at the expense of solidarity, and it is all in a state of flux because of the external pressures for change that we have been concerned to highlight. But to those who say the price was worth paying, or that there was no choice, that such developments were unstoppable, one might reply that it would be nice if we could have both. Adaptability and response capability as well as corporate cultures to which people can respond.

Not an easy task, but as was suggested in Chapter 7, it is made to look worse than it is because we are still in an age of transition; what we are experiencing now is endlessly compared with what we used to have. So the first thing is to work on the expectations people bring, particularly those who are newly joining. To say, in effect: 'We hope you join this organization; but we don't know how long it will be for; and you probably will be asked to change; but we will try to make that change manageable, and hope there will be some benefits.'

Then there are gains to be made with the announcement and implementation of change. Too often the advocates of change are confrontational, liking to speak of 'sounding wake-up calls' and suggesting if those who are going to experience this change had been made of the right stuff the organization would not be in the dire straits in which it currently finds itself. This kind of bombast is quite unnecessary. Environmental change may well call for change within companies, but that does not make present incumbents a bunch of dozy, pampered, washed-up has-beens.

So change needs explaining, and on occasion should be introduced in sorrow rather than anger. And often at times it can be done in an orderly way. That is to say, it can be planned, phased, scheduled and resourced. What is more, balance is important, the idea introduced at the end of Chapter 7 and taken from the Talent Foundation report. Balance, that is, in the sense of harmonizing the gearing up for the future, the demands of innovation, with the needs of the present. It is also seldom the case that an all in one go, instantaneous change is required. Telling people that from TOMORROW you will do this, this, and this, carries the highly demotivating implication that over the previous period they were misguided dumbos whose work contributed little of value.

Side by side with issues of presentation and implementation is the central consideration urged in Chapter 7, that exposure to change, experience of change, and learning from change, the EEL factor, have the greatest value for managerial and professional progress. This is not the age of silos and of 'getting your ticket stamped'. This is the age of general management, with companies 'bottom-slicing' themselves so that general management starts lower down the organization and occurs earlier in people's careers.

The ultimate will be not just reconciling change and culture, but making change a credible mainspring of culture.

LEVELS OF SERVICE

There is another paradox between the universal desire to raise the quality of service on the one hand and workforce flexibility on the other.

In the earlier discussion of increasing revenue in the face of generally more demanding customers we urged adding service to product, and service to service (ie, raising service quality), backed by examples from all sorts of industries and operations. And this really is a conscious priority for most companies. The paradox derives from the fact that such efforts are undermined by downsizing and particularly de-layering which tends to reduce direction and supervision, and even more by moves to non-core employee groups, temps, agency workers, part-timers, students, and even full-timers on fixed-term contracts excluded from some benefits and from organizational advancement. It is not just that all these developments call into play people lacking deep commitment and a long-term familiarity with the company's business, it also undermines what we have called organizational memory. These developments, non-core staff and attenuated organizational memory, in turn put greater demands on systems and initial training.

To take the strong version of this paradox consider that quality service in critical encounters is often the result of people with knowledge, experience, and discretion using all these to the customers' advantage. Tricky stuff for non-core staff! So look for any points where you can get leverage. After all:

▊ Some of the knowledge can be codified.

▊ The codification needs to take account of the exceptions, the situations that are non-routine.

▊ The experience cannot be codified, but it can be compensated by putting in (or putting back) enough experienced and supportive supervision.

▊ If you can pick the right front-line staff you can give them discretion, indeed privilege discretion over conformity.

But above all be aware of this tension between the goals of service quality and workforce cost reduction and flexibility. Just consider that a top-seeded international tennis star has an occupational life expectancy that is at least 10 times longer than that of an employee at a telephone call centre.

It is readily acknowledged that there are costs in quality service provision, costs of systems development, training, employee remuneration and management time. So to valorize the pro-service view it is worth rehearsing a few of the arguments for customer retention as opposed to customer creation. This is especially so given the universal approval and enthusiasm that surrounds new business, attracting new customers, winning key accounts from rivals and so on. All this tends to make customer retention seem a bit unexciting. Claims of the 'I didn't lose any customers today' kind are not the stuff of which CEO of the Year awards are made.

In view of this glamourization of new business, just think how cost efficient customer retention is. It is much more expensive to get what you haven't got than to keep what you have got. And the key to the retention is customer service. IBM have claimed that the repurchase rate for customers who have experienced no problems is 84 per cent, but for customers who have experienced a problem but believe it has been dealt with decently the repurchase rate is 95 per cent. This idea tends to be reinforced by cross-industry PIMS (profit impact of marketing strategy) data which suggests that service is more important than either product quality or price. That is to say, perceptions of poor service are five times more likely to lead customers to go elsewhere than price or product issues.

Add to this the fact that loyal customers tend to be more profitable than new customers, for a variety of reasons:

▌ They tend to spend more than new customers.

▌ It is easier and cheaper to service existing customers. This is particularly true of business-to-business operations where knowing the business, knowing what they want to do with their purchase from you, knowing what they are striving to achieve, is more important and often more complicated; being further down the learning curve counts for more.

▌ Loyal customers may be a source of referrals, generating more revenue.

▌ Loyal customers in particular are likely to ask for extras, customization, support services, all the things which command a price premium.

When you look at it from the provider's viewpoint, this is a magnificent scenario. What the surveys and consultancy databases are telling us is: it does not have to be cheap, it does not have to be perfect, it does not even have to be problem free, the provider just has to have a pleasing and effective response when a problem is reported!

It is sometimes suggested that a pervasive reason why companies do not cash in on this dynamic is that they have difficulties seeing it all from the customer's viewpoint, their policies are implicitly formulated to protect themselves against the putative 4 per cent of customers who will exaggerate complaints and inflate claims in the hope of getting something for nothing. If you want to try out the 'seeing it from the customer's viewpoint' idea, take something basic your company does and try to list the points of customer contact involved, and then imagine what could go wrong at these points, and in turn how problem points could be turned into successes. It can be done for business-to-business operations, but a consumer product/service example is probably more accessible. Consider Disney World, take the points for each attraction, as indicated in Figure 11.1.

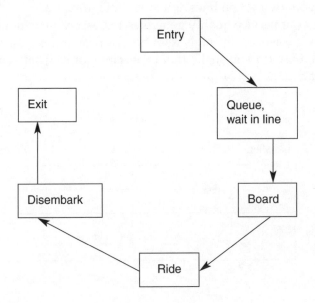

Figure 11.1

As soon as you put the process on paper you can see the critical service points. The queuing will be boring, may go on too long, and you will be harassed by your children. The boarding may be physically difficult for anyone too young or too short. Your family party might get split over two cars. And what about when you have waited in line for three-quarters of an hour and then your little daughter gets scared to get on, but gets over it as soon as you have forfeited your turn. There are counters to all of these, all of it can be managed, you just need to get the key points up on the screen.

Before we leave the discussion of service there is another idea which deserves to be mentioned. The one distinction that is always made is between customers who are satisfied and those who are dissatisfied. Fine, as it should be, but we could add a second dimension, consciousness. Whether it is good or bad, how aware is the customer? Remember that in business-to-business operations this question does not just hinge on the vagaries of individual psychology, though these are relevant, but on the often impersonal nature of the interface between two organizations. Crazy example: imagine British Airways, they obtain paper clips (office supplies generally in truth) via an Internet buying portal. Maybe they get really marvellous service from their paper clip supplier. But who will know?

When you add consciousness to satisfaction it generates a two by two table, with two action lines as shown in Figure 11.2.

So when your service quality generates widespread customer satisfaction, say measured by high retention, repeat orders, absence of complaints, how do you make them conscious of it? That is another trick that can mark you off from the competition.

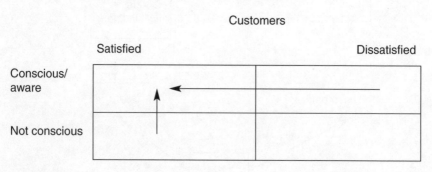

Figure 11.2

MARKETS NOT INDUSTRIES

It was suggested earlier that the focus of competition is the market rather than the industry. This is not just semantics, thinking market rather than industry will sensitize you to a wider range of opportunities and threats. On the threats side the most obvious is the entry of new players from another industry, and we offered examples of this phenomenon in Chapter 1. In financial services in particular the entry of non-industry providers has become very widespread.

There is also the issue of some once distinct industry boundaries disappearing, becoming porous, or embracing new elements – the move from publishing to multi-media and the size of the media conglomerates, for instance. Energy distribution (gas and electricity) in the UK would be another example. So would financial services again, with a running together of retail banking, insurance, mortgages, and loan finance. The leisure industry is another case in point with, in the UK, a merging of food chains, hotel chains, pub-restaurant chains, and health clubs. Such developments are a reason to be agnostic about the conventional notion of 'the industry'. Another twist to this is that just about every entity that has a distribution system wants to use it for extras going beyond the industry basics. But these are opportunities as well. A focus on the market is the first step to generating what we called cognate customer groups in Chapter 5, that is: groups that would become customers if you adapt the offering, or deploy the core competence in a somewhat different way; groups that are not (yet) customers, yet having the same presumptive needs as groups who are.

Putting it simply the market focus makes you think about what it wants, what you have got, how to bring these together, and about who else is likely to muscle in on the act.

POWER AND THE VALUE CHAIN

Again it was suggested earlier that in mature economies power seems to pass down the value chain, with companies at each stage putting pressure for better deals, discounts, delivery and service on other companies higher up the chain. We are bringing up the idea again simply to say it is important to be aware of this dynamic, especially if your position in the value chain is such that 'it will be done to you, but you won't get to do it to them'. Most vulnerable are suppliers to the corporate equivalent of 'the rich and famous'.

If you know your company is going to be at the receiving end you can try to protect yourself by:

▌ differentiating in terms of quality and know-how;

▌ hopefully emphasizing your scarcity value;

▌ locking them in with your grasp of their business;

▌ and knowing enough of their vulnerabilities for them to want to keep you 'inside the tent'.

ANOTHER LOOK AT BI-POLARIZATION

We have argued that there is an in-built trend towards bi-polarization, where big companies get bigger, small companies, typically serving some profitable niche also prosper, and the medium-sized companies in the middle are progressively marginalized. If you are in a medium-sized company this concerns you.

To shape the argument a bit more, the kind of medium-sized company that is in danger is one that is just like the big players in its industry, but on a smaller scale. It is the company that is not distinguished by anything much except size. Consider the following about such companies:

▌ They will find it more difficult to achieve the economies of scale and scope of the bigger players.

▌ They are less likely to achieve market dominance.

▌ They are not protected by industry entry barriers; clearly not, because others are already there, on a larger scale.

▌ They do not have the advantages of niche operations.

The companies in danger are those that get so far and no further, that are, say, regional when their rivals are national. If your company is in this middle ground the options are to:

▌ grow;

▌ differentiate;

▌ find some way of protecting your product-market, of locking in your customers, of raising the cost for would-be interlopers.

But even then, your company may still be bought.

In this brief discussion there is the suggestion that if you are a small niche-player, you are all right, in contrast to the 'caught in the middle' brigade. This is largely true, but there is a qualification.

This is that commercial viability does not always imply continued independence, a theme that has come up several times. So that in Italy, Fiat, for example, spent the 1980s acquiring just about every other Italian car company, some of them occupying quality niches, and they now live on simply as brands. Staying with cars, Ford more recently variously acquired Jaguar, Aston Martin, and Land-Rover – all of them serving up-scale market niches. Or again we have seen it in beer brewing, with large-scale brewers wanting to acquire distinctive, specialist niche operations – Interbrew with their Abbaye de Leffe, Anheuser Busch with Leinenkugel, and so on. What is more, most of these acquired niche companies have been run perfectly well by these big, generalist 'parents'. No one is saying that Jaguar went downhill because Ford bought them, or that enthusiasts are not still relishing that 'red lager from the Northwoods', Leinenkugel of Chippawa Falls, Wisconsin.

So the moral is that niche operations may well be commercially viable in the age of bi-polarization, so much so that top tier companies in size terms will come along and buy them. Only very occasionally does a niche company like Theakstons get bought by the generalist Scottish-Courage as it now is, only to be recreated as Black Sheep by the same family, a story told in Chapter 5. Do not bank on it.

The same 'health warning' applies to counter-concentration, the tendency for concentration in one industry in the sense of M&A activity leading to the dominance of a smaller number of larger players, in turn leading to concentration in related industries. Examples such as publishing and book retailing, builders merchants and builders, brewers and pub chains in the UK were offered in Chapter 2. Again the moral is: if concentration occurs in the industry next to yours in the sense of being connected by the value chain, expect concentration in your own industry. And if you don't want to experience M&A in the passive sense, you have to 'do it to them before they do it to you'.

M&A – MERGER AND ACQUISITION

So far we have tended to treat concentration as an impersonal trend, something that just happens to be going on out there. That treatment is justified, it is an identifiable trend and one that is consistent with the mature market, overcapacity state of much of the world economy. But we want to complement that by looking at M&A as a purposeful act on the part of real companies rather than as a statistical abstraction.

If you are a CEO or a business owner, acquiring another company is probably the most exiting thing you ever get to do; and that is its undoing. Probably the best advice one can give is try not to enjoy it so much! If it was not such fun CEOs might do less of it, or do it more prudently.

M&A also takes a variety of forms, and the earlier discussion of concentration has focused on one particular form, the horizontal form where like acquired like within a conventionally defined industry – BP and Amoco, General Motors and Saab, Astra and Seneca, Interbrew and Bass – leading to the much vaunted dominance of industries by a smaller number of larger players. But it may also be unrelated, deliberate diversification away from a core business about which one is apprehensive, of the Philip Morris/Kraft General Foods/Miller Brewing kind. And it can also be vertical, up or down the value chain, with retailers, say, acquiring (stakes in) logistics operations or internalizing their supply chain, manufacturers acquiring suppliers and so on. And it may on occasion be vertical and unrelated. Or it may even be the case that the acquirer simply wants to own another company in order to receive more profits, and does not seek or need any integration – strategic, cultural, or operational.

This spectrum of type and purpose is again part of the problem: there are possibilities there to excite just about everyone! It helps to make M&A irresistible, though in fact there is a battery of arguments against it, including:

▎ Just about all surveys suggest the majority of acquisitions fail, in the sense of not delivering the degree of cost savings, revenue increase, enhanced shareholder value and so on which was used to justify the initiative in the first place.

■ Indeed there is a cynical school that proclaims most acquisition strategies are post factum rationalizations.

■ Financial advisors are often paid by deal value; so they want a deal to happen, and they want a big deal.

■ This in turn may lead the due diligence operation to be hasty, shallow, or narrowly focused.

■ Also, big acquirers tend to be centralizers, which means that post-deal they dispose of the bits they do not want, which undermines employee morale and the integrity of the acquired business.

■ If and when the acquirer decides it has paid too much, it turns on controls and cost cutting, which is again alienating for the workforce.

■ A lot of CEOs find the deal exciting, but the implementation boring, so the deal maker moves on to the next target leaving the first 'undigested'.

There is a kind of diffuse vicious circle, as shown in Figure 11.3, waiting to happen.

This is not to say that cost cutting is wrong, even if there is a price to pay, but a lot of the deals are justified up front in terms of revenue growth, which tends to set everyone up for disappointment.

Sometimes the acquired company or the junior partner in a merger is grateful, seeing the acquirer as a white knight rescuing it from a worse fate. But more often people are apprehensive. Stories abound about how in the run-up to M&A employees come to spend two hours

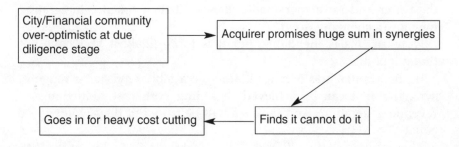

Figure 11.3

a day discussing their fate around the water cooler. One might add to such studies-cum-rumours a more targeted threat, that of headhunters moving in pre-acquisition. They will tend to go for: high tech people, with the company's intellectual property; marketing people with customer relationships thought to be portable.

How much better to get them while they are still in post and thus more credible to the next employer.

If these are some of the concerns, what are the counters?

BEFORE

Beef up the due diligence. Do not restrict it to the financials. Do not pressure advisors into doing it in 20 minutes.

Think critically about all the claims that get made in the enthusiasm of the battle, things like:

▌ We can integrate the two salesforces.

▌ We will save a fortune on IT.

▌ Cross-selling opportunities will be limitless.

And so on. Such claims may well be true, but they are not invariably true. How easy will it really be to integrate two salesforces? Customers are often dubious about continuing to deal with merged/acquired companies, feeling the new entity will not understand their need as well or that its commitment will be diluted. Apprehension of this kind may well be reinforced by interfacing with salespeople who are handling a product, service, or brand for the first time. The salesforces too will see it coming, some will leave, probably the better and most marketable ones so that in practice integrating may mean changing down.

None of this is inevitable, but it is more likely if you have not thought of it.

In the approach to M&A initiators invariably envisage a range of synergies that can be achieved regarding both cost reduction and revenue generation. And they may all be true. But they won't all be equal.

That is to say some will be easy to do while some will be more diffi-cult. Some may be achieved quickly, others will take time. Some will be risky. They may backfire, alienate powerful interests, produce unintended consequences and have to be abandoned, while others may be of the risk free 'won't hurt anyone' kind. And there are likely to be differences of scale. Some will be really worth doing if they come off; others are probably worth doing, but they won't make that much difference.

For sure no one is going to get all this right, it never works out exactly as you hope, but the odds in your favour are much increased if you think it through first, something that is often aided by having operational people on board as well as the 'big picture' ones. In short:

▍ Review synergies before the event.

▍ Try to screen out the do-able from the cosmetic rationalization.

▍ Among the do-able look for those that are:
   - quick;
   - easy;
   - risk-free;
   - large scale.

AFTER

If enthusiasm for the deal inclines people to rush into it, reality and complexity tend to slow them down when the deal is done. Probably better the other way round. Move fast while the situation is in a state of flux and things can be done. After a takeover you are going to have to do some things that will not be popular. The sooner these are done and people get used to the idea that these are not in the pipeline anymore, healing can start. There will also be decisions that have to be made in conditions of insecurity. Make them anyway. That is probably particularly true of personnel decisions; you cannot spend a year assessing the rival merits of the two finance directors, or whatever (I was once in a company in Denmark where they had waited seven years after an acquisition to decide whose IT system should be adopted!).

Side by side with this 'slow down before not after' dictum is the related issue of priority. Do not try to advance slowly and meticulously on a broad front. Prioritize. Pick out the few important things and go for them. It is the style of the US Marines that is needed, not that of the regular army.

Advising business

All my contacts with companies while preparing to write this book caused me to think about the work of those who advise businesses – banks of various kinds, law firms, accountancy practices, advertising agencies, consultancies of course, and in an indirect way even business journalists and sometimes management academics. It was not that I was dishing out advice myself, I went to learn and to understand, but I realized I had something in common with the armies of business advisers, that is to say, I was heavily dependent for my understanding on what they told me.

Mindsets

Listening is not the only way in. You can work on the accounts, engage in financial ratio analysis, run the numbers, peer into the quantified record of past performance, and even make comparisons with other companies in the industry that are objective in a way. But what they tell you, the briefing, the introduction, the overview, the summation, the definition of the problem, are still important. Also, what they tell you tends to shape the understanding you derive from some of the other sources listed above.

What I have come to think is that what they tell you is not purely a statement of objective reality, though there are chunks of objective reality in it, but rather the presentation of a mindset. This mindset is made up of:

▌ beliefs and values;

▌ causal arguments;

▌ 'facts';

▌ 'constraints'.

The beliefs and values are certainly worth knowing, especially when articulated by organizational leaders. The causal arguments bit is vital. This is where they say things like 'We're doing this because …', 'That course of action isn't possible for these reasons …', 'Business growth is being driven by …' and so on. It invariably makes sense, it is usually convincing, sometimes you do not know enough about the industry to judge, and occasionally you have doubts about it. But even on those occasions of doubt they are still expressing a causal connection which they believe in and which is shaping their decisional behaviour. The facts are sometimes real facts (whatever they are) things you did not know about the industry, things in the environment that are going to impact, quantifiable facts about changes in the market, and so on. And on those occasions when it sounds like 'facts' in inverted commas it is not so much that the numbers are wrong, but executives have picked out something, which might be factual, and emphasized it because it fits the causal argument or is consistent with the values and beliefs. One gets a lot of facts in this sense in the run-up to takeovers. The constraints come in all shapes and sizes and at all points on the objectivity–subjectivity scale. But they are important to the adviser, and fascinating for the outsider – typically something you could not have worked out for yourself.

If I were an adviser I would now stand back a bit from what they tell me, and shake it down into these four categories : OK, testimonies do not fit these four categories exactly, but even doing it approximately will enhance understanding. And it would probably enhance the quality of advice.

On being aware

Everyone who has dealings with companies mentally grades them. You put them on some good to bad, competent to incompetent, outstanding to dire continuum. But, one of my consultant friends urged, there is another equally important variable, and that is awareness. In short, do they know? If we take the negative option, are they aware of their shortcomings, do they realize that they would be judged incompetent by informed outsiders? More interestingly, if we take the positive option, and they are judged good or competent, are they aware of that? And in particular if they are good, do they know what it is they have got right, what they are doing well?

As soon as I heard this idea I found myself re-running 20 or more interviews in my mind, ones where I thought they were doing something remarkable but they were not aware of it, not sure of it, or if they suspected it they did not exactly know why. If this testimony sounds a little starry-eyed I should add that if you are an interested academic as opposed to a saviour/adviser, you don't get to see many incompetent companies because they won't let you in; also, especially with my smaller companies I made an effort to include in the study businesses that had already been objectively rated as above average performers.

If for ease we turn the formula into a two by two diagram, shown in Figure 11.4, perhaps the interesting thing is that there are several instances of directions in which advisers might seek to move companies, as shown by the arrows.

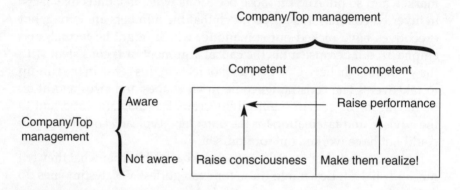

Figure 11.4

Finally, lest anyone should be misled, there is a certain bias in my interpretations. I am intrigued more by the intangible than by the finite, prefer *savoir faire* to systems, and discretion to control.

I am more excited by innovation and by what can be achieved with imagination than by administrative diligence. I think the best idea is one I have not had yet.

12

References

Barsoux, J L and Lawrence, P (1990) *Management in France*, Cassell Educational, London

Burke, M and Meredith, R (2001) Seeing red over green, *Forbes Global*, 26 November, p 34

Calori, R and Lawrence, P (1991) *The Business of Europe*, Sage, London

Cramley, B and Sancton, T (2001) Master of the Universe, *Time*, 6 August, pp 36–43

de Jager, J L (1998) *Albert Heijn: The life and times of a global grocer*, Peddleston Court, Herefordshire

Edwards, V and Lawrence, P (1994) *Management Change in East Germany*, Routledge, London

Ellwood, I (2000) *The Essential Brand Book*, Kogan Page, London

Evening Standard, 31 January 2000

Fayol, H (1916) *L'administration générale et industrielle*, 2nd edition, Paris. See also Fayol, H (1949) *General and Industrial Management*, Pitman, London

Financial Times, 6 July 2001

Fortune, Sam's Big Blue Challenge, Europe Edition, 27 August 2001, **67**, pp 52–55

Gamble, P R and Blackwell J (2001) *Knowledge Management: A state of the art guide*, Kogan Page, London

Guardian, M&S plays catch-up with fashionably fickle children, 30 August 2001

Guardian, The wheel of fortune spins again, 29 December 2001, p 24

Hammer, M and Champy, J (2001) *Reengineering the Corporation: A manifesto for business revolution*, (paperback edition) Nicholas Brealey, London

Hofstede, G (1980) *Culture's Consequences*, Sage, Beverly Hills, CA

Hollowell, P (1968) *The Lorry Driver*, Routledge & Kegan Paul, London

Ind, N (2001) *Living the Brand*, Kogan Page, London

International Herald Tribune, 16 March 2001

Kapferer, J-N (2001) *Re-inventing the Brand*, Kogan Page, London

Kanter, R M (2000) *When Giants Learn to Dance*, Simon Schuster, New York

Kellner, T (2001) Cybersleuth, *Forbes Global*, 26 November, pp 20–21

Klein, N (2001) *No Logo*, Flamingo, London

Lawrence, P (1984) *Management in Action*, Routledge & Kegan Paul, London

Lawrence, P, ed (1985) *Small Business Breakthrough*, Basil Blackwell, Oxford

Lawrence, P (1986) *Invitation to Management*, Basil Blackwell, Oxford

Lawrence, P (1991) *Management in the Netherlands*, The Clarendon Press, Oxford

Lawrence, P (1998) *Issues in European Business*, Macmillan, London and Basingstoke

Lawrence, P and Edwards, V (2000) *Management in Western Europe*, Macmillan, London and Basingstoke

Leonard, Devin (2001) Mr Messier is ready for his close-up, *Fortune*, 17 September, **18**, pp 26–33

Luttwak, E (1999) *Turbo Capitalism: Winners and losers in the global economy*, Orion Publishing Group, London

McRae, H (2001) Honey We've Shrunk the State, *Fortune*, European Edition 12, p 25

Meredith, R (2002) Under the skin, *Forbes*, 4 February, pp 22–25

Myers, A and Bajer J (2001) *Innovation, Adaptation and Business Success: Final Research Report*, The Talent Foundation, London

Peters, T J and Waterman, R H (1982) *In Search of Excellence*, Harper & Row, New York

Simon, H (1996) *Hidden Champions*, Harvard Business School, Boston, MA

Tanzer, A (2001) Pillfactory to the World, *Forbes Global*, 10 December, pp 26–30

Thurow, L (1996) *The Future of Capitalism*, Nicholas Brealey, London

Tomlinson, R (2002) Dethroning Percy Barnevik, *Fortune*, 8 April, 7, pp 38–42

Turrettini, J (2002) More than the sum of its parts, *Forbes*, 15 April, p 43

van Marrewijk, A (1999) *Internationalisation, Co-operation and Ethnicity in the Telecom Sector*, Eburon, Delft, Holland

Index